The Decisive Campaigns of the Desert Air Force 1942–1945

Other titles by Bryn Evans:

With The East Surreys in Tunisia, Sicily and Italy
1942–1945
(2012, Pen & Sword Books Ltd)

Air Battle For Burma
(2016, Pen & Sword Books Ltd)

Airmen's Incredible Escapes
(2020, Pen & Sword Books Ltd)

The Decisive Campaigns of the Desert Air Force 1942–1945

Bryn Evans

Pen & Sword
AVIATION

First published in Great Britain in 2014
and republished in this format in 2020 by
PEN & SWORD AVIATION
an imprint of Pen & Sword Books Ltd
Yorkshire – Philadelphia

Copyright © Bryn Evans, 2014, 2020

ISBN 978-1-52678-194-9

Typeset by Concept, Huddersfield, West Yorkshire, HD4 5JL.
Printed and bound in England by CPI Group (UK) Ltd, Croydon CR0 4YY.

MIX
Paper from
responsible sources
FSC® C013604

Pen & Sword Books Ltd incorporates the Imprints of Aviation, Atlas, Family
History, Fiction, Maritime, Military, Discovery, Politics, History, Archaeology,
Select, Wharncliffe Local History, Wharncliffe True Crime, Military Classics,
Wharncliffe Transport, Leo Cooper, The Praetorian Press, Remember When,
White Owl, Seaforth Publishing and Frontline Books.

For a complete list of Pen & Sword titles please contact
PEN & SWORD BOOKS LTD
47 Church Street, Barnsley, South Yorkshire, S70 2AS, England
E-mail: enquiries@pen-and-sword.co.uk
Website: www.pen-and-sword.co.uk
or
PEN & SWORD BOOKS
1950 Lawrence Rd, Havertown, PA 19083, USA
E-mail: uspen-and-sword@casematepublishers.com
Website: www.penandswordbooks.com

Dedication

For Jean,
and for all who have served in the blue of the RAF,
and other Allied air forces.

The Lost (extract):

Think of them. You did not die as these
caged in an aircraft that did not return.
Whenever hearts have song and minds have peace
or in your eyes the prides of banners burn,
think of these who dreamed and loved as you,
and gave their laughter, gave their sun and snow,
... To them this debt you owe.

Their lives are ended, but dreams are not yet lost
if you remember in your laugh and song
these boys who do not sing, and laughed not long.

Herbert Corby*

* *The Lost*, p. 80, from *The Terrible Rain – The War Poets 1939–45*, Brian Gardner, Methuen & Co. Ltd, London, 1966.

Contents

List of Plates

A top view of Spitfire Mk VB No. R6923, QJ-S of No. 92 Squadron RAF in 1941.

A small formation of Wellington bombers based at Malta.

A Vickers Wellington Mk II of No. 104 Squadron, Bomber Command, in April 1941.

Ground crew of No. 274 Squadron RAF overhaul Hawker Hurricane Mk 1, V7780, AB-M, at Landing Ground 10/Gerawala, during the defence of Tobruk.

Armourers work on a P-40 Tomahawk of No. 3 Squadron RAAF in North Africa, December 1941.

A Lockheed Hudson Mk V bomber of No. 48 Squadron RAF in 1942.

A Curtiss P-40 Kittyhawk Mk III of No. 112 Squadron RAF in 1943, with the red-painted propeller spinner of the Desert Air Force.

A Spitfire Vc/Vb, ER338 QJ-S, of Flight Lieutenant Neville Duke, No. 92 Squadron RAF, flying over El Nogra, Libya in December 1942.

In April 1943 Bristol Beaufighter V8318, F-Freddie, of No. 252 Squadron RAF, creates a cloud of dust as it moves out from its landing ground at Magrun.

Three Curtiss P-40 Warhawks.

A Hawker Hurricane Mk IV (No. KZ321) in desert camouflage.

A de Havilland Mosquito B Mk IV, DK336.

A Hawker Hurricane Mk IV of No. 6 Squadron RAF being serviced at Foggia, Italy, in July 1944 prior to a sortie over the Adriatic.

The Royal Palace at Caserta.

Flight Lieutenant Neville Duke standing with his Spitfire Mk V of No. 92 Squadron RAF at Biggin Hill in 1941.

Squadron Leader Lloyd Wiggins.

During the Battle of El Alamein on 26 October 1942, the Italian oil tanker *Tergestea* was torpedoed and sunk outside Tobruk harbour, by a formation of three Wellington torpedo-bombers led by Flight Lieutenant Lloyd Wiggins of No. 38 Squadron RAF.

Sergeant Alec Richardson, a Kittyhawk fighter pilot of No. 3 Squadron RAAF.

Members of the 64th Fighter Squadron of the 57th Fighter Group, standing in front of one of their Curtiss P-40 Warhawk fighters in Tunisia.

Squadron Leader H.S.L. 'Cocky' Dundas, commanding officer of No. 56 Squadron RAF, photographed on 2 February 1942 at RAF Duxford.

Captain James 'Big Jim' Curl, pictured with his P-40 Warhawk in Tunisia.

ACM Sir Arthur Tedder in December 1943 on the Italian coast.

Squadron Leader Bill McRae.

Brigadier General Michael C. McCarthy USAF (Rtd).

USAAF P-47D Thunderbolts of the 345th Fighter Squadron over northern Italy on 6 April 1945.

The personal message from General Sir Richard McCreery, commander of Eighth Army, to Air Vice Marshal William Foster, AOC-in-C of the Desert Air Force, on the morning of 3 May 1945, following the surrender of German forces in Italy on 2 May.

The personal handwritten letter from Air Vice Marshal William Foster, AOC-in-C of the Desert Air Force, on 3 May 1945 in reply to the personal message from General Sir Richard McCreery, commander of Eighth Army.

List of Maps

Acknowledgements

My very first acknowledgements must be to Roderic Owen and Sir Arthur Tedder GCB. In 1948, for his ground-breaking book on *The Desert Air Force*, Roderic Owen was fortunate to gain an interview with Tedder who, at the time, was Marshal of the Royal Air Force Baron Tedder of Glenguin. In the Air Ministry in London an apprehensive Owen was ushered in to the office of the Chief of the Air Staff. In response to a previously formal request, Tedder, who had been the architect of the Desert Air Force (DAF), gave Owen a draft text of a 'Foreword' for his book. Owen was both pleased and relieved to find it most appropriate and acceptable.

Owen, himself a veteran flyer of the DAF, recounted how he then asked if he could next write Tedder's biography. In his typically self-deprecating way, Tedder responded by asking, 'Why?' After discussion Tedder reluctantly agreed to Owen taking it on. One of the arguments Owen used to persuade Tedder was that an Air Force interpretation of the war was required, 'to counter those orthodox military and naval interpretations'.[1] Later, in 1966, Tedder would publish his own autobiography, *With Prejudice*. My efforts in writing *The Decisive Campaigns of the Desert Air Force* rest on many shoulders that have come before me, but none more so than those of Owen and Tedder.

There is another connection to those times, more than sixty years ago. Much of my underlying motivation for this book comes from my parents. My father Cliff served in RAF Bomber Command from 1939 to 1945. My mother, Tamar, told me of lying in bed in the months before I was born, and listening to the Luftwaffe bombers droning above as they flew over Doncaster on their way to bomb Sheffield's steelworks. Consequently, during my childhood in the late forties and early fifties in the UK, my parents imbued me with the deepest respect and awe for what the RAF had done to turn back the German bombing raids.

Before going any further I must make two important apologies. The first is to the Allied navies, whose operations I was unable to cover in the scope of this book. The Allies' naval forces were the foundation rock without which the North African and Italian campaigns could not even have been commenced.

The second apology must go to the ground support staff of the Desert Air Force, whose gruelling, round the clock work and dedication can never be understood fully and appreciated. From as early as 1942 until 1945 their sustained ability to keep DAF aircraft serviceable and flying combat operations, even on the very day on which they relocated to a new airfield hundreds of miles distant, is beyond comprehension.

I cannot begin to find the words to thank the many veterans of those times, to whom I have spoken in my research. In particular, I must sincerely thank Jack Ingate, Frank Jensen, Lloyd Leah, Bill McRae and Lloyd Wiggins, but the interest and support from everyone, veterans' families and friends, has been inspirational to me. And again I must apologize for not being able to include all the contributions I have received. Yet, without such help, I could not have written a word.

Once again I am indebted to my editor, the well-known military historian and prolific author, Richard Doherty, for his passionate advice and suggested revisions. Drawing on his encyclopaedic knowledge and his many books on the North African and Italian campaigns, Richard has uncovered some quite unique and invaluable research material. As with my previous book on the East Surrey Regiment, I am especially grateful to Brigadier Henry Wilson at Pen and Sword Books, for taking on my proposal for this book, and making me get it done!

I am particularly appreciative of the many military histories on the air war in the Mediterranean, North African and Italian theatres, and must sincerely pay tribute to authors Chaz Bowyer, Andrew Brookes, John Herington, Christopher Shores, Andrew Thomas and, of course, Roderic Owen and Sir Arthur Tedder. There are too many research sources to list in their entirety, but a special thanks goes to the Australian War Memorial in Canberra, Australia, the Imperial War Museum and King's College in London, and the Royal United Services Institute of Australia in Sydney for access to their archives and collections. I have tried to attribute the most influential sources I have consulted in my research, and I can only apologize if I have inadvertently missed any.

Above all I owe everything to my wife Jean. Her love, interest and encouragement have been indispensable to my writing of this book.

Bryn Evans
Sydney
January 2014

Note
Owen, *Tedder*, p. 9–11.

Author's Note

During the Second World War, and for many years after, certain German aircraft manufactured by Bayerische Flugzeugwerke (BFW), such as the Bf109, were commonly referred to as the 'Messerschmitt 109' or 'Me109', particularly by Allied pilots and air crew. The terms were derived from the well-known designer Willy Messerschmitt, and his partner Robert Lusser. Airmen from those days still use the term 'Me109'. I have used the technically correct, and now widely accepted, Bf109, except where direct quotes use Me109 from referenced sources.

Foreword

While researching a British regiment in the Second World War[1] I was troubled to understand a recurring conundrum. From the Battle of El Alamein and the Operation TORCH landings in north-west Africa shortly after in late 1942, as Churchill predicted, it was the turning of the tide. Allied armies fought their way from Egypt through Libya, Tunisia, Sicily and the length of mainland Italy, without any major reverse until final victory in May 1945.

This was despite the German forces and their defences being advantaged by the mountainous terrain, massively favourable to a defending army, first in Tunisia and then Italy. After Cassino the Allies' Fifth and Eighth Armies even lost some of their best divisions, transferred to Operation OVERLORD and the north-west Europe front. Yet it seems that histories of the campaigns and veterans speak consistently of the German soldiers' professionalism and training, and of their superior weapons and equipment. Most problematical of all is that the Allied armies hardly ever enjoyed a two-to-one advantage in ground troops, and were often outnumbered.

It can be argued that the Allies in North Africa and Italy, through the breaking of the Germans' Enigma code, had better intelligence, and overall employed greater flexibility and innovation in their tactics. Certainly the Allies' offensive strategy, compared with Hitler's 'defend to the last man' mindset, was an advantage. So, too, was the air superiority established by Allied air forces, of which the Desert Air Force (DAF) was a renowned leader.

The name 'Desert Air Force', itself sounds bizarre, suggesting a contradiction in terms, an incongruity, not unlike imagining for instance, an 'Army of the Sea'. In 1948 in his classic book, *The Desert Air Force*, Roderic Owen said, 'To trace the history of the Desert Air Force is to try and dissect the sinews of a myth.' Although the DAF origins can be said to have taken shape in 1940, it was only officially given the name Desert Air Force in May 1943, when it was about to leave North Africa and its deserts and never to return.

Marshal of the Royal Air Force Lord Tedder GCB, who was commander of the DAF for some of its early years, stated in Owen's book that the DAF played a lead role, and was '... the key to the ultimate victory' in Europe'.

Those readers who have never heard of the DAF, or know little of its history, I can imagine may be thinking, 'Can Tedder's statement really be valid?' When you listen to some of the pilots who flew in the air battles in

North Africa and Italy in the Second World War, you gain an insight into Tedder's belief.

One veteran I met in Sydney, Squadron Leader Bill McRae DFC AFC, who is now 101 years old, flew the first Wellington Mark VIII torpedo-bomber in July 1942 from the UK to Malta. It was equipped with the latest top-secret radar, to enable it to find and sink enemy ships at night.

Another veteran I visited in Adelaide, Wing Commander Lloyd Wiggins DSO, who is now closing in on his century in years, piloted one of those Wellington Mark VIII torpedo-bombers to snuff out Rommel's last hope during the Battle of El Alamein.

DAF was made up of both air force formations and individual airmen from nearly every Allied nation. From the early years Americans, Australians, British, Canadians, New Zealanders and South Africans were prominent, either in their own national wings or squadrons, or in RAF formations, within DAF. Later DAF embraced airmen from many other Allied nations, such as Czechs, Free French, Greeks, Poles and Yugoslavs.

Roderic Owen believed DAF gained its strength and *esprit de corps* from its very diversity of nations and cultures. A common cause welded them together.

When you hear of the experiences of men such as McRae and Wiggins, it transports you back to those times, when those campaigns hung in the balance. They paint a picture of the life and death struggles of airmen, as the DAF and Allied air power sought to subjugate the Axis air forces, and make the difference for Allied armies on the ground in North Africa and Italy.

The exploits of the many DAF airmen recounted in this book are but a tiny fraction of the thousands who comprised this legendary air force. But read the stories that follow, and you will better understand the history that they made. And you can be the judge as to whether the Desert Air Force was the Allies' leading tactical air force of the Second World War, and whether Lord Tedder was correct, and DAF was a fundamental key to the Allied victory in Europe.

The re-issue of this book in 2020 coincides with the 75 years since 1945, when on 2 May in Italy then two days later on 4 May in Germany, all Axis forces surrendered. In those campaigns the hard-won air supremacy of the Allies made a crucial and decisive difference.

Bryn Evans
Brisbane, Australia
June 2020

Note
1. *With the East Surreys in Tunisia, Sicily and Italy* (Pen & Sword, 2012).

Prologue

In Preston railway station in northern Lancashire, it was one o'clock in the morning on a cold November night in 1940. In the gloomy wartime black-out the queue of servicemen and civilians inched slowly forward towards a restaurant counter. Each person was probably dreaming of warming their hands, around a mug of tea or coffee. In the line was Air Vice Marshal Arthur Tedder. Following a meeting on a new 40mm aircraft gun with Rolls Royce in Barrow, he was waiting for a delayed connection to London.

Finally AVM Tedder arrived at the counter, paid for a mug of coffee, and took it back to a vacant table. As he bent to sip the steaming drink, a crumpled evening newspaper on the floor caught his eye – 'AIR CHIEF CAPTURED'. An RAF aircraft en route to Cairo, transporting Air Marshal Owen Boyd to take up the position of Deputy to Air Marshal Longmore, the Air Officer Commanding-in-Chief RAF Middle East, had made a forced landing in Sicily. There Boyd had been taken prisoner by the Axis authorities.

Only a few days earlier Longmore had requested London that Tedder be sent out to be his Deputy. Churchill had rejected Tedder, and approved the appointment of Boyd. Now the hazardous Mediterranean air route to Egypt had claimed another victim. The Germans must have thought Air Marshal Boyd was a choice prize to have fallen into their hands. If it had been Tedder, it may well have been, and the war may have taken a very different course.

Arthur Tedder was born on 11 July 1890 in Glenguin, Scotland. At Cambridge University he studied history, and gained a reserve commission as a second lieutenant in the Dorsetshire Regiment. On the outbreak of war in 1914, and after a short spell serving in the Colonial Service in Fiji, he returned to Britain and took up a promotion to lieutenant in the Dorsetshire Regiment. When he seriously injured his knee, he gained a transfer to the Royal Flying Corps, and gained his wings in 1916. He saw service as pilot, squadron leader and wing commander in France, Britain and Egypt during the rest of the war.

In the inter-war years promotions and senior appointments in the RAF followed, until he was promoted to air vice marshal in 1937, and in July 1938 Director General for Research in the Air Ministry in London. In 1939 his department came under the Minister of Aircraft Production, Lord Beaverbrook. Such were Tedder's considerable abilities and communication skills, he had a way of inspiring people, and his subordinates did not need his

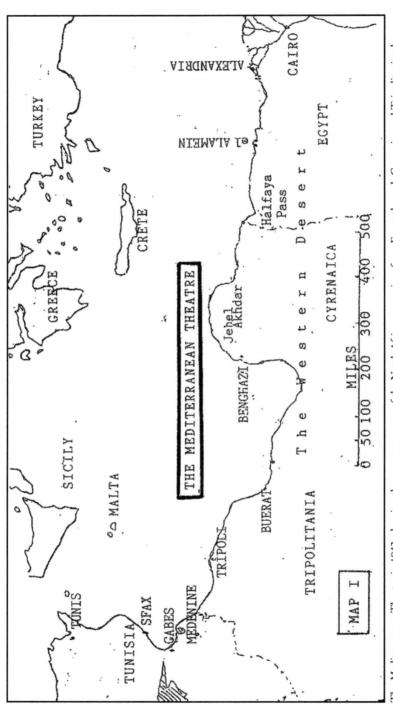

The Mediterranean Theatre in 1942, showing the enormous span of the North African campaign, from Egypt through Cyrenaica and Tripolitania, the Western Desert to Tunisia.

specific orders to follow his lead. With Lord Beaverbrook somehow they did not get on, and their poor working relationship was a factor when he was passed over by Churchill for Air Marshal Boyd.

Now, in that poorly-lit Preston railway station, Tedder's mind must have raced. When he arrived in London next morning, he may well find himself to be back in favour, and soon bound for Cairo after all.[1]

* * *

As Tedder had anticipated, on 30 November 1940 he departed London as Acting Air Marshal, on a flight to Cairo to be Deputy to Air Marshal Longmore. So as to inspect the airfields, facilities and arrangements for ferrying aircraft to Egypt, he was aboard an Imperial Airways flight via Lisbon, then Freetown, Lagos and Takoradi in West Africa, before flying west to the Sudan, and finally north to Cairo.[2]

It would be under Tedder's leadership in due course, that the Desert Air Force would be created. In the North African and Italian campaigns of the Second World War, the Desert Air Force (DAF) pioneered collaborative and close army-air support, which became the template for Allied forces, and an indispensable strategy for victory in both the European and Pacific theatres.

The Desert Air Force (DAF) was a blend of airmen and squadrons from nearly all the Allied countries. DAF airmen from a wide spectrum of cultures and countries, displayed a no-nonsense approach to their mission and operations. Uniforms were replaced with whatever attire was most practical and effective for the conditions, with a similar attitude to any bureaucratic processes and procedures. Everything became secondary to the priority of getting the job done.

The first formal origins of the DAF would come in November 1941, when Air Marshal Tedder appointed Air Vice Marshal Sir Arthur 'Maori' Coningham in command of a number of squadrons from No. 202 Group RAF in Egypt, to form the Western Desert Air Force (WDAF). Its charter was to provide close air support to Eighth Army in the Western Desert of North Africa, and in effect became the first Tactical Air Force of the RAF. In February 1943 it would absorb some of the squadrons which were supporting British and US forces in Tunisia, and be renamed simply as the Desert Air Force (DAF). From that time the DAF also formed part of the much larger North-West (Mediterranean) Allied Tactical Air Force (NWATAF).

* * *

However, in June 1940 when war commenced with Italy in North Africa, the main operational arm of the RAF Middle East was the small No. 202 Group, predominantly based in the Egyptian Delta near Alexandria. On 13 September 1940 six divisions of the Italian Tenth Army, which was around three times the size of British Army forces in Egypt, advanced from Cyrenaica in the east of Libya and crossed the Egyptian border. Despite being equipped with obsolete and few aircraft, mainly Gloster Gladiator bi-plane fighters and Bristol Blenheim bombers, 202 Group helped the British Army's Western Desert Force (WDF) to resist the Italian forces, and push them back from the border into Libya.

In December 1940 General Wavell, C-in-C Middle East, decided to go onto the offensive. In Operation COMPASS a strong armed reconnaissance force, under the command of General Sir RN O'Connor, crossed the border into Libya, and attacked the Italian Army. Despite some RAF squadrons having been transferred to defend Greece, two squadrons of Hawker Hurricane fighters had recently arrived from the UK. With the Hurricanes added to the remaining fighter squadrons of Gladiators and Gauntlets, Blenheims and Wellington bombers, 202 Group was able to give effective support to the WDF, and counter the Italian Air Force, the Regia Aeronautica.[3]

In the first week of Operation COMPASS, medium bombers such as Bombays and Wellingtons, hit Italian airfields every night. To protect its air bases the Italian Air Force had to weaken its patrols over its front lines. By the end of the first week the RAF had destroyed 74 enemy aircraft. O'Connor's force drove the Italians back across the Cyrenaica border, taking Sidi Barrani, then Bardia by 4 January, Tobruk by the month's end, followed by Benghazi, on its way to reaching as far as the border of Tripolitania. The new Hurricanes were prominent as the squadrons of 202 Group inflicted significant losses on the Italians' aircraft and airfields.[4] By the time Benghazi was taken, the number of Italian aircraft claimed shot down, found damaged or destroyed, had climbed to around 1,100.[5]

Also in December 1940 in another beginning, Acting Air Marshal Tedder took up his appointment in Cairo as Deputy to Air Marshal Longmore. Tedder's first task was to stand in temporarily for a sick Air Commodore Collishaw, as commander of 202 Group. It was timely for Tedder to see how, as the Cyrenaican coastal airfields were captured, and became available in January and February 1941, that for a brief period Hurricane fighters could fly direct non-stop to Malta. Shipping convoys to and from Malta were able to gain some measure of air protection.[6]

In February 1941, due to supply constraints and sheer exhaustion, O'Connor's advance came to a halt on the Tripolitania border. Soon after on direct orders from London, further elements of both Army and RAF were redeployed to defend Crete and Greece. Unfortunately around the same time, the first German forces under General Erwin Rommel were beginning to arrive in Tripoli, to reinforce the Italians. In the second week of February, Benghazi was severely bombed by the Luftwaffe, forcing the Royal Navy to pull out its ships, shore-based sailors, boats and other equipment from its port. The WDF looked at its depleted strength and made preparations to withdraw. In late March Rommel led his Axis Army, now with the Luftwaffe's support, in a counter-attack on the weakened British force.

Rommel's offensive soon forced WDF back into Egypt, leaving only Tobruk in a besieged situation. When German forces also completed their occupation of Yugoslavia, Crete and Greece, this conversely strengthened 202 Group, for it allowed some surviving aircraft to withdraw and return to Egypt. Further transfers of squadrons from East Africa, and a large delivery of Hurricanes from UK, provided some welcome relief and consolation for RAF Middle East.[7]

*   *   *

The fall of Crete and the Royal Navy's loss of ships to Luftwaffe attacks, proved a number of things in Air Marshal Tedder's thinking. Without the possibility of air cover from Cyrenaican airfields Crete had been doomed, and the Navy unprotected. Malta was now alone and in mortal danger. It meant that the Mediterranean sea passage was effectively closed to Allied shipping. Tedder could see that the age-old strength of sea power had been compromised permanently.

The conclusions that he drew were that, air power must be joined to sea and land forces in both strategies and operations, and that air power must be exercised jointly with the other two services. At the same time but with a pre-eminent priority, air power must be used to first win the air war with the enemy air forces.[8]

From the disastrous defeats in Greece and Crete, Tedder developed his view of a 'cycle of interdependence'.

> The safety of the shipping route depended upon the Army capturing the Cyrenaican airfields, from which aircraft could take off to protect naval vessels convoying merchant shipping. The capture of the airfields by the Army depended on the Navy, provided with air cover, escorting merchant vessels containing Army supplies to Alexandria, and upon the RAF providing air support for the Army as it advanced. The RAF could only provide efficient air support for the Army, or air cover for the Navy, if it had established a degree of superiority over the enemy air force, but the RAF, depended largely for its supplies upon the safe arrival of the merchant vessels, hence upon the safety of the shipping route.[9]

Tedder was asserting the committed doctrine and theory of the Chief of the Air Staff, Air Marshal Portal. The air war must be won first, to establish and sustain air superiority. To do this the RAF must be independent from the other two services, and retain its ability to be flexible and concentrate its operations as required to support either the Army or Navy.[10]

*   *   *

By June 1941 when WDF launched its Operation BATTLEAXE offensive, some squadrons of 202 Group had been re-equipped with American aircraft such as the Curtiss P-40 Tomahawks and Martin Marylands. The strengthening of 202 Group, also included the first South African Air Force (SAAF) squadrons.[11] Operation BATTLEAXE was an attempt to regain the Cyrenaican coastline, where airfields were essential to provide air protection for Malta and the sea routes through the Mediterranean. The Army demanded an air protection umbrella of fighters over the battle area, to which Tedder reluctantly agreed. However he sent the medium bombers in interdiction raids against Tripoli and Benghazi.[12]

Tedder was urged by the Army to take risks to provide army protection and support over the battlefield to a maximum possible level. On 11 and 12 June thirty-six Hurricanes were moved to forward airfields. When the offensive began on 15 June, 202 Group had tasked four squadrons of Hurricanes, two of Blenheim bombers, one of Tomahawks, and one of armed reconnaissance Hurricanes, to direct support of ground forces. Although the number of aircraft was still below that of the Axis air forces, Tedder thought it gave the RAF some level of air superiority.

In the event there was a paucity of information supplied by the Army, on which to direct bombing or strafing of Axis forces. Through maintaining fighter patrols over the battlefield, and in the face of much enhanced Axis air forces, thirty-three RAF fighters were lost. Tedder was concerned that the over-emphasis of such tactics, would lead to the Axis air forces gaining air superiority. He expressed his view that to maintain air cover protection over the battlefield indefinitely, or to use air attacks to turn back enemy ground forces, could only be contemplated if the Axis air forces were near totally eliminated.[13]

While WDF incurred heavy losses in tanks, and the RAF in aircraft, the Axis forces retained their positions. Only supply shortages restrained Rommel's Deutsches Afrika Korps from counter attacking. Both sides eyed each other as they rebuilt for the next battle.[14]

The failure of Operation BATTLEAXE in only a few days brought much Army criticism of the poor air support, as they saw it, arguing that the RAF should become subordinate to the Army. The disagreement went as high as Churchill, who gave his ruling:

> The idea of keeping standing patrols over our moving columns should be abandoned. It is unsound to distribute aircraft in this way, and no air superiority will stand the application of such a mischievous practice.[15]

Tedder's resilience, nerve and persuasive logic won the day. Operation BATTLEAXE was a failure, but it proved to be a catharsis, and a foundation for Tedder's greatest opportunity in the future.

Tedder appointed AVM Sir Arthur 'Maori' Coningham as the new commander of 202 Group, and he commenced transforming it into a tactical air force. In July No. 253 Wing was formed, with two squadrons of Hurricanes and one of Blenheims for close army-air support. A few months later in October/November 1941, with three more fighter Wings, 258, 262 and 269, the Western Desert Air Force (WDAF) was established.

On 18 November 1941 the new British Eighth Army attacked in Operation CRUSADER, supported by twenty-eight WDAF squadrons, which included six of Hurricanes and five of Tomahawks. The fighters were backed by Blenheim, Boston and Wellington bombers.[16]

For a week before the start of Operation CRUSADER, the RAF and the Navy struck at enemy ports and shipping, to prevent Axis supplies reaching Tripoli and Benghazi. WDAF bombing raids hit Tripoli and Benghazi, Axis supply lines to their front lines, and Axis airfields. Tedder took the long view that, it was by choking off the enemy's supplies, and building air superiority, the war in the Mediterranean would be won.

Despite it being alleged once again that the RAF was inferior in numbers to Axis air forces, Tedder insisted that the RAF would gain superiority. He believed, and again convinced the Army and London, that his strategic long view to gain air superiority to support the Army in North Africa, would in time be the difference to bring complete victory.[17]

When another campaign surfaced in the media for WDAF to be subordinated to Army control, Tedder strongly disagreed. He pointed out that protection for the Army's ground forces was but one element of a spectrum of air force operations. Tedder was not afraid to be blunt in rebutting the Army's criticism, that WDAF's inferior number of aircraft meant that the Axis had air superiority:

> I set little store by numerical comparisons of strength. Serviceability, reserves, supply, and morale are vital factors in any real comparison.[18]

Operation CRUSADER had three main objectives: to gain and occupy the Cyrenaican and Tripolitanian coastal cities and ports, so that the RAF could use their airfields to protect shipping through the Malta 'narrows'; to relieve Tobruk; and ultimately to drive the Axis forces out of North Africa, so securing Egypt.[19] Over two months Operation CRUSADER forced the Axis armies to withdraw to the west, and Tobruk was relieved.[20]

Regaining the Cyrenaican airfields enabled air cover to reach across the sea to Malta, and allowed three convoys through to the besieged island. The success of Operation CRUSADER brought an immediate reaction from Germany. In an ominous move the Luftwaffe transferred Fliegerkorps II from Russia to Sicily.[21]

In January 1942 WDAF put its first American P-40 Kittyhawks into operations with No. 3 Squadron RAAF, and in March the first squadron of Spitfire

Mark Vs took to the skies. Also in March AVM Coningham re-formed WDAF into two groups: 202 Group to oversee the squadrons and units based in the Egyptian Delta, and 211 Group to command the Wings and Squadrons over the front lines. Two Wings were re-numbered with designations they would make renowned for the rest of the war – 253 becoming 243 with four Hurricane and two Tomahawk squadrons, and 262 becoming 239 with three Hurricanes and three Kittyhawks.[22]

Although by early January Eighth Army had regained nearly all territory lost a year before, Rommel counter attacked almost immediately in late January. Once again Eighth Army had to retreat to the Gazala Line in Cyrenaica to make a stand. The Axis Panzerarmee once more in late May attacked breaking the Allied lines near El Adem. In early June 1942 Rommel instructed the Axis air forces to pound the Free French forces in the remote oasis of Bir Hakim into submission. Bir Hakim was a former Turkish fort, which the French gallantly defended from 26 May to 11 June, when they finally pulled back to join Eighth Army. The French had bought precious time. While the Luftwaffe diverted its efforts in this dubious strategy, Eighth Army was forced to retreat further from Gazala to Tobruk, but was able to do so virtually untouched by enemy aircraft attacks.[23]

Using squadrons such as Nos 3 and 450 Squadrons RAAF, with their recently introduced Kittyhawk fighter-bombers, able to carry 250lb and 500lb bombs, and medium bombers, WDAF was able to respond with attacks on enemy supply convoys and troop concentrations. In addition the small number of Spitfires, such as the Spitfire Mark VBs of No. 145 Squadron RAF flying as escorts for Hurricane fighter-bombers, were beginning to make their presence felt. It was fortunate, but also a sign that Tedder's strategy was beginning to pay off, that WDAF was achieving a measure of air superiority, enabling it to cut off many Luftwaffe and Regia Aeronautica attacks, and protect the retreating Eighth Army columns.[24]

Despite WDAF being much strengthened, close to its base airfields, and supplies in the Egyptian Delta, and with that advantage able to check the Axis air forces, Eighth Army was being pushed back again into Egypt. The delivery to WDAF of new and up to date aircraft was still highly susceptible to interception by Axis aircraft through the Mediterranean. Ferrying of aircraft from Britain remained mostly dependent upon the long and round-about route across Africa, which was slow and increasingly congested. A significant numerical advantage in aircraft over the Axis air forces still eluded WDAF.

A crisis point was approaching quickly. Holding onto the Cyrenaican ports to protect Malta and the sea routes, was now a lower priority. Eighth Army's very survival, and the whole Middle East was in the balance. By inference, Tedder's strategy that air power would make a crucial difference, and the future of the embryonic WDAF, were also approaching the acid test.

Notes
1. Owen, *Tedder*, pp. 121/2; Tedder, *With Prejudice*, pp. 32–4.
2. Tedder, op. cit., pp. 32–4.
3. Bowyer and Shores, *Desert Air Force at War*, pp. 6–9.
4. Bowyer and Shores, op. cit., p. 9; Owen, *Desert Air Force*, pp. 43–5.
5. Owen, *Tedder*, p. 134.
6. Tedder, op. cit., pp. 29–38.
7. Bowyer and Shores, op. cit., p. 10; Owen, *Tedder*, p. 136.
8. Owen, *Tedder*, pp. 138–9.
9. Ibid., pp. 139–40.
10. Ibid., pp. 140–1.
11. Bowyer and Shores, op. cit., pp. 10–11.
12. Owen, *Tedder*, pp. 142–4.
13. Tedder, op. cit., pp. 124–8.
14. Bowyer and Shores, op. cit., p. 11.
15. Owen, *Tedder*, pp. 142–4.
16. Bowyer and Shores, op. cit., pp. 11–12; Owen, *Desert Air Force*, p. 315.
17. Owen, *Tedder*, pp. 150–2.
18. Ibid., pp. 151–5.
19. Ibid., pp. 151–2.
20. Bowyer and Shores, op. cit., pp. 11–12; Owen, *Desert Air Force*, p. 315.
21. Owen, *Tedder*, pp. 151–5.
22. Bowyer and Shores, op. cit., p. 12.
23. Owen, *Tedder*, p. 160.
24. Bowyer and Shores, op. cit., p. 13; Vader, *Spitfire*, p. 108.

Chapter 1

Crossing Africa

Flight Lieutenant Lewis Bevis walked down the gangplank of an old Irish Sea cattle-boat in the port of Takoradi. It was September 1941 and he was ashore in the Gold Coast, West Africa. He had sailed from Greenock, Glasgow, first in a passenger liner to Gibraltar, before his second voyage south in the cattle freighter. Bevis, who was from London, had joined the RAF in 1940, gained his wings earlier in 1941 at Brize Norton and then trained on Tomahawk fighters.

Now he had to report to the Takoradi RAF base, and fly a Hurricane fighter thousands of miles across Africa to the Desert Air Force of RAF Eastern Command in Egypt.[1] The Desert Air Force (DAF), in its air war against the Axis air forces, and to support the embattled Eighth Army in the desert war against Rommel, was continually short of planes.

During 1941–42 in the North African campaign there were only three routes by which aircraft could be delivered to Egypt and the Middle East. By ship around the Cape of Good Hope, South Africa, then north to Port Sudan on the Red Sea was the most secure, but was the longest duration. Flying aircraft through the Mediterranean was extremely hazardous. The Luftwaffe had fighters based in North Africa, Sardinia, Sicily, Crete and other islands such as Pantelleria.

Irrespective of the threat of interception by Axis aircraft, RAF fighters from Gibraltar did not have the range to even reach Malta, although in early 1942 some did so by flying from aircraft carriers in the western Mediterranean, when they were within a one-way flight range of the besieged island. By ship to Malta or Cairo through the Mediterranean was far too dangerous to consider. In the first half of 1942, for instance, hardly any cargo ships completed the voyage to Malta, being sunk either by Axis aircraft or naval vessels.

The third route, flying via Gibraltar and the west coast of Africa across the Sahara to the Sudan and then north to Cairo, became the most dependable. Opened as a civil aviation route in 1937, it became a vital lifeline for delivering aircraft to the Middle East and in particular DAF in Egypt. In early 1941 the numbers of aircraft delivered on the cross-Africa route were, for example, 49 in March, 134 in April, 105 in May and 151 in June. The total flying distance for these aircraft was around 4,000 miles, broken up into stages for refuelling, before they reached RAF Eastern Command in Cairo.[2]

It may have become the most reliable and quickest route to ferry aircraft to Egypt, but it still presented both foreseeable and unforeseen dangers to pilots. The cross-Africa route was a daunting first-time flight across unknown terrain and skies, especially for the large number of inexperienced and recently trained pilots.

After a week or two of training and acclimatization at Takoradi, Bevis took off in a flight of six Hurricanes, on the first leg of the long haul to Egypt. The first day they followed a Bristol Blenheim in the lead for navigation, south to Lagos in Nigeria where they spent the night. Next morning they lifted off on a four hour flight to Kano in Northern Nigeria.

In the group with me was another Londoner, Rick. Petrol economy was important and we were instructed to fly at low revs and high boost to achieve this. After a little over an hour's flying, I developed engine problems with a loss of performance. I fell behind the flight and was advised by the leader to make my own way.

However, Rick decided to stay with me. Our flight was at 12,000 feet over thick cloud, when I explained to him over the R/T that if I descended below the cloud, I would not have enough power to regain height. He suggested that he should go down below the cloud and advise me of the terrain. Checking the course on my map, I saw that we could possibly be over mountains up to 5,000 feet, so I told him to wait. Rick did not do so and was found ten days later, dead, having descended into a mountain face.

I continued on, and no longer being in touch with Rick, decided I had to try to get below the cloud cover. I broke cloud at about 3,000 feet over high ground coming out just above the treetops, luckily to a landscape falling away in front. Being on course I was able to pick up the Niger river and, in time, landed at Minna where petrol reserves in 4-gallon cans were available.

The next day Bevis, with a full tank, was able to reach Kano. The ground crew there found that the Hurricane's engine required maintenance on its plugs, caused by the necessary over-boosting during the flight. This meant that he had to wait to join the next ferry flight of Hurricanes. When they arrived three days later, Bevis set off with them for the various stages via Maiduguri, El Geniena, El Fashr and Wadi Seidna across the southern Sahara to the Sudan. Despite Bevis and the other pilots having been flying since 0545 that morning, at the Wadi Seidna airfield the station officer made them refuel and take off on a seven-hour flight north to Luxor in Egypt. This next leg would be without the guiding Blenheim, which left on a flight to join a squadron in the Far East.

During the flight from El Fasher, Bevis had dropped his maps onto the floor of the Hurricane, intending to recover them on landing at Wadi Seidna.

Distracted by the orders of the station commander, he forgot to do so. Once airborne Bevis found himself thinking it would be easy to follow the other five Hurricanes.

After nearly an hour, we ran into a sandstorm, reducing visibility to nil. We got split up and now I was on my own. I made several attempts to land in the desert, pulling away at the last moment from rock-strewn areas. Finally I noticed a native village with a clear area nearby on which I landed. I was then able to recover the maps. While I was doing this, I was descended upon by a crowd of natives from the nearby village, riding donkeys and camels. While they gathered round, I pointed to place names on the map to establish my position. The name Abu Ahmed rang a bell with them, and that apparently was where I was.

The village headman gave Bevis a rope bed for the night, and he slept surprisingly well. In the morning by using sign language and pointing at chickens, he managed to get boiled eggs for his breakfast. However, when he reached the Hurricane, he found that the villagers had stripped it of the leather gun covers, his parachute and, among other loose items, his Very pistol, which was his only means of defence.

I started up the motor, surrounded by donkeys and camels. I had checked my fuel and the distance from Abu Ahmed to Luxor, and I reckoned I still had enough to get me there. I climbed to 8,000 feet and set course.

At a point some forty miles south of Luxor, where a low mountain chain crosses the Nile and there are river cataracts, the red fuel-warning light came on. I was shocked, very short of fuel, and wondering about the gauges. Looking around, I saw what appeared from high up to be a roadway.

However, when I got down to about 1,000 feet what had looked a suitable road from higher up was, in fact, a doubtful surface with banking on each side. Committed I made a good landing, but unfortunately hit a large boulder. This turned the aircraft off the road and onto its back, and I passed out.

Although unconscious for a while I was not seriously hurt. Eventually an Egyptian, an educated engineer working on the Nile, came to help me. He took me to a telephone. After some hours a truck arrived from Luxor with airmen seeing what they could recover from the Hurricane.

Bevis then returned to Luxor with the recovery crew, and in a few days was allocated another Hurricane in a group flight to Cairo.

On this last leg of the journey I flew into a *khamsin* (sandstorm). The desert sands are lifted by gale-force winds to heights of 10,000 feet. It gives you the impression of being just above the ground temporarily raised to 10,000 feet.

In the poor visibility once again I became separated from the rest of the flight. I climbed above the sandy murk to work out a plan, knowing that I required sufficient fuel to make a precautionary landing if necessary. With this in mind I decided that the best course was to try to land while I still had petrol in hand.

I let down into the sandstorm's cloud level, and immediately forward vision was reduced to nil. I continued to descend steadily by circling turns, all the while watching the air speed, gyro instruments and altimeter. At around 800 feet suddenly the colour around me changed from a reddish-brown to grey. This turned out to be the ground coming up. I levelled off, and landed into a 40mph wind. I rolled no more than a few hundred yards before coming to a stop.

I began to get out of the aircraft to look around, but as I was dressed only in shorts and a sleeveless shirt, I found the gritty wind stung too much, so I stayed in the cockpit. It was about 1500 hours. As the evening drew on, the storm abated as is usual in a *khamsin*. I took a look around in the dark, returning to the aircraft to try and get some sleep sitting up.

In the morning Bevis was able to walk around and inspect the area where he had landed. The storm began to regain its tempo, and he knew he needed to take off again soon.

I had landed in a small wadi with soft sand scattered through it. I started the engine and taxied to the far end. Several times the wheels sank ominously into the sand, making it feel as if the aircraft must go up on its nose. I then realized I would have to prepare a path. I began laying flat stones to try to make a firmer surface for take-off.

It was tedious back-breaking work. The temperature rose above 100. What little water I had in my flask I sipped economically throughout the day. By evening my confidence was slipping. I knew I was in for another night in the cockpit. I continued to gather stones for the take-off that I had put off to following morning. I also knew I was beginning to dehydrate.

Bevis spent another night sat upright in the Hurricane's cockpit. When he woke in the morning he realized his situation was desperate. His water was nearly all gone, and it was doubtful that he could last another day in the heat with no shelter. He had to get away at once. Otherwise he would die in this desert.

Then another blow struck me. When I pushed the starter button the engine wouldn't turn fast enough to fire. I now seemed to lose my power of reason. My mind started to wander back over past years. I thought of my early training – of school, Sunday school and God. Although I had been brought up strictly in the Church of England, I had in my late teens decided to be an agnostic. I reasoned this was the only way to be free and unencumbered with mythology. Yet now in my despair, I sought an answer from God.

Exhausted, demoralized, his lips burnt and tongue swollen with thirst, Bevis sank to his knees. He prayed for divine intervention.

I saw the faces of all those with whom I had argued and discussed religion. They seemed to scorn my present weakness, which drove me to my feet. I summoned the strength to unpack part of the tool kit and remove the engine cowling. I took out several plugs and, using my shirt dipped them into the petrol tank, I squeezed fuel directly into the motor.

Bevis knew that what he was doing was his last chance. Somehow his training kicked in and he concentrated on what he was doing, readying himself for the opportunity to fire up the Hurricane's engine, and lift the aircraft into the sky. He removed the copper wire on the throttle, intended only for emergency use, and then pressed the starter button. The engine turned, fired, but would it hold? For a few seconds the tension was unbearable. If the engine died, he was done for.

But the motor had caught properly. The airscrew was spinning. I put down 30 degrees of flap, held the stick back into my lap, and opened the throttle wide. The power was surging now, and the aircraft began to roll forward. Slowly, then faster, and faster. For the first 200 yards or so it was touch and go. The Hurricane bucked, but with the tail still held down I was airborne, hanging precariously on the prop.

Soon I was gathering flying speed. I kept the hood back and climbed into the still, clean air above the sand storm. After heading east for some forty minutes, I saw a town on the banks of the Nile. It appeared to be a military barracks and a landing strip beside it. It was Asyut, and I put down, and was taken to the Egyptian base hospital for a check-up.

Next day Bevis flew on to Kilo 8, his planned destination close to Cairo. Another Hurricane fighter with another pilot had arrived.[3]

* * *

In July 1942, unaware of the near disasters endured by pilots such as Flight Lieutenant Bevis and his Hurricane fighter, an all-Australian crew began a similar flight across Africa. They were to deliver a Hudson bomber to the RAF in Cairo.

18 July 1942: Delivery of RAF Hudson Aircraft FH372 from UK to Cairo

Transcript of log kept by Flying Officer John McKenzie (Navigator):

Day 1. 18 July 1942: Portreath (Cornwall) to Gibraltar

We took off at 0700 from Portreath, an all-Australian RAAF crew, Pilot Officer Murray Evans, Pilot Officer Peter Staughton, Flight Sergeant Don Baird (Radio), and myself. The Hudson's fuselage was jam packed with spare parts, even auxiliary fuel tanks in the cabin and bomb bay. A burned out Wellington at the end of the runway made me remember we had been restricted to just 300 rounds of ammunition. Over the Bay of Biscay we kept a vigilant watch out for Luftwaffe Ju88s or Arado Ar-196 reconnaissance float-planes. Whilst at the same time listening to our two engines cutting out for a period, when we heard our radio operator Don reporting that he was hearing German radio communications, we were all on edge.

After nearly six hours we struggled down through turbulence, to land at Gibraltar where the runway protruded out into the Strait. The main Gibraltar–Spain road crossed the runway's taxi path, and on the northern fringe of the aerodrome we could see the Spanish town of La Linea. The magnificent weather and colour of Gibraltar, and its availability of food and drink, made an impression on us compared with wartime UK.

Day 2. 19 July 1942: Gibraltar to Bathurst, The Gambia, West Africa

In good weather we left at 0700 on the longest leg of the trip, and were soon at a cruising height of 3,000 feet. We were following the coastline, with the desert country of first Morocco then Mauretania on our port side. With no radio or loop bearings, and me being too inexperienced to use sun shots capably, my navigation was not that respectable.

The high peaks of the Canary Islands poked out of clouds well to starboard. After several more hours above cloud cover, we decided to descend to have a look see. At 200 feet it was still as thick as pea soup, and there was a strong stench of the sea. We climbed back to 3,000 feet. Conditions began to clear, and the African coastline was still to port!

On sighting Dakar to port we watched for unfriendly Vichy French aircraft, then turned due east to the Gambia. We saw what we believed to be Bathurst aerodrome, and asked permission to land, and received approval. On our approach a herd of cattle straggled across the runway, and we had to go around again. We had taken eleven hours flying since departing Gibraltar.

Our plane was surrounded by African troops wearing slouch hats. We reported our landing to Bathurst control, to which we received the response, 'Where are you?' We had landed at the wrong aerodrome, and were told to stay put. The CO of the resident No. [200] Squadron RAF came aboard to fly our aircraft out. When asked why we had landed at the wrong aerodrome, we related that in Gibraltar we were briefed that there was only one aerodrome, and we couldn't miss it.

With a squall storm about to hit, the CO took off and flew us to the correct operating aerodrome. There we met some old Aussie mates with 200 Squadron. We put on our issued mosquito boots as malaria, scrub typhoid and other tropical diseases are endemic.

Days 3–10: Bathurst

On checking the aircraft compass we found it not working. With no spares available, we had to wait for a replacement from Gibraltar. We were allocated a batman, a young local boy named Lanning, who cooked breakfast for us, shone our shoes, made beds, prepared our bush showers etc. Seeing me in shorts, the Medical Officer told me to change out of my shorts into slacks, even though I had none with me, or he would put me on a charge.

I arranged to go to Bathurst in one of the Squadron's supply trucks, stepped aboard and sat down. Suddenly the loading of the truck by local natives, came to a standstill. For some reason, they were all staring at me seated in the truck. An irate Flight Sergeant appeared to sort out the delay. He took one look at me, and told me to take off one of my two wrist watches. I was wearing one navigator-issue watch, and another personal watch. Apparently the locals regarded someone wearing two watches, as being of great wealth and revered as awesome!

Our days were passed doing typical tourist things, such as swimming in the sea in the oppressive heat, seeing the sights, and taking photos. At last the spare parts and other gear arrived, and we reloaded the aircraft. The new compass was installed and tested, and we were ready to go again.

Day 10. 27 July 1942: Bathurst (The Gambia) to Takoradi (Ghana)

After saying our farewells to 200 Squadron RAF, and being briefed on the possibility of some severe weather, including line squalls, we took off at 0730 for our destination of Takoradi on the Gulf of Guinea. Once we were in the air we received a request to make a detour well south of our designated track, to search for possible survivors of a torpedoed ship, but we made no sightings. We arrived at Takoradi at 1700 after a flight time of 9.30 hours. It was mainly overcast and very humid, but we found our mess accommodation to be comfortable. We learned that Takoradi was the assembly point for Hurricanes being ferried to Egypt and the Middle East. The usual formation was 15–20 Hurricanes led by a Blenheim mother aircraft, which carried a navigator. The next day (Day 11) was a rest day in Takoradi, when we took a local bus for an outing to the nearest town, Sekonde. On our return to Takoradi, we retired early before our departure on the morrow.

Day 12. 29 July 1942: Takoradi to Kano (Nigeria)

At 0820 we took off. I saw that all the topographical maps on board were endorsed with the note – 'Not necessarily accurate – report inaccuracies on landing'. This was daunting for a relatively inexperienced navigator like myself. It was overcast below us, and remained so until we saw the junction of the River Niger, which in the clearer weather looked huge. The terrain gradually changed, tropical forests, to light vegetation, and then sparse as we neared Kano. We arrived at the Kano airfield at 1320, five hours flight time, landing on a very long runway. After we had checked into a spacious mess and quarters, we drove into Kano.

It was a big mud-walled city, and fascinating. A policeman decided to attach himself to us, and laid into the locals, who were all eager to touch us, with a heavy cane used to great effect. There was mixture of dress, colourful Nigerian and Arabian. There was a fantastic looking market outside the walls. Kano is a terminus for Arabs and East African traders, who arrive on camels. This brings a merging of races, complexions and attire. For very good prices, Peter bought a huge snakeskin, and Don some ebony wood carved bookends.

Day 13. 30 July 1942: Kano to El Geniena (West Sudan)

We took off at 0823, and once again I viewed the ominous warning on the charts regarding their accuracy. The terrain began to change to desert-like country. On my estimated time for arriving over what should be the huge Lake Chad, I was eager to see it and confirm our course. All the maps, if they were to be believed, showed Lake Chad as a big body of water, and I should have seen it by now. There was no sign of water anywhere. I nearly had a panic attack. I checked my navigation calculations, which seem correct, and peered down again looking for water. Then I realized Lake Chad was bone dry, with tracks across its desert-like bed.

We arrived at El Geniena at 1425 after six hours airborne, and made our first landing in desert conditions. We were under the impression we were landing at 15 feet higher than the desert runway, and hit the deck with a bone-jarring bang. In stinking heat, a huge Sudanese man in Arab dress welcomed us to the mess, where we were offered a tepid orange drink covered with flies. He had three vertical scars on each cheek, fairly common tribal markings. Egyptians refer to them as 'hundred and elevens'! Our aircraft suffered the indignity of being refuelled from four-gallon cans.

Day 14. 31 July 1942: El Geniena to Wadi Seidna (Sudan)

After taking off at 0800 in clear dry conditions, our flight of four hours and ten minutes was without incident. We arrived at 1210 to a busy aerodrome, and checked in to very comfortable permanent accommodation. There was some confusion as to our posting, with some crews being diverted to India. We were ordered to stay put until advised, and in the mess the local food had us guessing. For the first time we had contact with air crew of the US [Army] Air Forces.

When one of the Hurricanes being ferried to Egypt crashed in a near-by Muslim cemetery, the pilot survived, but in urgent need of emergency hospital care. We were ordered to fly him in our Hudson to Khartoum as gently as possible for hospitalization there. After arrival at Khartoum, and after we had seen him transferred safely to an ambulance waiting near the runway, we were thinking this could be a good opportunity for us to take trip into the Sudanese capital, and have a look around. Before we could disembark the AOC for the Khartoum area appeared and told us to 'Get that blankety-blank aircraft out of here!' Back in Wadi Seidna we found that confusion still reigned over our posting destination.

As the days drifted by, we got another opportunity to make a flight to Khartoum, which sits on the junction of the Blue and White Nile rivers. On this occasion we had the time to go into the city on the back of a unit supply truck. In the main street the rest of the crew hustled me into a store to buy me a topee hat, which was displayed in the window. They said it was because of my fair complexion. I objected, but the deal was done. Back on the back of the truck we drove on, but it was not long before my topee blew off, and was crushed by the following car. I had owned it for a full twenty minutes!

We had great fun buying ivory animal miniatures from the locals. In the bargaining we introduced them to 'double or quits', on the toss of a coin, which they loved. Then we were stupid enough to eat lunch in a local restaurant. Back at Wadi Seidna – disaster. Gyppy tummy, all of us for days. Also big black beetles appeared from somewhere. If they touched unprotected skin, blister formed. At one stage Peter Staughton was hospitalized with some suspected bug, but after several days discharged OK.

At last, after two weeks in Wadi Seidna, we were ordered to continue our flight north.

Day 29. 15 August 1942: Wadi Seidna to Wadi Halfa (Sudan), and then to Cairo, LG224

We took off at 0450 in clear conditions, following the Nile north. After three hours and twenty minutes, we landed at Wadi Halfa close to the Egyptian border. We were airborne again at 0945 the same day. After an uneventful flight we reached Cairo, and landed at 1410 at the nearby Landing Ground 224, finally delivering Hudson Bomber FH372.

While we were sent on some short leave, Don Baird was admitted to hospital with suspected malaria. He was back three days later on

18 August, when we flew the aircraft to LG108 Maintenance Unit for overhaul. This ended our delivery procedures. Our total flying time had been 56 hours and 30 minutes. Distance flown [from Portreath] was an estimated 7,900 nautical miles.

McKenzie and his crew then joined No. 459 Squadron Royal Australian Air Force (RAAF) based near Cairo, flying Wellington bombers on coastal patrols against Axis U-boats and other shipping.[4]

*   *   *

The first United States Army Air Forces' (USAAF) fighter formation to be deployed to North Africa, the 57th Fighter Group, also flew the cross-Africa route in July and August 1942. Some of their Curtiss P-40 Warhawk fighters came across the Atlantic on aircraft carriers to Accra, and were then flown from the carrier's deck to refuel at Accra RAF base, before, on the same day, in small groups with RAF bombers leading the way, flying to Lagos. From there they made the journey in stages similar to Bevis and his Hurricane to Egypt. By doing so they became the first USAAF group-strength unit to deploy into a combat area from the deck of a carrier and, once in Egypt became the first USAAF fighter group to go into action in North Africa.[5]

Other P-40 Warhawks were shipped to Accra in freighters, and re-assembled there. Lieutenant Mike McCarthy of 64th Fighter Squadron was one of those who flew the cross-Africa route from Accra, first north to Kano, then via Fort Lamy, El Fasher, Khartoum and Wadi Haifa to Cairo. McCarthy was a first generation Irish-American from Boston. He signed up for the Aviation cadet programme after Pearl Harbor in December 1941 and, at twenty-one years of age, gained his wings.[6]

In mid-1942 such was the dire situation with Eighth Army in North Africa being driven back by Rommel's Axis army that some aircraft were routed through the Mediterranean to Cairo. This decision was also taken presumably because of congestion on the cross-Africa route.[6] To deliver the latest Wellington Mark VIII torpedo-bomber to Cairo, and bolster the interdiction campaign which was seeking to blockade Rommel's supplies, it was decided to take the risk.

In the UK in July 1942 an Australian flight lieutenant, Bill McRae, had recently completed his final training as a pilot of a Wellington bomber, and was wondering what would come next. He and his crew, second pilot, navigator, wireless operator, rear and front gunners, were awaiting a posting to an operational squadron. Out of the blue and with no operational experience, they were given an unexpected and critically important mission.

We were handed a brand new Wellington Mark VIII, and ordered to fly to Cairo via Gibraltar and Malta. Wellingtons were normally used for bombing but this was rather a special one – festooned with radar aerials, associated instruments and equipment, and modified to carry torpedoes. It was to be used to locate and attack enemy vessels at night. At the time the equipment was highly secret and we were briefed on how to destroy the aircraft should we be forced down in enemy territory. I must say the thought occurred to me that my RAF superiors were taking a bit of a risk in entrusting this aircraft to me.

A ferry flight they called it! The later part of the flight would be at night into Malta to hopefully avoid enemy fighters, and I must confess I was none too confident of my ability to fly in the dark. My night flying training in England had been limited, first in winter with the reflected light from snow on the ground and a moon, then later on in summer when there were only a few hours of darkness.

Bill McRae was a twenty-nine-year-old from Sydney, Australia. At the outbreak of the Second World War he was working for the Bank of New South Wales in London. He joined the Royal Artillery and, in November 1940, was temporarily attached to the RAF with whom he learned to fly light aircraft for directing artillery. This included a spell with D Flight RAF in 1940 at Old Sarum, where trials were being conducted with Air Observation Post (AOP) aircraft. A year later, and impatient to be flying operations, McRae transferred permanently to the RAF, and in April 1942 commenced training as a pilot of Wellington bombers, which was successfully completed by the beginning of July 1942.

At 0800 on 29 July 1942 we departed Portreath in Cornwall, and reached Gibraltar at 1600. No problems, except for a little excitement when we first sighted the Rock. It was after I had asked my navigator to leave his office, and come up front to see the end result of his labours. Suddenly the aircraft began to behave in the most peculiar manner. The airspeed fell away and we began to lose height. I had to open the throttles fully to maintain height, and had visions of ditching in the sea.

After a couple of minutes on full power trying to maintain height, I realized that the flaps were fully down. The navigator had accidentally put his hand on the flap lever, when he was leaning over to get a better view. After England, Gibraltar was another world, sun, clear blue sky, hot weather, plenty of food and drink, cigarettes and even chocolate. We got little sleep that night as we were in a hut next to the runway, and there were constant landings and take-offs.

At 1600 the next day we took off on the 1,000 mile hop to Malta. At the briefing we were told to keep radio silence, and call up Malta about half an hour before reaching the island. They would come back with a course to steer to reach the aerodrome. Then just before we were due, they would switch on some searchlights. We were warned that the enemy might intercept our wireless message and reply with a course to take us to Sicily, which was only some eighty miles north of Malta.

On arrival in Malta we were advised to leave someone on board the aircraft, otherwise emergency rations, parachutes and anything moveable would be stolen. As we left we were joined by another Wellington, flown by a friend with whom I had been training for nine months. Not long after take-off we were surprised to see him turn back. Because of keeping radio silence we did not know why.

McRae's flight in the latest Wellington Mk VIII, equipped with secret radar instruments, was uneventful until they neared the island. On calling Malta they were duly given a course, but then were enveloped in low cloud, and unable to see the ocean or the horizon.

We were at 3,000 feet and there was a half moon. But with the cloud there were no searchlights from Malta to be seen. After circling around for ten minutes, we thought we spotted them through the cloud. Keeping in mind we might be over Sicily, and also aware there were hills reaching up to 700 feet in Malta, we carefully descended. Suddenly there was break in the cloud, and an island off the Malta coast appeared. Then we caught sight of the aerodrome flare path. We touched down at 0100 on 31 July, and my night landing was reasonable.

When we reported to the aerodrome control officer, the first thing he said was, 'You seemed to be wandering around a long time. We were beginning to get a bit worried.' I felt like replying, 'So was I'. He told us to taxi the aircraft away into a blast shelter, and be back at daybreak. We then went into the mess for a cup of tea and ran into a party. The boys were celebrating the escape of a Beaufort torpedo-bomber crew, who had been shot down by the Italian Navy.

The chaps in the mess were a mixed bunch – English, Australians, Canadians and New Zealanders. One of the Canadians was Flight Sergeant Beurling, who was something of a local hero, a Spitfire fighter ace with some twenty victories. They were a happy crowd and morale was high. One could sense the special bond that exists between those who go to battle in the sky. We went back to the aircraft and tried to sleep.

Next morning McRae and his crew took a trip into the main town of Valetta, took a ride in a horse-drawn 'taxi', saw the bomb damage, air raid shelters in the cliffs, the lean and hungry look of the locals, and endured a couple of air raids accompanied by bursts of fighter gunfire.

We reported back to the aerodrome and at a briefing at 1700 for the flight to Egypt, we were not told much. The main thing was to keep an eye out for some units of the Italian Navy. It would be unhealthy to fly straight over them. We were told to taxi out half an hour before darkness and to leave at last light. However, if an air raid began, to get off the ground immediately and fly south at low altitude.

We duly taxied to the take-off runway, switched off, disembarked and waited outside in the warm air. At this point three passengers turned up – a submarine commander and two Dutch seamen, whose ships had been bombed in Malta. About ten minutes before darkness the air raid sirens went and the aerodrome controller started flashing a green light; this meant 'Get going fast!'

We scrambled aboard, and once I had hurried the Wellington on to the runway, I pushed the throttles fully open. Unhappily there was a cross wind blowing, and after a couple of hundred yards the aircraft swung off the runway. I had to stop, turn around, taxi back and start again. By the time we took off, searchlights were sweeping around, and guns beginning to flash. Looking on from a couple of miles out to sea the view was spectacular – flares, flashes, heavy flak and searchlights, like a large fireworks display.

Not far off Alexandria we sighted a submarine on the surface in the half light of dawn. When it signalled us I had visions of it being in distress. I told the wireless operator to stand by to report their plight. Their message was, 'Good morning'. Soon after we turned in over the mouth of the Nile and soon the Pyramids stood out in the now clear morning light. One could not have wished for a better landmark at journey's end. I flew around them and landed at a nearby aerodrome.

I think the most lasting impression of the flight was the meeting with those pilots in Malta. Being my first flight out of training, it was the first time I had mixed with, and been accepted by, operational types. It gave me the feeling of being a member of a select brotherhood. As a crew I think we realized that the long haul of training was behind us, and ahead lay the excitement and dangers, and the exhilaration (sometimes), the fears (always), and the cruelty (often) of wartime operational flying. As a crew we had suddenly come of age.[7]

Later McRae would learn why his pilot friend flying the other Wellington had turned back, shortly after they had left Gibraltar. The hatch over the pilot's seat had blown open, and could not be closed in flight. He then completed the flight to Malta on the next evening. There he was commandeered by RAF Malta. On a subsequent bombing operation from Malta he was forced to make a crash-landing. While attempting to free his rear gunner who was trapped in his turret in the burning aircraft, he was badly burned and his rear gunner was lost.[8]

McRae and his screw had delivered the latest Mk VIII Wellington torpedo-bomber, which would play a critical role in the El Alamein battles. He did not know it at the time, but it would be another Australian pilot who would use this new weapon to great effect in the final struggle with Rommel's Axis forces.

Notes
1. Veteran's account, F/Lt Bevis.
2. Tedder, *With Prejudice*, pp. 35–168.
3. Veteran's account, Bevis, op. cit.
4. Veteran's account, F/Lt McKenzie, No. 459 Squadron RAAF.
5. Molesworth, *57th Fighter Group*, pp. 15–16.
6. McCarthy, *Air-to-Ground Battle for Italy*, pp. 16–18.
7. Tedder, op. cit., p. 355.
8. Veteran's account, S/Ldr McRae, Nos 104 and 146 Squadrons RAF.

Chapter 2

El Alamein, July 1942: the four-month air war begins

It was late in the day on 3 July 1942 near El Alamein. The Axis Panzerarmee Afrika was making a major thrust at a protruding salient in the British Eighth Army's line which was held by the 1st South African Division. From the west, out of a dying sun, a line of Junkers Ju87 Stuka dive-bombers grew larger, as it headed for the smoke and dust of the battle. They were intent on blasting a hole in the Eighth Army defences through which the German armour might surge. Unbeknown to the Luftwaffe pilots, their flight direction and their bombing run had been tracked.

That first week of July 1942 saw what is now called the first battle of El Alamein. After a 400-mile advance that had finally taken Tobruk, Field Marshal Rommel was intent on continuing the drive of his Axis Army to gain final victory in Egypt. Once there the problems of his over-extended supply lines would disappear. Close to Egypt's north coast, the desert war of over two years seemed to have reached a tipping point. The British Eighth Army had been forced back to within some sixty-five miles from Alexandria. From there the Nile delta was only a few miles to the east, and a rail line ran south to Cairo.

Even as the Stuka dive-bombers began to peel off to commence their screaming dives, a squadron of Hawker Hurricane fighters of the Desert Air Force (DAF) caught them in the act. The Stuka dive-bomber, apart from its terrifying steep dive, had a poor top speed at no more than 255mph in the Ju87 types D and G. In contrast, the Hurricane had a maximum speed of around 320 to 330mph. In addition, the Hurricane was far more manoeuvrable, with a faster rate of climb, a higher service ceiling, a tighter turning capability, and was better armed.

For the German flyers the situation was even more unfavourable. In a supreme irony they were in the gun-sights of No. 1 Squadron SAAF, and the South African pilots knew that their mission was to protect their countrymen on the ground. Like a flock of startled seagulls attempting to evade swooping birds of prey, the Stukas dumped their bombloads and dived towards the desert floor. The South African squadron leader followed and made the first kill. His fire probably hit a fuel tank, causing the Stuka in his sights to explode in front of him.

One by one the Hurricanes, now coordinated by their Squadron Leader on radio, pounced on the fleeing Stukas. Above them 274 Squadron RAF had engaged the Luftwaffe's top cover of Messerschmitt Bf109 fighters. Only one Hurricane was lost and one damaged, as the two DAF squadrons shot down thirteen Stukas and one Bf109. It was the highest haul of downed Stukas in one day, and the RAF's C-in-C Middle East, Air Vice Marshal Sir Arthur Tedder, visited 1 Squadron SAAF to congratulate the pilots.[1] Within the overall desert war the engagement may have been a small aerial battle, but in the culminating struggle for North Africa the DAF victory was not just a straw in the wind.

*   *   *

The Allies' underlying strategy in North Africa was to strangle the Germans' sea and air supply routes from Sicily and southern Italy. As yet it had not stopped Rommel's onward drive, attacking the Gazala Line in late May, to push Eighth Army back towards Egypt. On 21 June Tobruk surrendered, and a week later on 28 June Rommel's forces captured Mersa Matruh. Eighth Army lost some 5,000 casualties, and around 40,000 men taken prisoner.

These victories, besides gaining the port of Tobruk and an overall advance into western Egypt, brought Rommel some welcome alleviation of increasing supply shortages. It was estimated that the Axis forces captured around 2,000 vehicles, 1,400 tons of fuel, and 5,000 tons of other supplies left behind by Eighth Army. It was enough for Rommel to press on, and force Eighth Army into a 300-mile retreat to El Alamein in Egypt.[2]

Throughout June the DAF had maintained operations from dusk to dawn, Wellington bombers by night and Bostons every hour during the day, to check Rommel's armoured columns. In escort top cover and fighter-bomber roles, fighter squadrons were flying as many as seven operations a day. Some individual fighter pilots even did five sorties in a day.

When pilots returned to their airfield and their mess, often just a makeshift tent, frequently one or more would be missing. Carefree young men were no longer that. Adrenalin fed boisterous remarks from some, but the strain in their faces betrayed what was inside. They had confronted fear, and knew what it was, what it meant. Those who had returned had conquered that fear, multiple times. Until the next time. New pilots with no combat experience arriving at a squadron would look at the experienced flyers, and wonder if they could prove themselves.[3]

The forward pressure of Axis forces on the ground meant that the safety of DAF forward landing grounds was at risk. Withdrawals by Eighth Army led, on 18 June, to DAF and Eighth Army HQs being forced to separate. Then, on the evening of 26 June, Tedder and Air Vice Marshal Arthur Coningham, C-in-C of DAF, learnt that an enemy column had outflanked Eighth Army lines to the south of Mersa Matruh. It was within only twenty miles of DAF fighter airfields.[4]

It was too late for squadrons to take off and reach more easterly landing grounds, so Coningham sent out DAF's own armoured cars to try and act as a delaying screen. Luckily the German tanks did not push forward during the night and at dawn next day, 27 June, Coningham had his fighter squadrons and Advanced Air HQ flying farther back to airfields inside the Egyptian border. It would prove to be a wise decision.[5]

In yet another retreat DAF ground staff of all ranks once again did a great salvage job, leaving little or nothing for the enemy. Tedder himself watched on 28 June as around 100 men managed to lift a Spitfire manually onto a truck. The plane was unfit to fly off, and no-one wanted to leave it for the Germans. Some fighter wings also claimed to have developed the ability to move, forward or back to another airfield within fifteen minutes. Despite having to watch DAF retreat with Eighth Army, Tedder still felt that the strategy of continuous attacks on Rommel's supplies must ultimately bring a decisive crisis for the enemy's lengthening supply lines. Benghazi and Tobruk would now become the main Axis ports to be targeted by DAF.[6]

Also in those final days of June, an early morning reconnaissance flight from DAF's No. 450 Squadron RAAF, found Axis forces near Fuka concentrating ready for Rommel's next offensive. Then for two days the whipped-up sand of a *khamsin* restricted the movement of ground forces, as well as air operations by both sides.[7]

* * *

The first battle of El Alamein began on 1 July. German panzers and motorized panzergrenadiers attacked the north-east of the British lines, and during the night Field Marshal Rommel went forward to the HQ of the 90th Light Division of Afrika Korps. The German offensive was met by a massive bombardment from Eighth Army artillery and DAF bombing operations. Rommel himself was personally pinned down with his chief of staff in the open for two hours by the shelling and bombing.[8]

Even at night DAF gave Rommel's attacking columns no respite. As they approached the Axis lines, pilots of Wellingtons and other light bombers peered expectantly into the dark. They knew that in a few minutes they would see flares burst over the target area, and illuminate Axis tanks and vehicles. Night after night Fairy Albacores of Nos 821 and 826 Squadrons from their airfields of the Royal Navy's Fleet Air Arm near Alexandria, would go in first as pathfinders. They dropped their flares over the target area, approximately timed to be fifteen minutes before the arrival of the Wellington bombers.[9]

The aerial bombardment included a squadron of Boston light bombers of 3 Wing SAAF, who had been sustaining daily sorties without a break for seven weeks. For four days the Bostons maintained a 'shuttle service' of an eighteen-bomber raid every hour, nicknamed the 'the Boston Tea Party'. The Eighth Army artillery's new 6-pounder anti-tank guns, the introduction of the American Grant tank with its 75mm main gun, and DAF's bombing and strafing, caused significant losses to the 15th and 21st Panzer and 90th Light Divisions. For four days DAF struck at both the thrust by the Panzerarmee Afrika, and Axis reserve movements.[10]

On 5 July Rommel conceded that his planned attack was in disarray, and called a halt. For the rest of July it enabled Eighth Army, still under the direct command of General Auchinleck, to initiate a number of counter-attacks. Some came to naught, as when the inexperienced 23 Armoured Brigade were nearly destroyed by 21st Panzer, and an Australian infantry battalion was cut off by panzers and forced to surrender.

However, many attacks against Italian infantry not only were successful and brought the capture of many prisoners, but also caused German units to re-deploy rapidly to plug breaches in the Axis lines. By 28 July Auchinleck found Eighth Army also in dire need of fresh troops and put an end to offensive operations. Although the first battle of El Alamein had ground to a stalemate, at least the Panzerarmee Afrika had been stopped.[11]

*   *   *

During the air war in July other factors, in addition to the Axis' shortage of fuel and other supplies, coincided to prevent the final defeat of Eighth Army. In support of Rommel's gains prior to July, the Luftwaffe and the Regia Aero-nautica (Italian Royal Air Force) had over-extended themselves. A deteriora-tion in Axis aircrew capability, and aircraft serviceability, allowed Eighth Army to withdraw, re-position and recover, without any significant enemy attack from the sky. At the same time Air Vice Marshal Tedder ordered every type of bomber and fighter from RAF Middle East Command, together with growing support from USAAF, into a round-the-clock ground attack on Axis forces.[12]

Tedder's response was only to be expected. He himself had been central in the development of air force strategic thinking and, in respect of support for the army, the identification of three principal needs. These demands on which to base decisions on army support were: speed of information, speed of decision, and centralized control to avoid dissipation of air resources. In late-1941 Prime Minister Churchill issued clear guidance in an air support directive:

> When the General Officer Commanding-in-Chief advises that a land battle is in prospect, the Air Officer Commanding-in-Chief will give him all possible aid irrespective of other targets, however attractive.[13]

Although the arrival of some Spitfires was a morale booster, the superior performance of the Luftwaffe's Bf109 over Hurricanes and Kittyhawks, despite the latter's ability to out-turn a 109, meant that Allied pilots fought on with inferior aircraft. Despite having lost 202 aircraft in the six weeks to 7 July, with some fighter squadrons having suffered 100 per cent losses and most at only 50 per cent strength, in the final week of July DAF alone flew 5,458 sorties.

Overall, in response to Tedder's orders, in the four weeks to 27 July the RAF in Egypt and Palestine flew more than 15,000 sorties, without counting anti-shipping operations. Besides better serviceability and a numerical advantage in aircraft sorties over the efforts by the Axis air forces, the DAF did enjoy another benefit. The time elapsed between a request from Eighth Army for air support, and scrambling an aircraft into the air in response, had been reduced to an average of only thirty-five minutes.[14]

The result was that during July 1942 the Army and RAF together had rebuffed Rommel's plan to drive through to Alexandria, Cairo and the Egyptian delta. From both radio intercepts and interrogation of prisoners, it was also learned that the efforts of the RAF, DAF and Royal Navy across the Mediterranean were choking off the Axis supplies. On the ground Rommel's supply lines now stretched back to Tobruk. However, Tobruk and long-haul vehicle convoys from its port were being heavily bombed by DAF. Bringing supplies overland from farther west, Benghazi and even Tripoli, was even more tenuous. Despite Alamein being only sixty-five miles from Alexandria and 150 from Cairo, the Luftwaffe was short of both aircraft and fuel. Together with DAF's better supplies situation and close proximity of airfields, it meant that Rommel dare not risk launching an air raid on British bases and airfields in the rear.[15]

In London Churchill told the House of Commons that in Eighth Army's retreat from Tobruk, it was the DAF that had saved the day, and telegraphed Tedder:

> I am watching with enthusiasm the brilliant exertions of the Royal Air Force ... The days of the Battle of Britain are being repeated far from home. We are sure you will be to our glorious Army the friend that endureth to the end.[16]

For any further offensive, Rommel had to wait for re-supply. With a burgeoning ascendancy in the air, DAF and RAF Middle East must prevent any such thing. As well as continuing to bomb and strafe the withdrawing Axis columns, DAF and other Allied air forces re-focused their operations not only on bombing Axis airfields, but also on interdiction of the Axis life-lines, bombing air and sea transport on supply routes from Sicily and mainland Italy.[17]

To mount and maintain ever-widening air interdiction operations against Axis shipping, U-boats and aircraft across North Africa, the Mediterranean,

Sicily and southern Italy, the sustaining of the morale of air crew was essential. In the face of the ever present and inevitable losses, the possibility of air-sea or desert rescue of a downed crew was an important morale booster, and something airmen could cling to.

*   *   *

As well as rescuing pilots and their crews who were shot or forced down either in the desert or at sea, RAF air-sea rescue squadrons played a crucial role by supplying, and occasionally transporting, patrols of the Long Range Desert Group (LRDG) of Eighth Army. Sometimes these missions, regularly flying only 200 feet above the sea or the desert floor, could require a hazardous landing in a remote desert location.

Besides the designated Royal Australian Air Force (RAAF) squadrons in DAF, such as Nos 3 and 450 Squadrons of Kittyhawk fighters and fighter-bombers in 239 Wing RAF, many Australians and other nationalities served with RAF squadrons. Australian Flight Lieutenant Frank Jensen was twenty-five years old and from Sydney, first attached to 230 RAF Squadron as a pilot of Sunderland flying boats, then in 294 Squadron RAF flying Wellington bombers in air-sea rescue. On a flight to find and rescue the crew of a downed aircraft, Frank faced the hazardous landing on remote desert sands.

I landed the Wellington, a twin-engined medium bomber which was nicknamed in the RAF as a 'Wimpey', on a flat expanse marked out on the ground by the downed crew. We pulled up easily and quickly in the soft sand. The trouble was that we would need a much longer stretch to take-off again, ideally around 900 yards to reach lift-off speed.

While the downed crew including some casualties were boarded, I paced out what was available for take-off. At about 600 yards I came to a sharp steep drop into a wadi, about twenty feet across. That was it, about 600 yards, no more. It seemed nothing like enough.

I had to think quickly. We could not sit around wondering what to do. We were sitting ducks for any Luftwaffe fighters, or a chance Axis ground patrol. It was late morning, the heat building up, and we did not want to be trying to fly back when darkness fell.

Once everyone was aboard, I told them all to sit or lie as close as they could to where the wing struts joined the fuselage, to make the tail of the plane as light as possible. Then I started the engines, warming them up fast. I needed to reach maximum speed and momentum quickly, before we came to the end of that 600 yards.

Revving the engines well beyond the recommended maximum, I pulled up the rudder but kept the brakes on. With the engines screaming, and everything vibrating, I let go the brakes. We lurched forward, and I fought to stop the nose powering into the ground. In no time we were tearing across the sand, and the wadi was coming up at an alarming rate.

Suddenly reaching over the edge of the wadi we were airborne, but not climbing. Luckily the ground on the other side of the wadi was a bit lower. We dropped and hit the deck and bounced up. Then we hit the ground again, and bounced up a second time.

Those rescued crewmen in the back were lucky they could not see out. I held the throttles on full power and prayed. Slowly, gradually, barely above the sand, we began to climb. As we gained some height a cheer rang out from the back of the plane. It had been a near thing.[18]

Rescuing a downed air crew may seem to have been a minor operation but it was invaluable for the spirit of Allied airmen. The squadron's other pilots and ground crew would wait and hope the missing crew had beaten the odds. And news of a successful rescue would quickly spread.

* * *

By August 1943 the Allies' interdiction of Axis sea and air supplies had begun to seriously blunt Rommel's offensive capability both on the ground and in the air. Because of over-extended supply lines and reduced supplies, not only in North Africa but at their bases around the Mediterranean, the Luftwaffe was being starved of maintenance parts, equipment, replacement aircraft, fuel, food and supplies of every kind.

At the beginning of July at their airfields in Greece, Crete, Libya, and Egypt, the Luftwaffe had some 720 aircraft of all types. Because of their supply constraints however only about 33 per cent were serviceable at any one time. It all meant that over the El Alamein battlefield they could put only a maximum of some 100 fighters and dive-bombers in the air at any time.

In contrast, with more reliable and shorter supply lines in Egypt, the Allied air forces enjoyed a serviceability rate of close to 70 per cent for more than 900 aircraft. Furthermore they could also call on the long-range Liberator bombers of the RAF and USAAF Halverson detachment, the Beaufighters of 201 Naval Co-operation Group, and the Royal Navy's Fleet Air Arm. The result was that Allied aircraft were able to fly around a peak of 360 sorties, in a mix of medium and light bombers, fighters and fighter-bombers, producing a numerical advantage of up to four to one over the Luftwaffe.[19]

Allied aircraft from both Malta and Egypt hit ports in Sicily and Italy, enemy shipping heading for North Africa, and Axis-held ports such as Tobruk, Benghazi and Tripoli. DAF bombing and strafing on road convoys eroded further the reduced supplies that did get through. Increasing operational dominance allowed Allied air forces to extend and intensify interdiction sorties.

Those wide-ranging operations demanded more and more a continuing pipeline of replacement aircraft and crew, so that DAF could support Eighth

Army as it struggled to hold off and stem Rommel's advance.[20] Despite congestion delays, the circuitous ferry route across Africa from Takoradi was beginning to pay off in feeding through both new aircraft and aircrew. During August, after flying their P-40 Warhawks over the trans-Africa route, pilots from the USAAF 57th Fighter Group began joining DAF in Egypt to gain combat experience, flying with squadrons operating P-40 Kittyhawks and Tomahawks.

In this period DAF became ever more integrated with Eighth Army. Its squadrons, administrative and other rear units such as Maintenance and Supply, had developed a capability to sustain operations for as long as three weeks without any re-supply. Air Vice Marshal Tedder expressed the view that the increasing air dominance of the DAF, together with the curtailment of Axis supplies by sea or air through the Mediterranean, had been the decisive factor in beating back Rommel in the first battle of Alamein.[21]

However, the situation did not translate well into reports to Allied High Commands, or in the media. In London Churchill and his government were facing dissatisfaction with defeat upon defeat, not only in North Africa but around the world. From a distance the stalemate of the first battle of Alamein did not look much different from another defeat.

General Auchinleck, as well as being C-in-C Middle East, had taken direct command of Eighth Army since sacking Major General Ritchie. After the first appointee to take over command of Eighth Army, Major General Gott, was killed in an air crash, Churchill appointed General Bernard Montgomery to take up the position. On 12 August Montgomery arrived in Egypt to command Eighth Army, but at first was reporting to Auchinleck. Three days later, on 15 August, Auchinleck was relieved by General Alexander.

One of the first actions taken by Montgomery was to move his main HQ forward to Burg el Arab on the coast, closer to the front lines. Co-located together in command tents only a short walk apart were General Staff (Operations), General Staff (Intelligence) and the combined Army Air Support Control. Around the same time Army Air Support Control No. 5 (AASC No. 5), arrived at Burg el Arab to join AASC No. 2, with whom it had trained in UK. A joint G (Operations/G (Air)/G (Intelligence) operations room was established in Army HQ, which was reminiscent of a fighter control room.

Placing these main command groups together so far forward did more than foster collaboration. It demonstrated a confidence in the coming offensive and in DAF's increasing air superiority over the Luftwaffe. Montgomery was in full agreement with Tedder on the need to win the air war first and that DAF and Eighth Army must fight as one entity.[22]

On the night of 30/31 August Rommel launched another attack to the south of El Alamein, aiming to outflank Eighth Army defences in the Ruweisat and Alam el Halfa ridges. Known as the Battle of Alam el Halfa, or the Second Battle of El Alamein, it was with hindsight a reckless gamble. The

Panzerarmee Afrika had only 200 German tanks and 281 Italian medium or light tanks, to take on more than 700 of Eighth Army. It had requisitioned 6,000 tons of fuel for the attack, but received less than a third, which was only enough for one week.

Rommel himself was sick, with a nose infection and a swollen liver, which confined him to his vehicle. In contrast Montgomery was fresh. He was also supremely confident and stated that there would be no more retreat. However, his description of Eighth Army's soldiers as demoralized is not one with which many of them would have agreed; Alexander's assessment of them as 'brave but baffled' was more accurate – after all they had just defeated Panzerarmee Afrika and brought it to a standstill. Eighth Army also had much shorter supply lines from the Egyptian delta, and not least the increasing edge in effectiveness of the DAF in the air war.[23]

*   *   *

In the background to the main struggles on the ground and in the air at El Alamein, an apparently minor contest in the air was taking place, which would have far-reaching and significant consequences. From about June 1942 the Luftwaffe began using high-altitude reconnaissance aircraft, three specialized Junkers bombers, Ju86Ps, which were able to make a weekly incursion over Eighth Army's positions.

In response a number of DAF Spitfires were modified to form a High Altitude Flight, of No. 103 Maintenance Unit based at Aboukir near Alexandria. At first, however, it was found that, even a lighter and highly-tuned Spitfire VB restricted to just two machine guns was at the limit of its range to intercept a Ju86P, which was able to operate at around 40,000 feet.

Because the Spitfire had little time to engage, on 29 August a new tactic was introduced; two Spitfires would hunt as a pair. Pilot Officer Eric 'Jumbo' Genders and Pilot Officer Gold climbed their Spitfires up to a Ju86P. In the event, perhaps two pairs of eyes meant that they had found the intruder quicker. Closing on the Ju86 Genders had time to hit it with a brief burst of machine-gun fire. It was enough to force it to ditch in the sea.[24]

Rommel had chosen 30/31 August, a moonlit night, to launch his attack on Alam el Halfa, now seen as the second battle of El Alamein. Once again Albacores from naval air stations near Alexandria, dropped parachute flares to add to the light from the moon over the enemy's armoured advance. Bomb-aimers in the follow-up Wellingtons could pick out the German panzers and support vehicles in silhouette against the pale desert sand.

To achieve victory on the ground Montgomery gave a very high priority to there being the utmost co-operation between the Army and the RAF. Only two weeks into his command, and in his first battle with Eighth Army, Montgomery was depending heavily upon DAF and RAF Eastern Command to repay his trust. Another defeat and retreat would put Rommel at the gates of Alexandria and Cairo. It would be a catastrophe for both Montgomery and the Allies.

Notes

1. Owen, *The Desert Air Force*, pp. 128–9.
2. Terraine, *The Right of the Line*, p. 375.
3. Wellum, *First Light*, pp. 100–1.
4. Tedder, op. cit., pp. 304–5.
5. Ibid., p. 375.
6. Ibid., pp. 306–11.
7. Owen, op. cit., pp. 127.
8. Ibid.
9. Terraine, op. cit., pp. 375–7.
10. Smith (AASC No. 5), *Air Support in the Desert*, Ref. McNeill, 1983–86, King's College London, p. 6.
11. Bierman, and Smith, *Alamein*, pp. 204–7.
12. Terraine, op. cit., pp. 375–7.
13. Smith, op. cit., p. 3.
14. Terraine, op. cit., pp. 375–7; Tedder, op. cit., p. 317.
15. Owen, op. cit., pp. 128–9.
16. Ibid.
17. Ibid.
18. Veteran's account, F/Lt Frank Jensen.
19. Owen, op. cit., p. 131.
20. Ibid.
21. Ibid., pp. 131–6.
22. Smith op. cit., pp. 5–7.
23. Barnett, *The Desert Generals*, pp. 260–6.
24. Thomas, *Spitfire Aces of North Africa and Italy*, pp. 9–12.

Chapter 3

El Alamein, the Second and Third battles, and the first No Fly Zone

Before dawn on 31 August, in the Battle of Alam el Halfa, DAF bombers were in the air. The combined aerial and artillery bombardment, which continued throughout the day, slowed the advance of the German armour, and prevented the Panzers from driving beyond the Eighth Army minefields. Over the next two days, 1 and 2 September, Allied bombing raids were mounted round the clock, reaching 668 bomber and fighter sorties on 2 September. The Axis troops had no respite day or night, particularly suffering from Allied bombs which were fitted with extended nose rods to detonate above ground. With losses mounting and no reserves of fuel, on the afternoon of 3 September Rommel had to order a retreat.

The three columns of withdrawing tanks, guns and vehicles were harried from the south by 7th Armoured Division, from the north and east by artillery shelling, and overhead by the ever present DAF aerial bombing. The only recourse for the Panzerarmee was to pull back into defensive positions, and wait once again to be re-supplied. In a message of thanks to the RAF, Montgomery stated that without their magnificent cooperation the battle could not have been won.

In the Alam el Halfa battle the Panzerarmee lost thirty-six German and eleven Italian tanks, and seventy-six tanks damaged although recovered. Worse was the loss of 370 'soft skinned' vehicles, which DAF was targeting to further exacerbate Rommel's supply shortages. Overhead, where the Hurricanes escorting the bombers were inferior to the Bf109s and Macchi 202s, DAF lost forty-three fighters and thirteen bombers. Axis air forces lost twenty-two fighters, plus eighteen 'probables', and twenty-six bombers, of which around a half were Stukas pounced on by Spitfires. [1]

Although Rommel withdrew on the ground, the air battle for supremacy went on unabated. On 6 September another Luftwaffe Ju86P reconnaissance flight was spotted, and Pilot Officers Genders and Gold scrambled. The Junkers bomber was about fifty miles east of Alexandria, but when it saw the fast closing Spitfires, it turned back out to sea. Increasing their speed, Genders and Gold gave chase.

Genders caught up with the Ju86P first, and machine-gunned its fuselage and starboard engine, which gave out smoke. With only three gallons of fuel remaining, and now 100 miles out to sea, Genders had to turn away. At a few thousand feet lower altitude, Gold watched the crippled Junkers bomber as it lost height, then finished it off.

While Gold had sufficient fuel to return to Aboukir, Genders ran empty when still out of sight of land. He baled out, somehow survived his dumping into the sea, and began to swim southwards. For twenty-one hours he swam, before being washed up onto an empty Egyptian beach. After an amazing open sea swim, he luckily found help, and returned to his base at Aboukir. Genders and Gold had downed two of the three Ju86Ps in nine days. The two pilots had reduced the Luftwaffe's high altitude reconnaissance operations over the rear of Eighth Army to an ineffective level.

By the end of August and the start of the battle for Alam el Halfa, DAF had three squadrons of Spitfires with an edge over the Bf109s and Macchi 202s. At the time the Bf109 had a maximum speed of around 350mph, and the Macchi 202 up to 370mph. Although the Spitfire Mark VB had a top speed of 378mph, the need to fit a tropical filter in North Africa reduced this maximum. However, other superior attributes of the Spitfire, such as its acceleration, turning and manoeuvrability, together with the skill of the pilot, were able to give it an advantage.

Not surprisingly, on 7 September came the first Spitfire pilot to claim five victories in North Africa. Flight Lieutenant Bruce Ingram, a twenty-one-year-old New Zealander of No. 601 Squadron RAF, shot down a Bf109 to become the first Spitfire 'ace' of the desert war.[2]

*   *   *

By mid-October 1942 at El Alamein, the interminable desert war seemed to have reached another impasse. Many in Britain must have thought that for the Eighth Army, once again with its back up against Alexandria and the Egyptian delta, its final defeat by the Panzerarmee Afrika was not far away.

By contrast the British HQ Middle East maintained a confidence that their victory would be the eventual outcome. In particular, Tedder believed that supply shortages would doom the Panzerarmee. Rommel continually pressed the German High Command for re-supplies and reinforcements, with which he could finally defeat Eighth Army. He was aware however that he was at the end of a long logistical train, subject to interdiction, and low on the scale of Berlin's priorities.

Despite severe supply shortages and increasing manpower losses through both battle casualties and sickness brought on by reduced rations, Rommel's Axis forces stood fast in strong defensive positions. They were dug in behind two belts of minefields, which stretched some seventy miles from the Qattara Depression in the south, to the only east-west road near the Mediterranean coast just north of El Alamein.

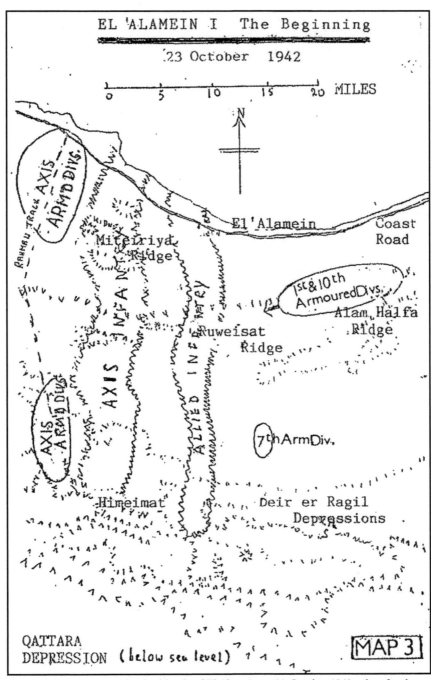

The ground deployments at the third battle of El Alamein on 23 October 1943, when for the preceding four days DAF had in effect imposed a 'No Fly Zone' on the Axis air forces. This had enabled the bringing forward of additional Eighth Army troops and armour, without detection by the enemy.

Although Rommel was for the moment desperate and impatient for new supplies and the strength to attack General Montgomery's Eighth Army once more, he held the Afrika Korps' 15th and 21st Panzer Divisions in reserve. Despite the Axis' supplies route stretching back to Benghazi and Tripoli, the Panzerarmee was maintaining its offensive positions. Rommel was confronted by Eighth Army's well prepared line of defences, which were the last remaining obstacle to conquest of the Egyptian delta. After that the Panzers could race for the oilfields of the Middle East. Their capture would turn the war Hitler's way.

As if oblivious to the static armies on the ground, in the air the battle for supremacy was constant. On 13 October Sergeant Alec Richardson, a twenty-six-year-old Australian from Sydney, was flying his P-40 Kittyhawk with No. 3 Squadron RAAF in an interception operation.

It was a funny day. Eighteen of us including six Yanks sent to intercept what turned out to be eighteen 109s flying high above us. The Kitties were usually flown at their best height, 13,000 feet, which meant being jumped out of the sun. The 109s kept circling above us and one Yank could not stand it any longer, and said over his radio telephone (RT), 'Why don't you come down and fight, you yellow bastards?' He got his wish as soon as they had the sun behind them, and it was positively dangerous with thirty-six planes filling the air in one big dog fight.

About twenty minutes later it suddenly finished, and I found myself alone in the sky. A very lonely feeling and I turned full bore for home. When I saw another Kitty ahead, I tried to catch it. When I saw Rod Mackenzie later I said, 'Why didn't you wait for me?' He said, 'I thought you were a bloody 109.'[3]

It had been a typical, sudden and chaotic aerial battle that, for every pilot on either side, was a life or death struggle.

* * *

While Rommel waited for fresh supplies and reinforcements, Montgomery planned to go on the attack. First it would be with infantry in late October in the north, to clear paths through the minefields before using armour. For such a frontal attack to succeed, against the still powerful and well dug-in Axis army, the element of surprise was essential. However, infantry and tanks must be brought forward for the attack without any knowledge by the enemy that an attack was imminent.

The problem was: how could this be done? Deep trenches were dug so that on the final day before the attack, troops brought forward would have to spend the daylight hours concealed in a trench. Yet the only real way to keep preparations from observation by the Germans was for DAF to deny both the

Luftwaffe and the Regia Aeronautica any offensive capability, and curtail to a minimum any attempted reconnaissance by Axis aircraft.

On 20 October DAF commenced their bombing campaign and mounted continuous fighter patrols round the clock. Air raids went in one after another on the German airfields at Fuka and Daba, using bombers and fighter-bombers, with separate fighter cover, without pause for four days and nights.

Under DAF command and control were some 200 light bombers, Bostons, Baltimores and B-25 Mitchells in No. 3 Wing SAAF, 232 Wing RAF and the USAAF 12th Bombardment Group, and around 500 fighters, Spitfires, Hurricanes, Kittyhawk and Warhawk, both variants of the Curtiss P-40 fighter, in 233, 239, 243, and 244 Wings RAF, No. 7 Wing SAAF, and the USAAF 57th Fighter Group. All wings or groups of wings had an Army Liaison Officer (ALO) with a W/T (wireless telephone) link to the Air Support Control section at Eighth Army HQ.[4]

The designated D Day for the land battle was 23 October, for which it was vital to maintain total air dominance, and as far as possible quarantine the airspace over the Allied lines and rear areas from Axis aircraft. On 21 October 'Jumbo' Genders, although now flying a standard Spitfire Mark VB, was still patrolling against any reconnaissance intruders over Eighth Army's rear positions. Over Heliopolis to the north of Cairo, Genders spotted a lone Ju88 and pursued it into cloud. Firing from astern, Genders hit one of its wings, causing an engine to fall off; the Ju88 eventually crashed behind German lines. It was Genders' tenth kill.[5]

Sergeant Alec Richardson was also in the air again on 21 October, with No. 3 Squadron RAAF in a bomber escort operation.

We were escorting Baltimores to bomb Daba, the 109 base, when we were attacked by some 109s. In a short fight I fired at the leader of a pair, and saw my tracer hit, and the plane start diving, but I lost sight of it as I went into a spin. By the time I pulled out there wasn't a plane in sight and I headed for home at full speed.

After a while I noticed four dots in the distance behind me and kept an eye on them. To my amazement they came up on me as though I'd been standing still, and when the first of the Macchi 202s peeled off to attack I turned into them and from then on, no matter what I did, I had one sitting on my tail and shooting. Every so often I'd pull the plane into a steeper turn, and it would flick over and I'd catch it, and do a steep turn the other way, only to find another one behind me.

The vertical reversements that I was unintentionally doing made me think my tail was being shot to pieces as it kept flicking upwards. It was bad enough worrying about my tail but when one Macchi bored down in a head on attack, I had to concentrate on him and forget my rear. I drew the plane up so we would hit, and fired and fired thinking the first to fire would win. I was amazed when the Macchi did not catch fire from my six 0.5 inch guns, especially as the tracers were all over him, including the cockpit.

I kept thinking, 'We don't give way', and did not. Had it been a 109 I would not have been here today, as they had a cannon through the nose, and the Germans read the same type of books. Anyway as we were about to hit, the pilot calmly dipped a wing and went underneath me with a roar like an express train. As if once wasn't enough one of them had a second try, which was a replica of the first, and I still failed to shoot it down.

Anyway my position was not improving – still four of them and I did not have time to radio for help. It suddenly struck me that they might have been playing with me, and they would get me when I ran out of petrol. Along the coast there was a great bank of cumulous clouds, probably reaching up to 25,000 feet, and I made a run for them. Eventually I had the wonderful feeling of the clouds closing right over me.

As soon as I was safe I throttled back to cruising speed, and opened the hood, in case I had to bale out thinking my tail was riddled and might fall off. I looked all around before checking my instruments, which were exactly where they should be. I shook the plane to make sure they were working. No sooner had I settled down when I came to a break in the clouds. There on my left and slightly to the front, only about twenty feet away or even less, was a Macchi with its pilot looking ahead.

I was tempted to let him have a burst, but thought if he blew up he might take me with him. And then I noticed 50 yards ahead and to the right, another Macchi waiting for me to show outside the clouds. As I couldn't see the other two I thought discretion was the better part of valour, and flew straight into the next bank of clouds. When I judged I was over our lines, I dropped down, until our drome appeared, and I landed exhausted.[6]

* * *

For the DAF the absolutely critical goal was to establish and control at any cost, what is now called a 'No Fly Zone', and eliminate the Luftwaffe and Regia Aeronautica from the skies. Typical of the whole DAF effort, over four days the two RAAF squadrons in No. 239 Wing, 3 and 450 Squadrons, flew 168 sorties either as fighter cover or fighter-bombers. Even before El Alamein, in June 1942 the exceptional performance of the two RAAF squadrons had been recognized, in a personal note from Air Chief Marshal Sir Arthur Tedder, C-in-C Middle East Air Force, to 3 Squadron Commander Nicky Barr: 'Congratulations on most efficient and successful fighter operations past two days. The bombers did very well because of the secure protection by 450 and No. 3 Squadrons.'[7]

On 23 October, the day before D Day, the same two squadrons were aloft at 0710 to raid El Daba once again. In a typical example of DAF morale, Sergeant Prowse of 450 Squadron and Sergeant Caldwell of 3 Squadron, despite making forced landings on their return, still found their way back to their base, and managed incredibly to fly twice more that same day.[8]

The Spitfires of 145 Squadron RAF were also up in the air at 0700 on 23 October, in the first of three missions. Around noon, near the Luftwaffe's El Daba airfield, their American pilot Flight Sergeant 'Mac' Powers gave chase in pursuit of two Bf109s heading west. Powers closed in on the nearest 109. His fire sent it into a dive, trailing both black and white smoke, before it hit the ground in a burning wreck.[9]

On the night of 23 October eighteen DAF light bombers in regular raids every ninety minutes dropped some 500 250lb bombs on Axis forces. During the ensuing day of 24 October they deposited some 700 more, equivalent to over 200 tons of explosive. Fighter-bombers also attacked tanks and gun positions, particularly soft-skinned vehicles which were much more vulnerable to a near-miss-bomb explosion. On the night of 24/25 October another 100 tons of bombs were dropped.[10]

While DAF fought for mastery of the skies, Eighth Army moved two armoured and four infantry divisions up to the El Alamein start lines, without any enemy knowledge. Late in the evening of 23 October the infantry would attempt the first and all important incursions into the German minefields.

At 2140 the Eighth Army artillery opened up. At 2200 the infantry, with each man trying to stay five yards from the next to present a scattered target to the German machine gunners, began their walk. When daylight came three gaps had been opened up in the minefields. Further back, however, German anti-tank gun positions remained. They had to be destroyed before the armoured divisions could surge through.

On 24 October 239 Wing flew 200 sorties, escorting 232 Light-Bomber Wing in attacks on these enemy gun positions. The typical formation comprised eighteen Baltimore or Mitchell bombers, six Kittyhawks with bombs and six without. Slightly behind and above were twelve more Kittyhawks, flying as escorts. From their forward airfields they flew first north over the Mediterranean, then westwards, parallel to the coast, before making their bombing runs in a north to south approach to their targets.

The combination of DAF bombing and artillery shelling created such huge dust clouds on 25 October that the troops in the front lines could see so little of the enemy they were unable to request air strikes on identifiable targets. The light bombers were then used to bomb the general area in front of X Corps, which included some estimates of likely places where the Panzers might be likely to pull back at midday for their regular practice of refuelling and brewing their coffee.[11]

The USAAF 57th Fighter Group was now operational in its own right and making an immediate impact. In a raid on 25 October on the Luftwaffe's airfield LG20, a Bf109 base, Lieutenant Lyman Middleditch Jr, of 64th Fighter Squadron, was in a group of eight Warhawks. As they pulled away after dropping their bombs, they were attacked by five Bf109s. Middleditch took on two 109s on Lieutenant Hartman's tail, pulling a tight turn to hit one of them with a full burst, sending it crashing into the sea. Two days later, on 27 October, he was flying top cover in an eight-plane formation when they engaged two approaching formations of Bf109s. Middleditch hit one 109 on his first pass and saw it pour smoke and fall into the sea.

Instantly three more 109s were on to him. He kept turning into the enemy fighters, using the advantage of a Warhawk in a tight turn against a 109, and hit another to see it too crash into the waves. Middleditch caught one of the other two 109s with a burst into the centre of its fuselage, flipping it into a cartwheel dive and a watery grave. The remaining 109 soon fled. A few weeks later Middleditch was awarded the DSC by Major General Lewis H. Brereton, Commander of Ninth Air Force, and AVM Arthur Coningham, Commander of the DAF. Later he went on to become an ace in early 1943.[12]

For many men whether in army or air force, the El Alamein battles would bring death, wounding or capture by the enemy. Flying his Kittyhawk in a second operation of the day on 25 October with 3 Squadron RAAF, Alec Richardson found the fates stacked against him.

On my return from an early morning sortie escorting Baltimores and Mitchells I collected a gallon of water and had a sponge bath. Pilots were allowed this luxury as they returned soaked to the skin with perspiration. For the next show Ken Bee was selected which was unfair as he had not flown for a month as he had been in hospital after being hit by a 109's cannon. Lucky for him the shell hit the armour plate behind his head and back, but he collected stray pieces of shrapnel in his legs. I was doing my daily letter writing, when I glanced at the flight board and saw that my name had been substituted for Ken's.

The flight started disastrously and did not improve. I checked the gun reflector sight – no image – the ground staff took a globe from Bobby Gibbes' plane parked alongside – still no image. Just then we were given the signal to take off, and I said, 'Don't worry, I won't try and hit any-thing,' and took off in someone's dust on instruments. At 80mph I pulled out of the dust.

Richardson was unaware that three other Kittyhawks had had to abort their take-offs. They were to have been part of the top cover.

We escorted the bombers to Fuka, the drome of the Italian Macchi 202 squadron. This target was always considered a 'sticky do', as we had to pass the German drome at Daba to reach the Italians, and very often lost someone. Furthermore the Macchi fighters could turn with us, and always had the height advantage like the 109s.

In an ensuing fight one of our planes was in dire straits with a Macchi very close behind him, but I needed the reflector sight in case I hit the wrong aircraft. The Kitty had a fixed ring and bead on the side. Never having used it before, I found it difficult to line up. It took my attention off my rear long enough for a Macchi to sneak up and put one burst into my plane. My reaction was instantaneous, and I dived from 7,000 feet to ground level. A wheel had dropped which meant the oil line had been hit.

I tried to retrieve the wheel without success whilst diving at 350mph plus. There was a notice on the dashboard warning pilots not to dive these planes at more than 360mph, but as I did not have time to worry about that I could have easily exceeded it. When I flattened out just above the ground, and going like the clappers, I decided to make sure he hadn't followed me down. Watching the ground very closely to avoid hitting it, I did a steep tight turn. At that very moment he fired, and I watched his tracer just miss me. We now had a situation where both of us were doing steep turns just above the ground, both doing about 350mph, and neither being game to tighten the turn further to get the necessary reflection to use the guns. In the middle of this all my instruments fell off and the engine seized.

I knew I had to get down, but was maintaining the speed without an engine. In the end I decided to ignore the Italian and flew straight and level, fish-tailing the plane to take off the speed, and when it was about 170–80, I whacked it on the ground wheels up. It hit pretty hard, slewing about because of the wheel hanging down and, after a few bumps, I came to rest. The canopy top had slammed shut, and I thought I was caught in the cockpit, but was pleasantly surprised when I had no difficulty opening it. I don't remember turning off any switches, especially the petrol switch, but I must have as I remembered to press two buttons on my IFF set (Identification, Friend or Foe), before jumping out. To my horror I then saw the Macchi boring down on me.

Just as I thought he was going to fire, I ducked down behind the engine, the only solid cover in sight. After amusing himself a couple of times he flew off. I collected an extra water bottle and twelve loose Sao biscuits from the luggage compartment, and ran north. To go east at 1430 was too obvious until nightfall. I only got 400 yards when a truck and five Germans bore down on the plane.

By this time I was flat on the ground, and only rose with my hands up when one of the Germans ran straight towards me with a revolver pointing at my heart. Everything except my left leg was quite brave, but it would not stop shaking. Once the German had taken my revolver, which was still wrapped up, he was quite friendly, and I found he spoke English, as [did] one of the others. I was a prisoner of war.[13]

It was just one of the many fighter engagements and dogfights which went on every day, unseen other than by the pilots themselves, striving to kill, or avoid being killed.

* * *

Four weeks before the third battle of El Alamein, on 23 September, Rommel had handed over command to his deputy, General Stumme, and because of bad health had flown back to Germany for treatment. After eighteen months continuous command in North Africa, he was suffering from liver and blood pressure problems, and no doubt general fatigue. His doctor wished him to have a lengthy period of recovery. During a brief stop at Rome he had remonstrated with Mussolini that his demands for supplies, 30,000 tons in September and 35,000 tons in October, must be met as a minimum: otherwise the campaign for North Africa would be lost. Following meetings with the German High Command and Hitler, he went to stay at Semmering, a mountain resort near Vienna.[14]

Rommel's recuperation was disrupted on the afternoon of 24 October when he was telephoned by Field Marshal Keitel. He was told of the massive attack at El Alamein by Eighth Army the previous evening. General Stumme was reported missing. Keitel asked him if he was well enough to return to his command immediately. Rommel said he was ready, and left at once by road to the airbase at Wiener Neustadt. Soon after midnight he received a call from Hitler, asking him to fly back to Africa and again assume command. At 0700 next morning 25 October Rommel's plane left for Rome.

On arrival in Rome in late morning, he was met by General von Rintelen who was attached to the Italian forces. He heard from Rintelen of how the British attack had broken through their lines south of Hill 31, were still pushing forward, and that General Stumme remained missing.[15]

General von Rintelen also informed me that only three issues of petrol remained in the African theatre; it had been impossible to send any more across in the last weeks, partly because the Italian Navy had not provided the shipping and partly because of the British sinkings. This was sheer disaster, for with only 300 kilometres worth of petrol per vehicle between Tripoli and the front, and that calculated over good driving country, a prolonged resistance could not be expected; we would be completely prevented from taking the correct tactical decisions and would thus suffer a tremendous limitation in our freedom of action.

I was bitterly angry, because when I left there had been at least eight issues for the Army in Egypt and Libya, and even this had been absurdly little in comparison with the minimum essential of thirty issues. Experience had shown that one issue of petrol was required for each day of battle; without it the Army was crippled and could not react to the enemy's moves.[16]

Rommel left Rome after midday on 25 October in his single-engined Storch. By the time he landed at his HQ in Egypt it was twilight. Even at that time he had a feeling of impending defeat. In the evening he was briefed by General von Thoma and Colonel Westphal. The fuel shortage was preventing any significant redeployment, and only localized tactical counter-attacks could be mounted against the British offensive. Better than anyone else, Rommel must have recognized that his army's greatest strength, speed and flexibility of movement, was being nullified.

It confirmed for Rommel the imminent crisis level of fuel stocks across all Axis forces in North Africa. He had discussed this in his stop in Rome where he had demanded all Italian naval forces be tasked at once to ensure the immediate shipment of petrol and ammunition to Axis-held ports. At his HQ Rommel also learned of the growing air superiority of the RAF, the Luftwaffe's inability to stop the bombing raids, and how the new DAF fighter-bombers were countering the dispersal tactics of Axis motorized units, to hit individual tanks and vehicles. Rommel felt that the supply situation was now approaching disaster.[17]

* * *

The Allies were well aware that Axis supply shortages remained desperate. With the Eighth Army offensive under way, it was critical that the aerial blockade of Axis-held ports was tightened. RAF Eastern Command and DAF re-doubled their interdiction operations against shipping.

Operations Record Book, No. 38 Squadron RAF, 24/25 October 1942:
Summary of Sortie Details

On 24 October at 1800 Wing Commander Pratt of 38 Squadron, led four Wellingtons in an operation to locate and attack an enemy convoy, which was known to be heading for Tobruk. They were first ordered to rendezvous with a specially equipped Wellington of 221 Squadron. Severe electrical storms forced the abandonment of the operation without finding the convoy.

At 23.30 Flight Lieutenant Wiggins and Sergeant Taylor of 38 Squadron, in two stand-by Wellingtons, took off in a second attempt to find and strike the enemy convoy. Sergeant Taylor managed to find a break in the weather, but could not locate the convoy in the designated target area. Flight Lieutenant Wiggins was unable to penetrate the storms, and on return was forced to land at a closer airfield. Wiggins' aircraft suffered a burst tyre on touch-down, resulting in a crash landing in the early hours of 25 October.

However, Liberator bombers were able to track the convoy during the rest of the night. This enabled another attack operation to be mounted on the morning of 26 October. At noon five Beaufort and four Bisley bombers of No. 47 Squadron RAF, attacked the escorted convoy of cargo ships making for Tobruk. Their attack on the convoy included a direct hit on the oil tanker *Proserpina* (4,809 tons), which caught fire. The *Proserpina* had been carrying 2,500 tons of petrol.

So critical was the supply situation for the Axis ground forces that both sides were committing every resource possible in the struggle over Axis supply channels. Six of the ten attacking aircraft were lost to either enemy fighters or anti-aircraft fire from the ships. A second operation by Beauforts failed to locate the remaining ships, which were still on schedule to reach Tobruk, before night-flying Wellington torpedo bombers would be available to intercept. Since these supplies were so crucial for the Axis army, it was decided to risk an operation by 38 Squadron for the first time at dusk.[15]

Operations Record Book, No. 38 Squadron RAF, 26 October 1942:
Summary of Sortie Details

At 1540 Flight Lieutenant Wiggins led three Wellington bombers in formation, with Pilot Officer Bertran and Sergeant Viles in Nos 2 and 3 positions respectively. The weather and visibility were good, with minimal cloud. The three aircraft proceeded at 100 feet until they were about 60 miles out to sea. They then turned westward, and proceeded parallel to the coast until they were approximately 60 miles north east of Tobruk. Navigation was perfect and they were able to make an immediate approach in formation.

In the first dusk attack ever attempted by 38 Squadron, the three planes headed straight for a large merchant vessel, the *Tergestea*, thought to be carrying both army supplies and fuel, and lying perhaps two miles outside Tobruk harbour. There were many destroyers escorting the *Tergestea*, but they were taken completely by surprise. It was not until the aircraft were beginning their run within two miles of the *Tergestea* that frantic signalling took place from the destroyers to the merchant vessel.

All three aircraft dropped their torpedoes at a distance of around 500–600 yards from the target. The three torpedoes were seen to be running straight towards the *Tergestea*, which appeared to be stationary, perhaps at anchor in the water. One or more torpedoes hit the ship causing an enormous explosion. The aircraft crews then observed a huge column of black smoke, surging up from the *Tergestea* to an estimated 3,000 feet.

After dropping his torpedo Flight Lieutenant Wiggins chose to take his aircraft climbing straight over the top of the *Tergestea*, attracting the greatest concentration of anti-aircraft fire from the escort destroyers. Despite his aircraft suffering multiple hits, Wiggins was able to maintain his escape flight beyond the range of the destroyers' guns.

Sergeant Bertran was able to turn away to starboard, and received lighter anti-aircraft fire. After releasing its torpedo, Sergeant Viles' aircraft was seen to stagger, probably from receiving fire from the destroyers. The last that was seen of Viles was his aircraft breaking away to port. Both Wiggins and Bertran completed their return flights safely to base.[19]

Wiggins' bombing run came in with a dark sky behind the three Wellington bombers, whereas their target, the *Tergestea* stood out against the sun setting in the west. Of six torpedoes launched, three ran well, striking the motor vessel *Tergestea* (5,890 tons). The cargo of the *Tergestea* comprised 1,000 tons of petrol, and 1,000 tons of ammunition. A further operation that night reported that there was no sign of the *Tergestea*, which must have sunk. Nothing remained of the convoy except for the tanker *Proserpina*, now settling low in the water and still burning after the earlier Beaufort attack.[20]

General Montgomery expressed his gratitude for the outstanding efforts of 38 Squadron and 201 Group RAF, to assist Eighth Army's offensive.

> Recent attacks carried out against enemy ships so vital to his effort were a wonderful achievement. I would be grateful if you would convey to those responsible our gratitude for operations carried out which must be epic against ships at sea.[21]

After grabbing only a few hours of sleep Rommel was up at 0500 on 26 October and in his command vehicle. He was briefed that RAF bombing raids had continued right through the night. During the afternoon attempted operations by German and Italian dive-bombers against British vehicle convoys, were intercepted by some sixty DAF fighters. Some Italian aircraft jettisoned their bombs over their own lines to get away, and suffered heavy losses against the faster DAF fighters. On the battlefield Axis troops were becoming fatigued and dispirited from the incessant DAF bombing raids throughout the day.[22]

Rommel felt that the supply situation, by constraining his actions, was making his position increasingly untenable.

> The tanker *Proserpina*, which we hoped would bring some relief in the petrol, had been bombed and sunk outside Tobruk. There was only enough petrol to keep supply traffic going between Tripoli and the front for another two or three days, and that without counting the needs of the motorized forces, which had to be met out of the same stocks.[23]

With sufficient petrol supplies Rommel would have moved substantial forces from the south to mount a major counter-attack in the north. As it was he only risked moving 21st Panzer to the north, knowing they could not return. He also reported directly to Hitler's HQ that unless supplies improved significantly the battle would be lost. That evening he wrote to his wife that the situation was critical.[24]

On 27 and 28 October Rommel wrote to his wife again, in a near defeatist mood, and doubting that he would survive. When he heard of the loss of the *Tergestea*, coming only twenty-four hours after the destruction of the *Proserpina*, Rommel must have been despondent. His last hope of any extra fuel supplies, in time to make a difference to his army's plight, was gone.[25]

Flight Lieutenant Wiggins thought that the loss of the *Tergestea* was probably the last straw for Rommel, and had condemned his Panzerarmee to retreat. Wiggins, of course, had a personal interest. He knew that Australian troops were fighting and dying on the Alamein battleground.[26] What Wiggins did not know, was that there was also another Australian connection. Three months earlier it was also another fellow Australian, Flight Lieutenant Bill McRae, who had flown out to Egypt, the first radar-equipped Wellington Mk VIII torpedo-bomber.

*   *   *

On 27 October above the desert's Kidney feature in the northern sector of the Alamein front line, Australian Flying Officer John Waddy in a Spitfire of RAF 92 Squadron, shot down an Bf109. Waddy had previously become an 'ace' with five kills flying Kittyhawk fighters, and this was his second Spitfire victory. His victory occurred above where his compatriots in 9th Australian Division were hanging on grimly to incursions they had made in the Axis lines.[27]

Down on the ground that same day a breeze cleared some of the dust from the shelling and bombing, so that a daringly low level flight by 208 Squadron of Tactical Reconnaissance RAF spotted the Afrika Korps west of the Rahman track, positioning for a counter-attack against X Corps. The Rahman track ran along the enemy front between the Qattara Depression and Sidi Abd el Rahman, providing a very useful 'bomb line' beyond which were the enemy targets. Thinking that the Eighth Army deployments in the south were a decoy, Rommel had summoned to the north 15th and 21st Panzer Divisions, 90th Light Division, and the Italian Littorio and Ariete Armoured Divisions, to counter an attack by X Corps.

The desert's dust returned on 28 October. Nothing could be seen at ground level nor at normal reconnaissance height. Mid-morning DAF took the only remaining option, and flew a reconnaissance at very low level, along the Rahman track and through blisteringly intense flak. Luckily the flight was successful, and discovered the Afrika Korps near Tel el Aqqaqir concentrating for an attack. From 1430 to 1700 seven waves of eighteen light bombers dropped more than 800 bombs on the Axis forces, and another 550 at night. Direct hits were not that many, but the bombardment forced the enemy's columns to maintain dispersal distances of some 100 yards. This caused secondary but serious effects such as deterioration of morale, and wasted time and fuel for all movements. The counter-attack was stopped before it could begin, forcing a withdrawal.[28]

During the day on 31 October, DAF put in heavy raids in preparation for the Australian troops in the north to attack across the coast road that night. Because from a certain height in a desert landscape there were often no distinguishing landmarks, coloured smoke was used to identify the Australians' front lines, to assist the bomb aiming. It enabled the bombardment to be accomplished successfully, nearly 300 bombs during the day and 560 more at night, as near as 1,000 yards from the Australians' start line.

On the night of 1/2 November, at 0105, Eighth Army launched the break-out offensive in the south, Operation SUPERCHARGE. Rommel had no alternative and on 3 November decided to withdraw his forces from Alamein some fifty miles west to Fuka. Some Axis troops who still had access to transport on that night 3/4 November began to pull out under cover of darkness. Rommel informed Hitler that a break-out by Eighth Army on 4 November could not be stopped, and that he planned to retreat fighting rearguard actions until he could be reinforced, or his forces evacuated from North Africa. Afrika Korps had perhaps only thirty serviceable tanks at this time. He informed Hitler and Mussolini that the lack of fuel prevented him from making any significant move on the battlefield. Eighth Army would destroy his forces gradually, with their greater numbers, of tanks, guns, ammunition, aircraft, fuel and other supplies.[29]

Following the sinking of the *Proserpina* and *Tergestea*, more, smaller Axis freighters had continued to try to reach Tobruk with supplies. On 28 October the tanker *Luisiano* (2,552 tons) was sunk, and an accompanying ship damaged and turned back, by torpedo-bombers based at Malta. On the night of 31 October-1 November Wellingtons and Beauforts struck again, sinking the *Tripolino* (1,071 tons) and *Ostia* (348 tons), before they could reach Tobruk.

Two ships, *Brioni* (1,987 tons) and *Lara* (1,976 tons), were within fifty miles of Tobruk harbour on the morning of 2 November when they were found and attacked by Beauforts of No. 39 Squadron RAF. While Beaufighters engaged some escorting enemy fighters, the Beauforts damaged both freighters. The *Brioni* was able to continue and reach Tobruk, only to be blown up in its berth by a Liberator bomber. The disabled *Lara* also continued slowly, and was within twenty-five miles of Tobruk when it finally sank. The Axis halted any more shipping for Tobruk. Out of eleven ships which tried to make the voyage, seven, including the largest tankers, had been sunk, and three damaged.[30]

Mid-morning of 4 November DAF sent its light bombers into attacks on the retreating Axis forces. However, their effectiveness was limited. A pattern bombing raid against a stream of motor vehicles only had an effect where the bombs cut the line of road traffic. The few vehicles destroyed and the casualties could be quickly moved aside, or the motor traffic make a short detour over the sand. The fighters and fighter-bombers struggled to keep within effective range with logistics, tactics, and equipment, to mount an effective pursuit of the retreating Axis columns. There was a continuing demand to get ground crews, support and supplies forward to airfields to keep within range of the enemy fleeing westwards.

Although AVM Coningham had officially expressed his confidence that DAF would be able to inflict massive losses on Rommel's forces as they withdrew across the Libyan desert, he also emphasized the need for control. He told the DAF wing and squadron commanders to exercise caution, and referred to past episodes when the Luftwaffe and Regia Aeronautica fighters had punished reckless attacks. Coningham was wary of the Axis air forces flying in more fighters from Tunis and Sicily.

Rommel did receive a response from Hitler, telling him that he must stand and fight. It was victory or death. There was a promise of more support from the Luftwaffe, but no mention of anything to provide more petrol supplies for the army. On the evening of 4 November, under threat of total encirclement if they stayed put, Rommel ordered a general retreat. On the night of 5 November he withdrew his Fuka HQ, and his only fighting groups which remained effective, 15th Panzer and 90th Light Divisions, farther west to Matruh. Because of lack of fuel 21st Panzer came to a halt at Qasaba halfway to Matruh. On the next night, 6 November, they were forced to destroy most of their tanks and guns, and then drive west in light vehicles.[31]

Rommel's Axis army, drained by DAF of its life support before the battle of El Alamein, had been starved of guns, ammunition, vehicles, fuel, food, men – everything. They had no more options. Now they could only retreat westwards in the face of Eighth Army's advance.

With the benefit of hindsight the sinking of the two supply ships carrying significant fuel for the Axis armies, the *Proserpina* and *Tergestea*, was the death knell for anything other than retreat for Rommel's forces. Together, the two ships carried 3,500 tons of petrol, probably enough for six days' operations in battle conditions. If they had got through at such a critical time of the battle, it would have resulted in some significantly changed tactics by Rommel. What such tactics might have been, and what might have been their effect is unquantifiable. On the other hand, without the fuel from *Proserpina* and *Tergestea*, he and his commanders must have always had in the back of their minds the need for conserving enough fuel to make a withdrawal. Certainly Rommel recognized the inevitable, and that all other options had been closed off, except retreat.

What clearly can be said is that both before and during the third battle at El Alamein, DAF had dominated the skies. Interdiction of Axis supplies, in which DAF and the other air forces of RAF Eastern Command were crucial airborne enforcers, had severely weakened the enemy. In the air Axis air forces had been subjugated so that Eighth Army could carry out its offensive on the ground. DAF fighters, particularly the Spitfires, had won their battles against the Luftwaffe and Aeronautica fighters, and Allied air power had won the air war over El Alamein.

Notes

1. Smith (AASC No. 5), *Air Support in the Desert*, Ref. McNeill, 1983–6, King's College London, pp. 9–11.
2. Thomas, *Spitfire Aces of North Africa and Italy*, pp. 9–12.
3. Veteran's account, Sgt Alec Richardson.
4. Smith op. cit., p. 13.
5. Thomas, op. cit., p. 13.
6. Veteran's account, Sgt Alec Richardson.
7. Dornan, *Nicky Barr, An Australian Air Ace*, p. 123.
8. Brown, *Desert Warriors*, p. 178.
9. Thomas, op. cit., p. 13.
10. Smith, op. cit., p. 14.
11. Ibid., p. 15.
12. Molesworth, *57th Fighter Group*, pp. 27–9.
13. Veteran's account, Sgt Alec Richardson.
14. Liddell Hart, *The Rommel Papers*, p. 292.
15. Ibid., p. 304.
16. Ibid., pp. 304–5.
17. Ibid., pp. 305–6.
18. National Archives (NA) UK, AIR 27/399/19; Veteran's account, S/Ldr Lloyd Wiggins.
19. NA (UK), AIR 27/399/20; Veteran's account, S/Ldr Lloyd Wiggins.
20. Herington, *Air War against Germany & Italy 1939–43*, pp. 372–3.
21. Ibid., p. 373.
22. Liddell Hart, op. cit., pp. 306–7.
23. Ibid., pp. 307–9.
24. Ibid.
25. Ibid., pp. 309–10.
26. Veteran's account, S/Ldr Lloyd Wiggins.
27. Thomas, op. cit., p. 14.
28. Smith, op. cit., pp. 15–22; Smith (AASC), *Blue Skies and Desert Dust*,
29. Ibid.
30. Herington, op. cit., p. 373.
31. Smith, op. cit., pp. 15–22.

Chapter 4

Allied air power lights the flame of Operation TORCH

As axis forces retreated from El Alamein westwards across Lybia, the sea off Algiers harbour on 9 November 1942 was covered with a forest of ships. Small boats and landing craft were shuttling back and forth with troops, tanks, vehicles, and other equipment and supplies of war. High above the ships a Ju88 reconnaissance bomber probed daringly into the Allies' airspace. Two Spitfires quickly found the enemy intruder, and sent it into a smoking dive into the waves. The fighters' interception would prove to be too late.

As twilight gathered later that day, three waves of Ju88s and Heinkel He111s began their bombing runs over the anchored invasion fleet and above Maison Blanche airfield. Spitfires from No. 81 Squadron RAF and Hurricanes from No. 43 Squadron RAF scrambled to intercept. More Spitfires from No. 242 Squadron RAF, who were escorting two B-17 bombers flying US General Mark Clark from Gibraltar across to Algiers, were also called on to attack the enemy raiders.

The Luftwaffe bombers were soon in disarray. Pilots of 242 Squadron claimed their first victories, Sergeant Mallinson an He111, Pilot Officer Goulding and Sergeant Watling a Ju88 each, while Flight Lieutenant Benham and Pilot Officer Mather shared a Ju88 kill. Five other pilots claimed half-kills and damages on the German aircraft.

Squadron Leader 'Ras' Berry, Commander of 81 Squadron, and his section shot down an He111 over Maison Blanche airfield, and fellow pilot, Canadian Flight Lieutenant James Walker, did the same for a Ju88. Having achieved two previous victories in the skies of UK and Russia, it was Walker's third kill, and perhaps a unique record in those three theatres of air warfare.[1]

* * *

The Spitfires' engagement with the Ju88s came a day after Allied landings in North-West Africa.

At around midnight on 7/8 November 1942, Operation TORCH, the first major Allied operation of the Second World War invaded Morocco and Algeria. Only a few days after the start of the third battle at El Alamein on 26 October, the Anglo-American invasion fleets had sailed from the east coast of USA and the west coast of Scotland. The enormous task force was in excess of 100 ships, and over 107,000 troops.[2]

Although the battle of Stalingrad was an immense distance from the Middle East, the German Army's struggle to overcome the Russians' stubborn and desperate defence was not immune to the impact of Eighth Army's victory at El Alamein, nor to the Operation TORCH invasion. Despite their defeats on the Russian Front, the Germans felt forced to transfer their Luftflotte II (Air Fleet) to Italy and Tunisia. If Rommel, or any others in Hitler's Reich, still harboured dreams of dominating the Mediterranean, and occupying the oilfields of the Gulf, Iraq and Persia, they were now collapsing.

Operation TORCH was made up of three invasion fleets – the Western, Central and Eastern Task Forces. The Western Task Force, commanded by Major General Patton, and under the protection of the US Navy, sailed from east coast USA to land at Casablanca. US Navy aircraft carriers, off Casablanca and Oran, provided the air cover with ship-borne fighters. The Central Task Force, with some British but predominantly American troops, set out from Britain under the command of Major General Fredendall, heading for the port of Oran on the north-west Algerian coast.

The US Army's Twelfth Air Force, commanded by the already legendary Brigadier General Jimmy Doolittle, also provided air cover for the Oran-bound fleet. General Doolittle had commanded the first US air raid on Japan after Pearl Harbor, when B-25 Mitchell bombers took off from aircraft carriers, without sufficient fuel to return. After releasing their bombloads over Japan, the B-25s flew on westwards to land at friendly bases in China.

The closest landing to the Tunisian border, by a convoy despatched from the Clyde in Scotland, was to be made by the Eastern Task Force. Although it carried a small number of US troops with designated officers to assist negotiations with the Vichy French authorities, this invasion force comprised elements of the British First Army under command of Lieutenant General Kenneth Anderson. While the Royal Navy escorted both the Oran and Algiers invasion fleets, air support for the Algiers landings was provided by the RAF Eastern Command. To strengthen air support at Algiers, on 6 November two DAF squadrons, the Beaufighters of No. 272 Squadron RAF and the torpedo-carrying Wellington bombers of No. 221 Squadron RAF, flew from Egypt to Malta.

One of those pilots in 221 Squadron was Australian Flying Officer William 'Bill' Stocks from Sydney. After a period in the Empire Training Scheme in Canada, Bill had arrived in Britain in November 1941 and, after training on Wellington bombers, in April 1942 he joined No. 221 Squadron at Sidi Barrani. In one anti-shipping operation with 221 Squadron, at a height of around 500 feet, Stocks made two severe hits on an enemy vessel. In another interdiction flight his wireless transmitter, rear turret and petrol gauges became unserviceable. Despite great difficulties he continued and completed the operation successfully. In what seems so typical of so many bomber pilots, Stocks' leadership, coolness and efficiency would in due course see him become a squadron leader in No. 28 Squadron RAF, and be awarded the DFC.

Despite the widest dispersal of troop landings over 130 miles north and south of Casablanca, General Patton's US Western Task Force encountered the stiffest resistance. The Vichy French were alert to the invasion. At approximately 0700 on 8 November their naval air force, *Aeronavale*, had their Dewoitine fighters strafing the landing beaches. However, in three days the Vichy French lost 119 aircraft out of 200, as well as having their airfields put out of action. The US Army Air Forces lost only forty-four aircraft out of 164, and all the US Navy aircraft carriers remained intact. Early on 11 November the French Commander in Casablanca surrendered and signed an armistice.

At Oran in Algeria at 0100, also on 8 November, the US 1st Infantry and 1st Armored Divisions went ashore. Before dawn the Royal Navy's aircraft carriers, HM Ships *Furious*, *Biter* and *Dasher*, launched ten Seafires, eight Albacore torpedo-bombers, and twelve Sea Hurricanes. During 8 and 9 November considerable air combat ensued with the Aeronavale over Oran's la Senia and Tafaraoui airfields.

This provided cover for American tanks to capture Tafaraoui on 9 November, which then enabled a Hurricane squadron and some Spitfires from the RAF's 31 Fighter Group to fly in from Gibraltar. When one Spitfire was shot down on its landing approach by a Dewoitine fighter, a quick response claimed three of the French fighters. The surviving French aircraft at la Senia took off and escaped to Morocco.

Later, when the Tafaraoui airfield came under fire from an approaching column of the French Foreign Legion and its artillery battery, the Spitfires were again called up. Their strafing attack blew up a truck carrying troops, spattering one Spitfire with body parts, and causing the French to withdraw quickly. By the end of the day on 9 November the French authorities declared a cease-fire to end any threat to the la Senia and Tafaraoui airfields.[3]

* * *

Farther east along the coast near to Algiers, also in the early hours of 8 November, the troop landings of the British First Army went ahead. Operation TORCH gambled on a land spearhead that in the main comprised only 11 and 36 Brigades of the 78th Battleaxe Division, some light tank units of Blade Force, and an American field artillery battalion. The task force, under command of 78th Division, was being used in an urgent but risky drive to occupy Tunis.[4]

While all three landings were equally important in order to occupy northwest Africa, in the short term those at Algiers were critical. A proposal to land farther east at Tunis had been rejected because of the threat of Luftwaffe and Regia Aeronautica attacks from their bases in Sicily. Yet the immediate goal of the Allies' ground forces was to squeeze the Axis armies in a pincer movement between Operation TORCH and Montgomery's Eighth Army. A rapid advance was planned to gain control quickly of the major port of Tunis before German forces could be landed there, and before the start of winter and the rainy season in late December.

The decision not to land at Tunis itself, or even the Algerian port of Bone near the Tunisian border, was driven by a fear of enemy air attack. Axis bombers based in Sicily could easily reach both Bone and Tunis with fighter escorts, whereas the British and American air forces could offer little support to any landings there. Even after air bases were established at Algiers and Bone, Allied fighter aircraft would be at the extremity of their range to reach Tunis, which would allow little time over the battlefield to support ground forces. In the event the capability of the Germans to react quickly and transport well-equipped troops, tanks, guns and aircraft to Tunis, was grossly underestimated by the Allies.

At the moment of the landings, there were no garrison troops in Tunis, and the German and Italian High Commands were taken completely by surprise. But Axis reaction was swift, and effectively assisted by the conduct of Admiral Esteva, the French Resident-General. The first German troops arrived by air at El Aouina airfield, near Tunis, on November 9, only a day after the Allied landings.

They seized the key points of the two cities; they executed or imprisoned the known and suspected Allied sympathizers; they took over the ports of Sousse, Sfax and Gabes and the inland town of Kairouan. Within a week there were 5,000 front-line troops in and around Tunis and Bizerte; they had tanks; and they were still flying in Messerschmitt and Focke-Wulf fighters.[5]

The landings at Algiers were not only the most crucial to the Operation TORCH strategy. They were the most risky, and no-one knew what the Vichy French authorities would do. The French possessed dangerous squadrons of both fighters and bombers at their Algiers airfields of Blida and Maison Blanche. In addition, while the Allied ships and troops were going ashore, they would be within range of Luftwaffe bombers.

When a French Douglas DB-7 bomber from the Blida air force base threatened the invasion fleet, two Seafire fighters from the aircraft carrier HMS *Formidable* shot it down. Successive flights of Martlet fighters from HMS *Victorious* then attacked Blida airfield in waves, shooting up aircraft on the ground and those attempting to take off. Around 0830, when the Blida air base signalled its surrender, naval fliers landed and took control.

Luckily bad weather had kept many French aircraft grounded, such as fifty Dewoitine fighters, and six Potez bombers, preventing them from causing mayhem amongst the invading forces. The French Air Force base of Maison

Blanche, where there had been no order to hold fire, was captured by 0900. Apart from a failed attempt to capture Algiers harbour, troop landings along the coastal beaches went well. Many Vichy French army units had been ordered not to resist.

During the morning of 8 November Hurricanes of No. 43 Squadron RAF, and Spitfires of 81 and 242 Squadrons RAF, flew from Gibraltar and landed at Maison Blanche. But, as the day neared its end, a Luftwaffe raid of fifteen Junkers Ju88 bombers attacked the ships off Algiers, damaging three Seafires on a carrier.

On the ground at the Maison Blanche air base, relations between Allied forces and the Vichy French were tense. British troops stood guard over parked French fighter planes. The newly landed Hurricanes and Spitfires remained on the tarmac for lack of fuel. Cold and hungry, their pilots huddled by their planes facing a Tunisian winter's night.[6]

Next day, 9 November, fighters of both 43 and 81 Squadrons had enough fuel left in their tanks to scramble against another Luftwaffe raid and were joined by Spitfires of 242 Squadron, already aloft, to disrupt and fight off the German bombers. When the fighter pilots returned to Maison Blanche their combat stress was no doubt quickly forgotten when the first food since their earlier arrival from Gibraltar was awaiting them.

The decisive impact of Allied air power in support of the Operation TORCH landings has not been well recognized. Even with a large number of inexperienced pilots, within two days Allied air forces had overwhelmed their French counterparts across Morocco and Algeria. Most important of all, the airfields at Maison Blanche and Blida near Algiers, and soon after at Bone, the closest to the Tunisian border, were captured with little damage. French ground forces, with their air support eliminated, and their leaders in disarray with conflicting loyalties, were left with no options. Allied forces were pouring in by air and sea. On 13 November General Eisenhower reached a final agreement with French authorities in Algeria under Admiral Darlan and hostilities came to an end.

The Royal Navy aircraft-carriers lost a total of forty-five aircraft over Oran and Algiers – fifteen Sea Hurricanes, eight Martlets, eight Albacores, two Fulmars and at least twelve Seafires. Despite a large number of inexperienced pilots, they had destroyed or driven the Vichy Air Force from the skies. Allied air power was clearly a huge factor not only in protecting the invasion fleets and troop landings, but also in gaining air superiority to force the early cease-fire by Vichy French Authorities.[7]

Although it was not known at the time, the early successes in Morocco and Algeria had a consequence. By the end of November there would be some 20,000 Axis troops in Tunis, specifically the 334th Infantry Division, the Italian 1st Division, and 10th Panzer Division. The Germans continued building up and, on 8 December, General von Arnim arrived in Tunis to take command of their forces which, on that date, were designated the Fifth Panzer Army. Perhaps the German reaction to Operation TORCH had been foreseen by the Allies as a possibility, but with a hope that it would not happen so fast.

In contrast, the Allies' initial attacking force from 78th Division with the two brigade groups and Blade Force to make the first thrust at Tunis totalled only 12,300 men. It was recognized as a gamble. With air bases close to Tunis, as anticipated the Luftwaffe quickly established air superiority in Tunisian airspace. It meant that Allied ground forces came under regular attack from enemy fighters and dive-bombers.

* * *

Unlike the Desert Air Force (DAF), which had been based in Egypt, and had experience in extending its supply lines and moving to temporary airfields with Eighth Army, the air force squadrons sent from the USA and Britain to support Operation TORCH had to be self-sufficient on arrival. In comparison, the Germans were flying in ground forces and aircraft from Sicily, only about 100 miles distant from Tunis, to all-weather airfields close to the port of Bizerte and the Tunisian capital, such as Blida and Maison Blanche.

In early-December winter rain and mud made many dirt airfields inoperable. To support the army's advances with air support and get within range of Tunis, Allied squadrons had to make use of temporary landing grounds and often had to roll out a dirt strip themselves. As the British First Army moved to within striking distance of Tunis, their closest operable air base was 114 miles to the rear at Bone. This meant that Spitfires were at the limit of their range, resulting in restricted patrol time over Tunis and German positions before having to turn for home.

RAF photo reconnaissance flights on 12 November revealed at least 120 Luftwaffe aircraft at Tunisian airfields, including forty Stukas and some Fw190s at Bizerte and Tunis. The Focke-Wulf Fw190 was fast, with a maximum speed above 380mph, well-armed and, apart from the Spitfire, superior at that time to other Allied fighters in North Africa. In addition there were some 270 German bombers based in Sicily and Sardinia that were raiding Algiers every night.[8]

Basing themselves at first at the Maison Blanche airfield outside Algiers, the Spitfire pilots of No. 154 Squadron RAF, led by New Zealander Squadron Leader Don Carlson, quickly made their name known. On 15 November Carlson shot down a Ju88 bomber. Adding this to his four victories with 74 Squadron in 1941 it made Carlson one of the first Spitfire 'aces' over North Africa. In their first two weeks, 154 Squadron claimed nineteen Luftwaffe bombers shot down, and nine more at least hit and damaged.[9]

In mid-November 81 and 111 RAF Squadrons, with Spitfires, were able to move farther east to Bone, 275 miles from Algiers but only fifty miles from the Tunisian border. The Bone airfield, not much more than a landing ground, had been captured on 12 November by 300 British paratroopers, flown in by C-47 transports of the USAAF 64th Group. Next day more C-47s brought in anti-aircraft guns and fuel, which enabled the escorting P-38 Lightning fighters to land and base themselves at Bone. The airfield was very basic and under continual bombing and strafing attacks from the Luftwaffe bases at Bizerte.

For the Spitfire pilots the arrival of winter rain, together with the Spitfire Mk VC's inferior performance to the Bf109, made the life or death struggle in the air even worse. The fight for supremacy of the skies was a tenacious struggle which would have profound consequences for the armies on the ground.

On 14 November Canadian Flying Officer Harry Fenwick of 81 Squadron RAF began a momentous five days of dogfights when he was shot up by a Bf109. Luckily, he managed a forced landing with a leg wound. On 16 November he was back in the air, first inflicting damage on a 109, only to be shot up himself again by another 109. Once more he found a way to return safely to base. The next day he made his first kill with a Macchi 202 and on 18 November his revenge was complete when he shot down a Bf109.

Although two Spitfires at any one time were required to be in constant patrol over the Bone airfield, and two more fuelled with pilots in the cockpit ready to go, not all Axis air raids could be countered. Soon after arriving at Bone on 19 November, No. 72 Squadron RAF lost eight Spitfires to a bombing and strafing attack by twelve Bf109s.[10] On 20 November thirty Ju88s bombed Maison Blanche airfield heavily, destroying the RAF reconnaissance aircraft.[11]

On patrol on 28 November over an Allied convoy near Algiers, Flying Officer 'Paddy' Chambers of 154 Squadron sighted five Italian Savoia-Marchetti SM.79 Sparviero aircraft, which were beginning a bombing run at the ships. Chambers closed with the SM.79s from behind and above. One by one he picked them off, to send four spiralling into the sea. Out of ammunition and his plane damaged, Chambers broke away. Flying Officer Alan Aikman shot down the remaining bomber, so that in this engagement both pilots reached their fifth victory and became Spitfire aces.[12]

On 3 December, close to Tebourba and Djedeida and about twenty miles from Tunis, 78th Division was being driven back by German Panzers. Over the battle area Pilot Officer 'Robbie' Robertson of 72 Squadron spotted some approaching Fw190 fighter-bombers. Diving to attack them he was shot at mistakenly by an American P-38 Lightning fighter. Despite the friendly fire Robertson shot down an Fw190 for his fifth victory. His success in becoming an ace seemed to continue on 18 December when he accounted for another Bf109. Soon after on the same sortie he took a hit from a cannon shell in the cockpit.

A splinter penetrated one of Robertson's eyes, leaving him bleeding and half-blinded. Somehow, Robertson kept control of the Spitfire to make a forced landing, but he lost the eye to finish him as a fighter pilot. Yet Robertson and the other pilots of 72 Squadron had taken a toll of the Axis air forces. In four weeks the squadron had racked up a score of twenty-one enemy aircraft destroyed, and another eight damaged or worse.[13]

On 6 December Flying Officer Fenwick, with fellow Canadian James Waller, shared a kill of an Italian Reggiane Re.2001 Falco II fighter. Fenwick then shot down a Bf109 of his own. These two victories took both Canadians to ace status.[14] Every sortie could end in a life or death struggle, with the incidence of death or maiming of aircrew increasing on both sides. A pilot could become an ace one day, and then be dead or invalided out on the next.

*   *   *

It is a common but false perception that the Tunisian campaign was fought in the desert. In fact, the major part of the fighting took place in the mountains and valleys of northern Tunisia. Much of it was in the cold and rain of winter, and the icy winds of the Atlas Mountains. The bad weather also disrupted the Allies' longer range bombers, which were using airfields even farther away in Algiers.

Unaware of the enemy's gathering strength, by 27 November leading elements of 78th Division and Blade Force had advanced down the Medjerda River valley, through the strategically placed market town of Medjez el Bab to Tebourba. They were literally within sight of Tunis, no more hills could be seen, only a flat plain less than twenty miles wide lay between them and the Tunisian capital. Major General Evelegh, the 78th Division commander, hoped to be reinforced very quickly and even had thoughts of entering Tunis on the next day.

Before noon on 28 November such thoughts were gone when 10th Panzer Division counter-attacked with some fifty tanks. Also the Luftwaffe's near freedom of the skies at this time enabled their Stuka dive-bombers to hit troops of the spearhead 11 Brigade of 78th Division at will. As well as defending their build-up in and around Tunis, the Germans were also intent on driving the Allies back beyond Medjez. Although by 4 December the superior German armour with unchecked air support sent the Allies reeling back from Tebourba, a week of stubborn resistance by 78th Division, and the American forces, gave First Army time to withdraw, and consolidate stronger forces at Medjez el Bab.[15]

In response to the Army's desperate plea for urgent air support, on 4 December Wing Commander H.G. Malcolm led off ten Bisley light bombers of No. 18 Squadron RAF, in daylight without any fighter escort, to bomb a Luftwaffe airfield. They were intercepted and also outnumbered by Bf109s. The ten Bisleys, obsolete, slow and poorly armed, were all lost. It was an illustration of the many selfless efforts by Allied airmen to stem the German ground onslaught. Wing Commander Malcolm received the posthumous award of the VC.[16]

A lack of forward airfields, and almost non-existent co-operation processes between the Army and RAF spelled disaster. That same day, 4 December, twelve other Allied aircraft were lost, five P-38 Lightnings, a Boston bomber and six Spitfires destroyed on the ground. To add to the Allies' setbacks, on 6 December the rains came. 'It rained for three days and three nights,' said Cyril Ray the official historian of 78th Division. 'There was no cover for the men and the slit trenches filled with liquid mud.'[17]

Despite the Tebourba setback the Allies regathered in Medjez and planned another assault on Tunis. Political pressure intensified and the festive season was ignored. The offensive was to resume on the night of 23 December 1942 with a plan to capture Djebel el Ahmera, a mountainous ridge some six miles north of Medjez, known as Longstop Hill. Until it was seized nothing could move down the valley to attack Tunis.

The torrential rain swamped airfields, grounding planes. At times the mud was too heavy for even mules to move supplies. The Tunis offensive was cancelled. Even so it was decided that an attack on Longstop Hill must go ahead. During the night of 23 December and all of the next day, Christmas Eve, the Coldstream Guards and the US 18th Infantry Division fought in waves to gain Longstop's peak. And like the ebb and flow of the tides, they first gained the summit, lost it, recaptured it, and lost it again. On Christmas morning, after the second German counter-attack, the Allies withdrew to Medjez with over 500 casualties, and another bitter, and costly defeat.[18]

This failure to take Longstop Hill, combined with the rain and mud, brought the Allied advance to a shuddering halt. To add to that was the lack of close air support. It all meant that any further move on Tunis was impracticable. The forced back down from the plan to capture Tunis and the nearby port of Bizerte before the end of December meant that Rommel's Panzerarmee Afrika, which was retreating across Libya to Tunisia from the pursuing Eighth Army, was likely to join up with von Arnim's growing Fifth Panzer Army. The only option was for the Allies to build up their strength during the winter.

Air Vice Marshal Tedder knew that the Allies must first win the air war before a spring offensive on the ground could succeed. In their gamble to capture Tunis by the end of December 1942, the Allies' lack of air superiority in Tunisia had been a major contributory factor in the failure. Or in the converse perspective, if the Allies had enjoyed air superiority, the outcome may well have been different.

The battle for air superiority also now had to be fought and won on two fronts, over Tunisia and the Libyan desert. The DAF was continually on the move in step with Eighth Army, from one isolated desert airstrip to another.

While the Allies had lengthening supply lines and temporary airfields, the Axis had permanent airfields in Tunisia, Sicily and Sardinia. To undermine this advantage, air power and interdiction were seen as the key by choking off the enemy's supply routes, whether by sea freight or air transport across the Mediterranean.

Notes

1. Thomas, *Spitfire Aces of North Africa and Italy*, pp. 24–6.
2. Ford, *Battleaxe Division*, pp. 6–7; Evans, *With the East Surreys in Tunisia, Sicily and Italy 1942–45*, p. 5.
3. Perrett, *Winged Victory – The Army Air Forces in World War II*, p. 184.
4. Daniel, *The History of the East Surrey Regiment, Vol. IV*, p. 150; Evans, op. cit., pp. 4–20.
5. Ray, *Algiers to Austria*, p. 6.
6. Shores et al., op. cit., pp. 12–13.
7. Ibid., pp. 13–21.
8. Perrett, op. cit., pp. 185–6.
9. Thomas, op. cit., pp. 24–6.
10. Ibid.
11. Perrett, op. cit., pp. 185–6.
12. Thomas, op. cit., p. 27.
13. Ibid., pp. 28–9.
14. Ibid.
15. Ford, op. cit., p. 49.
16. Terraine, *Right of the Line*, p. 393; Owen, *The Desert Air Force*, p. 60.
17 Ray, op. cit., p. 25.
18. Evans, op. cit., pp. 4–20.

Chapter 5

DAF to the rescue of French forces at Ksar Rhilane

Dust swirled in the wake of the German armoured columns. They comprised two groups of Panzers, half-tracks and support trucks as they powered across the desert. It was 10 March 1943 near Ksar Rhilane in southern Tunisia and General von Arnim had sent the Panzer force racing to intercept the Free French forces of General Leclerc. The French had recently driven across the desert from Lake Chad to join General Montgomery's Eighth Army in a 'left hook' to outflank and help break the Axis defences on the Mareth Line. At about this time the combined Axis forces in Tunisia, now designated *Heeresgruppe Afrika/Gruppo d'Armate Africa* (Army Group Africa), were put under the command of von Arnim. He was desperate to prevent a link up of the British First Army of Operation TORCH with Eighth Army, which was pressing hard against the German-Italian Panzer Army (previously Panzer-armee Afrika) in the south of Tunisia.

Above the lines of German armour and motor transport, Pilot Officer Arthur Dawkins, of No. 450 Squadron RAAF, eased his Kittyhawk fighter-bomber around to survey the burning vehicles, which his bombs had just struck. He peered through the murk of smoke and dust for more targets which he could strafe. Then one of the trucks coming up in his flight path suddenly blew up in an immense explosion, enveloping him in a fog of black smoke, dirt and debris. It must have been an ammunition truck, he thought. Dawkins fought to keep control, feeling the plane being dragged down. Emerging again into bright sunlight, he was astonished to see, wrapped around one of his wings, a length of a truck's canvas tarpaulin. The base air-field at Nefatia some fifteen miles away, at once seemed much further distant.[1]

Kittyhawk fighter-bombers, twelve each from Nos 3 and 450 Squadrons RAAF, were bombing and shooting up the German armoured columns, while escorting Spitfires chased off some Stuka dive-bombers, which were heading for the French. Five attacks were made on the German forces, three by Kittybombers and two by Hurricane fighters of No. 6 Squadron RAF, known as the 'Flying Can-openers' due to their use of 40mm-cannon-armed tank-busting Hurricane IIDs (each Hurricane carried two 40mm cannon under its wings). The 250lb wing bombs, and the 500lb bombs under the fuselages of the Kittyhawks, together with the heavy cannon strafing of the Hurricanes, destroyed fifteen vehicles, and damaged others which were driven away by enemy recovery teams during the night. Despite losing six aircraft the fighter-bomber operation was a great success.[2]

* * *

In northern Tunisia during January and February 1943 the Allies' front lines, which in late December 1942 had been pushed back to the south from the edge of Tunis, remained entrenched close to Medjez-el-Bab in the Medjerda valley. In the face of the German offensive pressure, a lack of air support, and the onset of winter rain and mud, any renewed attack on Tunis had been postponed until spring. The rain turned many roads into quagmires, making them impassable for wheeled transport. The result was that the Medjez el Bab sector of the front became a salient protruding into Axis-held territory. A stalemate set in as both sides tested each other's lines while rebuilding.

Into January 1943 the Allied infantry companies had spread out into widely dispersed positions and taken on reinforcements in tough patrolling engagements. By being able to use local airfields near Bizerte and Tunis, the Luftwaffe exploited their air superiority in air-to-ground attacks, which meant that the infantry were often restricted to patrolling at night. German fighters had free range to fly through the valleys, attacking any vehicles or movement. General von Arnim repeatedly initiated attacks, sending in his troops and tanks to break through First Army's lines. In winter temperatures, which could drop to freezing, and even snow in the high hills, Allied troops spent many days and nights in cold, wet and hastily-dug trenches. Mountains and strongpoints were continually fought over, gained, lost, and regained, with no significant advance.

* * *

On 3 February 1943 Wing Commander Hugh Dundas DFC arrived at Souk el Khemis in northern Tunisia to take up a temporary position as commander of the Spitfire squadrons of 324 Wing RAF. Dundas was still only twenty-two years old, a decorated veteran fighter pilot of Dunkirk, the Battle of Britain and more than sixty missions over northern France with the legendary Douglas Bader. He was startled, as all pilots were at first, to see the airfields of bulldozed mud, and the primitive living conditions faced by squadrons and their pilots:

> The Spitfires were operating off strips of wire matting, laid on top of rushes which in turn had been laid on the mud. The strips were between 800 and 1,000 yards long and only 25 yards wide. They were connected with the squadron dispersal areas by more strips of matting, laid in narrow lanes. A pilot who put a wheel off the runway while landing – and

it was all too easy to do so when coming down in a gusty cross wind – was certain to capsize his plane. Alongside these makeshift airfields the squadrons' officers and ground crews lived and ate in tents.[3]

Hugh Dundas was from Barnborough in South Yorkshire and, on leaving school, first learned to fly in the Auxiliary Air Force. In May 1940, at only twenty years of age, he was in combat in the skies over Dunkirk and a few months later he was flying his Spitfire in the Battle of Britain. In those intense days of continual fighter dogfights he was shot down, cheating death by baling out just before the aircraft hit the ground. Once out of hospital he flew again in that aerial struggle for Britain's skies, and in more than sixty sorties in Bader's squadron over France in 1941, before his posting to Tunisia in early-1943.

By mid-February 1943, Axis aircraft strength in the Mediterranean region had risen to around 1,570, of which approximately 300 were based in Tunisia. Poor maintenance and supply difficulties, however, meant that only 50 per cent were generally serviceable for operations at any time. By contrast RAF Middle East, with under 1,000 aircraft, enjoyed a typical 75 per cent rate of availability. In addition Allied air forces were expanding rapidly.

On Eisenhower's instigation in early February all Allied air forces, including the USAAF across North Africa, were placed under the command of Acting Air Marshal Tedder, as AOC-in-C Mediterranean. In a series of discussions and meetings in Algiers, Eisenhower and Tedder had found a meeting of minds, for a working relationship and in their views of the role of air power. Tedder was appointed as Deputy to Eisenhower, and AVM Coningham took over as AOC Tactical Air Forces in North Africa. Tedder put great emphasis on maintenance and supply, which he saw as the essential backbone of air power.

Once Tripoli had been captured by Eighth Army on 23 January, RAF Middle East moved its whole maintenance and supply organization from Egypt to the Libyan capital. Maintenance and supply services, together with mobility and improvisation, were seen as integral and fundamental to maintaining the strike power of aircraft and their aircrew. The Axis air forces, on the other hand, suffered from supply shortages of every kind, particularly fuel, causing a lack of flexibility and an overall reduced number of sorties.

A major cause of Axis supply difficulties, as they had been for Rommel in the lead up to El Alamein, was the interdiction of Axis air routes and shipping by Allied aircraft. A typical example was provided by the two RAAF Squadrons, No. 454 flying Baltimores and No. 459 flying Hudsons, in the eastern Mediterranean. During March 459 Squadron undertook ninety convoy support sorties mainly at night, typically taking off soon after midnight, and 454 Squadron commenced operations against U-boats and E-boats.

*   *   *

In the first weeks of 1943, although the Allies continued to pour troops, guns and supplies into Algeria and feed them through to Tunisia, there was some disarray and indecision at the highest levels in London and Washington. In January Churchill and Roosevelt met in Casablanca, appointed General Alexander to command all Allied land forces in North Africa (18 Army Group) and as deputy to Eisenhower, and reaffirmed their resolve to win the Tunisian campaign.

There was a mixture of optimism and belief that it was only a matter of time before they would defeat the Axis forces by pinning them between Montgomery's Eighth Army and the Anglo-American forces of Operation TORCH. However, no-one could foretell how long it would take, or at what cost. The invasions contemplated by the Allies for Italy and north-west Europe rested upon first defeating the Axis powers in North Africa. There was fear of the Tunisian campaign dragging on and on. Under some criticism and pressure by the political leaders and high commands in London and Washington, Eisenhower made a brave statement to Churchill and Roosevelt by promising victory in Tunisia by mid-May 1943.

Whilst the Allied commands planned and reorganized during January, their fear of being bogged down in Tunisia threatened to become a nightmare. For Rommel and his German-Italian Panzer Army, with their long, controlled retreat across Libya and then into southern Tunisia behind them, had already begun to combine with General von Arnim's forces in the north. Rommel established strong defences on the Mareth Line, which had been built in the south by the French to guard against Italian attacks, to fend off Eighth Army. He was also intent on preventing the Americans from advancing from the Atlas Mountains in the south-west, and driving a wedge between his Panzer force, and von Arnim's Fifth Panzer Army in the north.

On 8 February Rommel met with von Arnim and Field Marshal Kesselring, who was in command of all German forces in the Mediterranean, and convinced them that the best strategy was a drive to the west to destroy the main Allied supply bases, at Tebessa in Algeria, and le Kef farther north-west inside Tunisia. Kesselring wanted to push the Allies back into Algeria, but Rommel and von Arnim agreed between them that it could only be a limited action. Rommel wanted time to focus on defence of the Mareth Line against Eighth Army.

At Sidi Bou Zid on the evening of 13/14 February 10th and 21st Panzer Divisions launched Operation FRÜHLINGSWIND (Spring Wind). This was a surprise night attack through the rocky terrain of the Faid Pass, previously thought to be unsuitable for tanks.[4] In two days, 14 and 15 February, they surrounded and then inflicted a crushing defeat on the US 2nd Armored Division, which lost 100 tanks, 88 half-tracks and artillery, and some 1,600 casualties.[5]

On 20 February 1943, after driving US forces into flight from Sbeitla, 10th Panzer Division then drove the Americans back some twenty-four miles west of Kasserine town itself, and gained control of the Kasserine Pass. Over the next three days, on mountainous roads threading through the western dorsal towards Tebessa and le Kef, the German Panzers with superior guns and tactics blasted their way forward through poorly-prepared American and British positions. By the close of 22 February at a height of 3,300 feet they were close to taking Thala, and only forty miles from le Kef.

The obvious and only option for an immediate counter was to turn to the DAF. As it always seemed to be, it was ready to respond. In day and night attacks DAF bombed Luftwaffe forward airfields, supply dumps, and troop concentrations on the Mareth Line and near Gabes. First Army began to move some forces down from the north to assist the Americans, and RAF wings in northern Tunisia sent fighter patrols to the area to counter Luftwaffe raids.

Wing Commander Dundas' 324 Wing was one of those ordered into these operations in support of US forces. Like all new pilots on arrival from UK, he faced an intense learning period in regard to both the climate and an unknown geographical terrain. Despite this, Dundas felt the need to quickly lead a two-squadron operation on one of these patrols. Once in the air he soon had some regrets that he had not prepared more thoroughly.

As Dundas led the formation of twenty-four Spitfires to the south, they flew into rain squalls and broken storm clouds, which hid the tops of mountains. Seeing the terrain for the first time, he found it hard to pick out the landmarks recommended at the pre-flight briefing. Their orders were to keep the ground under observation, so he had to resist the urge to climb to a safer altitude.

Aware that he must not make a mistake, which could be disastrous in the conditions, he dismissed a fleeting temptation to turn back. Dundas knew that such a decision would undermine his credibility so soon in his command. He kept going and they reached the designated patrol line without encountering any enemy aircraft. He turned the group around to the north on the homeward return leg, and into even worse weather.

Because of the mountains and the weather, radio contact with their base was disrupted. Even if a reliable communication could be made, Dundas also recognized that his fellow pilots would be expecting him to lead them home without having to resort to a request for a homeward bearing. He found himself praying to a higher authority that he was leading the group on the correct course. At last they emerged from the clouds to see the landing strips of Souk el Khemis ahead. By the time he had taxied to a stop, and switched off the engine, Dundas felt drained, as if he had survived a ferocious dogfight with an enemy fighter.[6]

Through those mountains below the patrolling Spitfires, Rommel's Panzers pressed on relentlessly, brushing aside inexperienced American troops. Once through the Kasserine Pass their Panzers were within one day's easy down-hill drive to le Kef, the Allies' major supply base. Despite American and British troops fiercely contesting the approach to Thala, the Allied command expected Rommel to launch the final attack on the morning of 23 February, and there was little confidence that it could be resisted. Then there would be nothing to stop the Panzers devouring the flat terrain all the way to le Kef. However, despite Kesselring flying to the front to urge them on, Rommel's advice to pull back was accepted.[7]

The Panzer columns had thinned themselves out in three separate thrusts. They lacked the strength to stretch out further without hope of reinforcements of men and supplies, and their extended columns were now running short of fuel. In the hours before dawn on 23 February Rommel turned the Panzers around, and returned to his defensive positions on the Mareth Line. Clearly the bombing by DAF of German bases and supply lines, and a counter-attack by the British 6th Armoured Division, added fuel to Rommel's fear of an attack by Eighth Army on his rear.

The flexibility, mobility and high serviceability of the DAF maintained by their ground crews, brought ever increasing capability for close co-operation with the army. In addition by March 1943 the numerical strength of the Desert Air Force over the Axis air forces, the Luftwaffe and Regia Aeronautica, had grown even greater.

DAF had become a unique mix of the Allies' national air forces. Both air crew and ground support airmen from Britain, Australia, Canada, New Zealand, South Africa and the USA, were to be found across the DAF squadrons. Postings and transfers increasingly ignored individual and national preferences, and responded to the demands of the front-line squadrons to replace casualties and meet operational demands.

In the Mareth area in March 1943 the main DAF groups, wings and other formations comprised:[8]

Wings	Squadrons	Aircraft Type/Details
232	55, 223 RAF	Baltimores
239	112, 250, 260 RAF, 3 and 450 RAAF	Kittyhawks
244	92, 145, 601, 73, 417 RAF 1 SAAF	Spitfires and Hurricanes
3 SAAF	12, 21, 24 SAAF	Bostons and Baltimores
7 SAAF	2, 4, 5 SAAF	Kittyhawks

57th Group, USAAF 12th Air Force	64th, 65th, 66th, 319th	Warhawks
79th Group, USAAF 12th Air Force	85th, 86th, 87th, 316th	Warhawks
12th Bomber Group, USAAF 12th Air Force	83rd, 434th	B-24 Mitchell
Other specialist units		Anti-tank, reconnaissance, night-fighters, air-sea rescue etc.

Although the Germans withdrew from Kasserine back to Gafsa, their Operation FRÜHLINGSWIND had inflicted a series of major battle defeats on the Americans, who lost more than 6,000 men dead or wounded, and another 3,000 taken prisoner out of 30,000.

Despite many brave Allied attempts to halt the Panzers, the Germans suffered fewer than 1,000 casualties, and only 201 dead.[9] The Allies were lucky to narrowly avoid a strategic defeat, and their main supply depots at Tebessa and le Kef remained intact. Nevertheless, there was to be no respite elsewhere.

On 3 March a recce flight over the Mareth Line by 239 Wing's 450 Squadron reported a build-up of German armour. Ignoring his supply shortages, Rommel did not intend to rely solely on static defence. Although the Luftwaffe had been unable to mount a preceding bombardment, on 6 March, supported by Focke-Wulf Fw190 and Me210 fighter bombers transferred from Sicily, German armour attacked Eighth Army at Medenine.

Acting upon the DAF reconnaissance information, Eighth Army's artillery was prepared, and positioned ready for the Axis thrust. First sandstorms, then cloud cover restricted overall air activity, but eight times on 6 March alone, DAF Kittybombers in three-squadron formations with Spitfire escorts, struck at the attacking Panzers. The combination of artillery pounding, and DAF's aerial bombing inflicted heavy losses on the German armoured columns, and forced the enemy's withdrawal. On 9 March an ill and exhausted Rommel, worn down from the constant attacks by Eighth Army in the long retreat from Alamein, flew home to Germany to recover. Von Arnim was forced to place all Axis forces onto a defensive footing. With hindsight it seems to have been a tipping point.

As a cover for Eighth Army's preparation to undertake a left flanking offensive around the Mareth Line, the Allies' Free French Force under General Leclerc began moving to the north from Ksar Rhilane. Early on 10 March they were threatened by approaching columns of German armour, supported by both Luftwaffe fighters and dive-bombers. Cloud cover had restricted DAF patrols and reconnaissance, but an enemy move against the French had been anticipated, and some squadrons were already briefed and on standby.

Once a signal was received from the French of the approaching German attack, squadrons scrambled into a combined DAF response. The preparations for Montgomery's 'left hook', a contingency plan to outflank the Mareth Line if it was needed, could only be protected by air power. Waves of DAF fighters and fighter-bombers rushed to the rescue. Kittyhawks and Spitfires, including the Kittyhawk of Pilot Officer Dawkins in 450 Squadron RAAF, forced the German armour to turn back and withdraw from their attack on the French at Ksar Rhilane. It was a remarkably successful intervention by fighter-bombers, which would have far-reaching implications for air power tactics and strategy into the future.

Yet the Mareth Line still held up a frontal offensive by Eighth Army. The fortified Mareth Line followed the northern edge of the Oued Zigzaou wadi for about thirty miles across the narrow coastal plain between the Matmata Hills and the sea. However, there was the possibility of a way around this Tunisian equivalent of the Maginot Line. Based upon information provided by the French, some patrols by Eighth Army's Long Range Desert Group had confirmed that the Tebaga Gap, a valley between the Chott el Fejaj salt lake and the Matmata Hills, was a viable route around the Mareth Line for troops and armoured columns experienced to desert conditions. To outflank the German defences, Montgomery decided to plan another version of his renowned 'left hook' tactic, and attempt to send a strong, armoured force onto these narrow mountain tracks to the west.[10]

Notes

1. Brown, *Desert Warriors*, p. 178.
2. Smith, op. cit., pp. 9–11.
3. Dundas, *Flying Start*, pp. 106–7.
4. Atkinson, *Army at Dawn*, p. 322.
5. Ibid., pp. 322–56.
6. Dundas, op. cit., pp. 108–9.
7. Atkinson, op. cit., pp. 322–56.
8. Shores, op. cit., pp. 125–36.
9. Atkinson, op. cit., pp. 384–90.
10. Smith, op. cit., p. 39.

Chapter 6

Fighter-bombers lay on an 'air blitz' at El Hamma

In early March 1943 Flight Lieutenant Neville Duke of No. 92 Squadron, 244 Wing RAF, who was already an ace from 1942 with eight victories, claimed six more, as the struggle by DAF to assert superiority over Axis air forces continued. On 1 March 1943 Duke shot down two Macchi C.202s, and claimed four more victories within a week. At times it seemed that every squadron's operation culminated in a clash of the opposing fighters.[1]

On every sortie each pilot faced a private battle, a battle against fear. And at the end of each day, if he had won that private battle, and also a battle against an enemy aircraft, he knew that there was no end to it. There was both physical and mental strain building continually for every pilot. A night's good sleep free from nightmares reliving the aerial combat, or a day or two off, could alleviate the physical fatigue. The mental stress for many fighter pilots often built day after day, no matter what. Every man had a breaking point at some indeterminate point, where time away for recovery was the only option. Of course, to get that opportunity he had to survive long enough.[2] Up to this time Duke had done just that, and much more.

Neville Duke, from Tonbridge in Kent, was twenty-one years old. Throughout his schooldays he had been an aviation enthusiast, and intended to apply for an RAF Short Service Commission once he was eighteen. This he did in June 1940 and in April 1941 joined 92 Squadron RAF, where he gained invaluable experience flying as No. 2 to Wing Commander A.G. 'Sailor' Malan DSO DFC. Duke was first posted to Egypt in November 1941, where he joined No. 112 Squadron RAF flying P-40 Tomahawks. After 161 sorties and 220 operational hours, he was ordered to take up instructor duties for a rest and recovery period, before, in November 1942, he gained a posting back to his original 92 Squadron, then based in Gambut, Egypt.[3]

On 19 and 20 March 244 Wing flew escort cover in close support for the fighter-bombers supporting Eighth Army as it moved into its offensives at El Hamma and Medenine. A few days later Duke and his fellow pilots were delighted when 244 Wing received twelve Spitfire Mark IXs, including six for the Polish Fighter Team of No. 145 Squadron RAF, and four for Duke's 92 Squadron. It was well timed, not only to support Eighth Army trying to break the Mareth Line, but also to counter the arrival of the Focke-Wulf

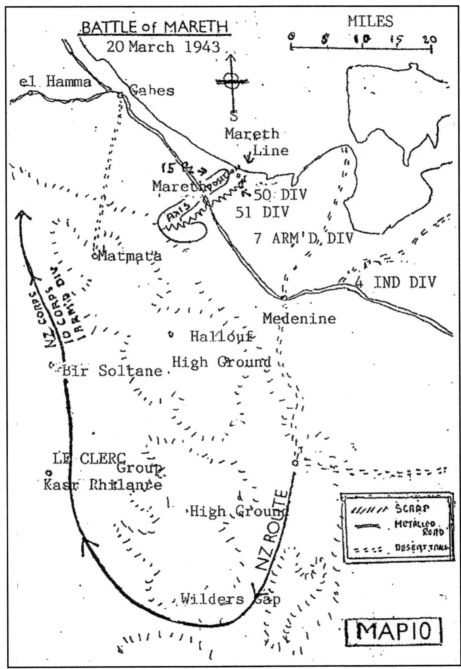

The Battle of the Mareth Line in southern Tunisia, 20 March 1943. The map shows the Ksar Rhilane and El Hamma battle locations, where close air support attacks by DAF assisted Eighth Army break through the Mareth Line with an outflanking left hook offensive.

Fw190. Air Vice Marshal Broadhurst, who had been appointed to succeed Coningham on 30 January, had persuaded the RAF in the UK to send out some of these latest Spitfires. The Spitfire Mk IX had a top speed of 408mph, a faster climb rate and a higher service ceiling than the Fw190. They out-classed the German fighters, whose pilots believed that DAF had been more widely re-equipped with Mk IX Spitfires.

Broadhurst by this time had also under his command two American fighter groups, 57th and 79th, both equipped with Warhawk fighters, the American name for the P-40, plus a bomber group with the B-25 Mitchell light bomber. Broadhurst persuaded the two fighter groups, approximately equivalent to RAF wings, to integrate their operations with the Desert Air Force under his command. For the Mareth air battles, because of the Americans' relative inexperience of air fighting or ground attack, a typical operational formation was half a squadron of Australian pilots in their RAAF Kittyhawks leading half a squadron of American pilots in Warhawks.[4]

*   *   *

In the mountains of northern Tunisia First Army continued its fight to gain control of the eastern dorsals of the Atlas range. They were still suffering from enemy bombing and strafing, since the Luftwaffe and Regia Aeronautica were flying readily from local airfields around Tunis. During the day Bf109 fighters and Ju87 Stuka dive-bombers often careered through the valleys, seemingly at little more than tree-top height, shooting up transport and anything that moved.[5]

In contrast, in the south, because of DAF forcing the German armour to turn back and withdraw from Ksar Rhilane, the next day, 11 March, the French were able to move up to their positions. From the Mareth Line 2nd New Zealand Division with other forces went westwards also without suffering any enemy strikes, despite the many miles of redeploying traffic, which would have been easily observed by Axis positions in the hills. The increasing dominance of DAF, due to its ability to operate from hastily pre-pared airfields close behind Eighth Army's front lines, was allowing the re-positioning of ground troops with impunity. It was a significant advantage over Axis forces, and meant that Eighth Army's plans for an attack outflanking the Mareth Line, through the Matmata Hills, were falling into place.

After the success of DAF at Ksar Rhilane, it was agreed that the US Twelfth Air Force and No. 242 Group RAF from Algeria and Tunisia, would concen-trate on bombing German air fields round the clock. DAF would confine itself to close support of Eighth Army, and its offensive against the Mareth Line, through a western out-flanking 'left-hook' tactic, to the west as well as a direct assault in the east.[6]

During the night of 19/20 March, 50th (Northumbrian Division) and 23 Armoured Brigade of XXX Corps began to move up for the frontal attack on the Mareth Line's formidable defences in the Wadi Zigzaou near the coast. Simultaneously 200 tanks and 27,000 troops of the New Zealand Division and 8 Armoured Brigade began the left hook around the south-west end of the line. When the French built the Mareth Line defences they thought the terrain of this area to be too difficult for any sizeable force to negotiate. The Free French on 19 March had taken positions across the Wadi el Outio, north of Ksar Rhilane, so that overnight on 19/20 March the New Zealanders skirted south and west around the Mareth Line, and then began to head north towards the Tebaga Gap.[7]

As Axis forces in response reacted to hurry west to meet the outflanking threat, on the evening of 20/21 March Eighth Army mounted a frontal attack on the eastern end of the Mareth Line. In support DAF commenced the 'shuttle service' bombing by light bombers on 21 March around Mareth. During the day fighter-bombers went out on armed reconnaissance searching for targets of opportunity, and the tank-buster Hurricanes of DAF's No. 6 Squadron did their work again claiming thirty-two hits on enemy vehicles.[8]

When Eighth Army's 50th Division had to pull back to the south side of the Wadi Zigzaou on 23 March they had suffered very heavy casualties with some brigades down by a third. Montgomery ordered 1st Armoured Division to reinforce the New Zealand Division, transferring the main impetus to his left hook.[9]

Having seen that Axis forces were being fully drawn into battle in the east, Montgomery ordered the left flank attack to press forward towards El Hamma. If successful this left hook would reach behind the Mareth Line, and force the Axis General Messe to pull back all his troops to the north. As the first attack on the eastern sector of the Mareth Line struggled to make a breakthrough, the 4th Indian and 1st Armoured Divisions moved to the west to bolster Montgomery's 'left-hook' tactic. The Luftwaffe, hammered by the bombing campaign against its airfields, was unable to attack the miles and miles of dusty columns. It confirmed that the Allies had gained air superiority, which allowed Eighth Army to redeploy its forces without fear of Luftwaffe attacks.

The problem with the 'left-hook' strategy was that Axis forces were entrenched in strong positions at El Hamma, in the Tebaga Gap's confined approach. Eighth Army's tanks would be vulnerable to the German 88mm guns, which were well dug-in, and lethal against armour. A direct frontal attack by Eighth Army could be a disaster.[10]

The New Zealanders were held up by very strong Axis positions which comprised extensive minefields and dug-in artillery, in a 6,000-yard-wide defile code-named the 'Plum'. The 'Plum' defile ran between Djebel Melaba on the north edge of the Matmata Hills and Djebel Tebaga, and Axis forces had also made use of a Roman wall which crossed the valley.

First Armoured Division began to follow the track now marked by the New Zealanders. It wound its way through the edges of the Matmata Hills for some 200 miles, and it would take two days. Meanwhile the New Zealanders called for DAF air support. At the same time there were concerns that the firepower of 1st Armoured when it arrived would be insufficient, and General Messe could reinforce Axis positions further in the meantime. Montgomery and Broadhurst agreed in principle to DAF mounting a ground attack operation to blast a way through the 'Plum', later to be referred to as the El Hamma Line (or 'Mareth switch-line'). An Army-Air conference on 24 March agreed that, instead of light bombers in formation attacks, fighter-bombers and strafing attacks would be used in front of the ground attack.[11]

The DAF success in attacking Axis armour at Ksar Rhilane must have impressed Eighth Army's planners. For the first time it was decided that the full DAF attack role would change. Instead of their typical tactics of strikes against supply columns and dumps, airfields and troop concentrations, DAF fighter-bombers would fly sorties in close collaboration with Eighth Army's ground attack. The plan was for the Kittyhawk fighter-bombers to go in low, bombing and strafing enemy lines, in the direct path of, and ahead of the 2nd New Zealand, 4th Indian and 1st Armoured Divisions. In terrain so favourable for the defenders, it was really the only hope for Montgomery's plan to succeed.[12]

The reasoning for using the fighter-bombers was based upon a number of factors, including the light bomber crews not knowing the new battle area, and that the effectiveness of pattern bombing against dug-in targets was doubted. It was thought that the fighter-bombers would be better at pinpointing enemy positions, and their use would allow the light bombers to continue with their night-bombing raids in the east. Perhaps the most influential factor was that Broadhurst wanted the fighter-bombers, with their bombs and cannon, to lay on a 'low flying blitz'.[13]

The modification of fighters so that they could carry bombs, either under their fuselage or wings, in a fighter-bomber role, was a recent development. It was controversial, with conflicting arguments for and against. Flying with 450 Squadron RAAF of 239 Wing RAF at this time was Flight Lieutenant Reginald 'Rusty' Kierath from a rural area in New South Wales, Australia. Kierath was one of a number of pilots who had flown a Kittyhawk in a fighter-bomber role, known as a Kittybomber, in the action at Ksar Rhilane. The first trial of a Kittyhawk in such a role had been undertaken in early 1942 by a fellow Australian, Clive Caldwell, a fighter ace with No. 112 Squadron RAF. On 24 March 1943, the lives of the spearhead troops, and the turning of the Mareth Line, depended upon the likes of Rusty Kierath and other flyers in DAF to deliver the cutting edge of the new air - ground support tactic.[14]

Besides tactical considerations on the ground, there were unavoidable strategic reasons for mounting an air blitz. Having been unable to break the Mareth Line near the coast in a frontal attack, to try again there invited further defeat and heavy losses. The only other possible way was through the defile at El Hamma. Yet the Axis had been able to reinforce its defences to make the El Hamma gap just as unattractive. To sustain its supply needs Eighth Army must break through, keep moving forward, and reach the main port of Sfax farther up the coast to open up easier access to shipping cargoes.[15]

The El Hamma strongpoint sat in a funnel of a valley, with German gun positions on the hills either side, and protected by mines and countless dry river beds. DAF was being called upon to destroy the trap.[16]

The proposed plan for an 'air blitz' by DAF in support of Eighth Army caused a reaction from AVM Coningham, who was now AOC-in-C of Northwest African Tactical Air Force (NATAF). NATAF comprised the Desert Air Force, XXII Air Support Command and the Tactical Bomber Force (TBF). Coningham was resistant to committing fighters to major ground attack operations. It was against established RAF doctrine, because of the risk of losing large numbers of fighters, and consequently air superiority. Coningham sent his senior air staff to remonstrate with Broadhurst, who was not deterred. Backed by Montgomery, Broadhurst got his way.

Immediately after the Army-Air conference on 24 March, fighter-bombers and the tank-destroyer Hurricanes attacked the enemy's tanks and transport, which were confronting the New Zealanders. Also more detailed planning for the 'air blitz' to break the El Hamma Line of the Axis forces got under way at once. With the stalemate at Mareth, the Axis 21st Panzer and 164th Infantry Divisions, already at El Hamma, could be reinforced by 10th and 15th Panzer. The principal elements of the air support plan drawn up for the El Hamma blitz were:

25/26 March: Night raid bombing on Axis HQs and telephone centres to keep the enemy awake and confused.
26 March 1530: Attacks on tank concentrations first by Hurricanes of the tank-buster No. 6 Squadron, followed by two squadrons of fighter-bombers.
26 March 1600: A creeping artillery barrage behind which 8 Armoured Brigade and New Zealand infantry would begin to advance.

The creeping barrage would create an advancing bomb-line. From sixteen fighter-bomber squadrons available for the operation, two squadrons at a time would bomb and strafe the enemy positions in front of the bomb-line for more than two hours continuously.

On the ground a large letter E marked the infantry's start line, with red and blue smoke next to it. As the troops moved forward they would indicate their positions with yellow smoke. Although this would be of use to enemy artillery in the valley's hillsides, there was a real concern to avoid the blitz hitting Allied troops. The New Zealanders provided locations of Axis gun positions, which Allied artillery would target regularly with smoke shells to further help strafing and dive-bombing by DAF fighters.[17]

The 'air blitz' plan called for continuous strikes by Kittyhawk fighter-bombers, commencing thirty minutes before the Army ground attack, to be maintained in two-squadron formations at a time for two hours. Could this revolutionary new tactic work? To break the Mareth Line the 'left hook' attack of Eighth Army must succeed. If the new DAF tactics did not achieve the planned effect, the ground attack would almost certainly be repelled. If it failed, it would take a more drawn-out offensive to drive the Axis forces back from the Mareth Line. General Eisenhower's commitment to London and Washington to defeat Axis forces in Tunisia by May 1943 and subsequent plans for the invasion of Sicily would be in tatters.

To assist the DAF bombing runs, smoke and army vehicles were deployed on the ground approaches: red and blue smoke for the start point, trucks drawn up in the form of code letters for DAF pilots, yellow smoke for Eighth Army positions, and white smoke shells bursting onto enemy positions. The first ever experiment of Army/Air wireless communication was instigated, using selected flight lieutenants with radios sitting in armoured cars in the front lines.[18]

On the morning of 26 March dust storms allowed the New Zealand troops and 1st Armoured Division, to concentrate for the attack with good cover against enemy observers. At 1530, in a late change, an unscheduled wave of light bombers of 3 Wing SAAF pattern-bombed enemy positions. When the dust and smoke from this raid cleared the anti-tank Hurricanes of 6 Squadron went in against 21st Panzer. Despite intense flak no aircraft were lost.

At 1600, as planned, the creeping barrage began, with smoke shells targeted as indicators on Axis gun positions. Then the waves of Kittybombers began their attacks, about 400 aircraft continuously over more than two hours. Squadrons would first drop their bombs on enemy positions, then dive down again to strafe with cannon and machine guns. By the end of the onslaught 21st Panzer and 164th Infantry Divisions had suffered significant losses of artillery guns and 'soft skinned' vehicles, as against thirteen Kittybombers lost.[19]

Over 24 to 26 March, day and night, DAF light bomber strikes had pounded Axis positions again and again south of El Hamma. On the afternoon of 26 March, despite serviceability constraints brought on by those two days of low-flying, DAF threw in 412 sorties in pattern-bombing against enemy telephone communications. Before the German troops could begin to re-organize, DAF fighter-bombers struck again, bombing and strafing at low level. The DAF bombing campaign, culminating in the fighter-bomber attack, fully achieved its aim of keeping the enemy's heads down before the ground attack.[20]

At the end of the air blitz 8 Armoured Brigade and the New Zealand infantry drove through the enemy minefields and defensive positions. First Armoured Division carried out a considerable advance in the hours of darkness, to ensure that the valley's natural features could not be used to mount an ambush on the tanks.[21] Over the next two days Axis forces fought rearguard actions, until they could retreat north with 15th Panzer from Mareth. As well as destroying large numbers of guns, tanks and other transport and imposing a toll of dead and wounded, by 28 March the Allies had taken 700 prisoners. The combined DAF and artillery blitz had turned the Mareth Line, and the Axis troops could hold no longer.

DAF lost seventeen Kittybombers in the operation, out of some 400. To achieve the major success of breaking the Mareth Line at El Hamma it was an acceptable loss. Those who were involved had no doubts about the worth of this innovative use of air support. Yet Broadhurst's decision to use fighter-bombers was still criticized in higher circles. Perhaps most important was the demonstration it gave of how fighter-bombers in close army-air support, where circumstances were favourable for their use, could change the tide of battle on the ground.[22]

By late-March and early-April 1943 the rains began to lessen. Planning and preparations were underway again for the spring offensive to take Tunis. With temperatures on some days around a maximum of 25–28°C, it allowed the bringing forward of more troops and supplies.

At the same time as the First Army infantry fought in the Oued Zarga mountains in the north, in the south on 7 April the first forward detachments of General Montgomery's Eighth Army made contact with leading patrols of II US Corps. The Allied pincer movement was beginning to close in on the Axis forces. Speed was now critical on all fronts to exploit the encirclement, and prevent the enemy from controlling his retreat and withdrawing his forces to Italy.

*   *   *

The struggle for air supremacy in early-April continued unabated. DAF squadrons began to come within range of RAF airfields in Tunisia, and all Allied air forces were put under the unified command of AVM Coningham. Every avenue was being explored to strengthen air superiority and Wing Commander Dundas of 324 Wing was presented with orders to undertake a bizarre mission. At the Bou Saada oasis in the desert, some 250 miles south of Algiers, a Vichy French air force unit remained isolated. They had been resisting all entreaties to collaborate with the Allies. Besides the opportunity to add another wing-size group to Allied air power, there was a demand to eliminate any threat they might pose. As the Allies ratcheted up the pressure on the Axis, and closed on Tunis, the last thing they needed was a rogue strike on their rear areas by some disgruntled Vichy French flyers.

Dundas' orders were to fly down to Bou Saada and talk the French CO into joining the Allies. He was to offer them the temptation of being re-equipped with Spitfire fighters. For a long flight over desert and the Atlas Mountains, and to guard against one of them having to make a forced landing for engine trouble or some other unforeseeable event, he took with him a Canadian, Jimmie Grey, commander of No. 243 Squadron RAF. In their two Spitfires they finally located the landing strip, close to an oasis settlement. The green palms and white of the houses and Foreign Legion fort sparkled in the sunset against the surrounding desert. As they descended Dundas saw a figure emerge from a tent and peer skywards:

> I told Jimmie to go on circling while I landed and taxied in. I would call him if I wanted him to follow. With great caution – and a little trepid-ation – I landed and taxied over to the tent. The man I had seen ran towards me, waving and smiling. I called Jimmie and told him to come down. Our one man reception committee was a young lieutenant in the French Air Force. He was evidently astonished to see us, but he was courteous and friendly.[23]

So as to portray his authority to negotiate Dundas introduced himself to the young French lieutenant as a lieutenant colonel, accompanied by Com-mander Grey. The young French officer was astounded that they had attained such senior ranks at their youthful age and was very envious. He then drove Dundas and Grey to his HQ where they met the French commander, a major well into middle age. Without enquiring the reason for their visit, he invited Dundas and Grey to dine with him and other senior French officers. During the dinner the focal point of the conversation was the Spitfire fighter, and their desire to get into the action.

> Maybe it was the wine working on me, but I decided that they were the sort of people we wanted with us, and I told their CO that I was autho-rized to offer them the opportunity to come and fight alongside us in the final liberation of Tunisia from the 'sale Boche'. This information aroused great enthusiasm – maybe the wine was working on them too ...[24]

Next day Dundas and Grey made an uneventful return flight to their home base but without gaining any clear indication from the French commander of his intentions. Further communications took place at a senior level between the Free French authorities and the Allies and, in due course, the French airmen from Bou Saada joined the Allied cause. They duly got their Spitfires and were flying operations in the final battle for Tunis.

Despite the growing evidence that Allied air power was winning the air war, for the troops on the ground, to most of whom the air force was an unseen hand, it was not at all clear where and when a final victory in Tunisia would come. The problem remained: how and where could the Allies break through to close the trap? In the far north, on the coastal approaches to Bizerte, the Americans were held up at mountain strongpoints such as Green Hill and Bald Hill. In the south the armoured strength of Eighth Army after the breakthrough at El Hamma had become neutralized by Axis defences in the hills around Enfidaville to the south of Tunis.

In the central north, in the Medjerda river valley, there seemed to have been little change since December. North of Medjez el Bab the Germans were immoveable. On ridges such as Djebel Bou Aoukaz and Longstop Hill, they stubbornly endured every attack by the Allies' First Army. With the terrain favouring the enemy's defences, the fear was that for some months yet the Axis could grind out a lengthy war of attrition before they succumbed.

Notes

1. Thomas, op. cit., pp. 21–2.
2. Bowyer, *Men of the Desert Air Force*, pp. 177–86.
3. Wellum, *First Light*, pp. 100–1.
4. Private collection – Communication from ACM Sir Harry Broadhurst to General Sir Charles Richardson.
5. Evans, op. cit., p. 24.
6. Owen, *The Desert Air Force*, pp. 169–70.
7. Smith, op. cit., p. 39.
8. Owen, op. cit., pp. 169–70.
9. Smith, op. cit., pp. 39–48.
10. Owen, op. cit., pp. 169–71.
11. Smith, op. cit., pp. 39–48.
12. Owen, op. cit., pp. 170–1.
13. Smith, op. cit., pp. 39–48.
14. Owen, op. cit., pp. 170–1.
15. Smith, op. cit., pp. 39–48.
16. Owen, op. cit., pp. 170–1.
17. Smith, op. cit., pp. 39–48.
18. Owen, op. cit., pp. 170–1.
19. Smith, op. cit., pp. 39–48.
20. Owen, op. cit., pp. 170–1.
21. Doherty, *British Armoured Divisions and Their Commanders 1939–1945*, pp. 106–8.
22. Smith, op. cit., pp. 39–48.
23. Dundas, op. cit., pp. 210–13.
24. Ibid.

Chapter 7

Interdiction, an air blitz and a 'No Fly Zone' to take Tunis

High above the island of Malta, Australian Flight Lieutenant Bill McRae of 104 Squadron RAF wrestled with the controls of a twin-engined Wellington bomber. He was taking off to raid Sicily's capital and major port of Palermo. In gusty winds and low cloud, groaning and creaking in its slow climb, the bomber dropped then surged upwards. Bill recalled that:

> Shortly after take-off we ran into turbulent cloud. Our course was over the sea on the east of Sicily, then a turn west through the straits of Messina and along the northern Sicilian coast to Palermo.

At the outbreak of the Second World War, Bill McRae was working for the Bank of New South Wales in the UK. As there were no Australian forces in Britain, he first joined the Royal Artillery before transferring to the RAF to train as a pilot. On completion of his training he had flown the new Wellington Mk VIII torpedo-bomber to Cairo, and later he was posted to Malta. On that night bombing raid to Palermo, despite the increasingly poor weather, Bill was aware of the pressure to get the job done.

> As we approached the north coast of Sicily, the cloud cleared and we were able to identify some islands, and work out the bombing run. We circled off the coast at 10,000 feet until 'blitz' time, then hugged the shoreline towards the target, Palermo Harbour.
>
> I began to lose height down to 8,000 feet, and increased speed to 160 knots. With the nose down I had a good view, and saw a ship moored at the wharves. At first there was not a lot of flak. We had no trouble in identifying the target and let the bombs go in one stick.
>
> Then I opened the throttles, and with the engines screaming at maximum revs, did a steep climbing turn, trying to get through the flak bursts, which were now targeting the aircraft. When we were back to 8,000 feet, I eased back on the throttles, and pushed the nose down to level off.
>
> Both engines suddenly cut out. In that instant, it seemed that time stood still. It flashed through my mind that we had been hit. Then, after a couple of seconds, the engines picked up.

As usual, when getting clear of a target, Bill found his mouth had gone completely dry. In another operation for McRae and his crew, to cut off German supplies, the target was the port of Sfax in Tunisia.

We took off in daylight, at 1700 hours, and I was delighted to be at the controls of a Wellington, which I was very familiar with from our Egypt based operations. We flew south low over the sea and then turned 90 degrees right towards our target. It was dark as we neared Sfax, and we were able to pin point our position on some islands to the east of the town. We had climbed to 6,500 feet and Ian had obtained the wind for the bombing run. The weather was clear and the buildings in the port were easy to identify.

As we began our run in exactly on the 'blitz' time, another aircraft dropped a string of flares. Ian did a couple of bombing runs, and with no guns firing at us, he thought he was back home on a training exercise. Turning over the sea for another run, with the light from the flares we spotted a ship a few miles off shore. We circled round to line up on it but the flares went out. We had our own flares, but Ernie found there were problems with their ripcords not working, which should pull off a cap, and arm the flare. I even took the laces out of my desert boots, and sent them back to Ernie to see if that would help. He launched three more, but none of them lit up.

That ship had a lucky escape. We returned to Sfax and got rid of the remaining bombs. On the way home the aircraft ran like a bird. It seems she must have known it was her last trip, as she went missing the next night along with its pilot, my good friend Flight Sergeant Iremonger, and crew.[1]

* * *

The raid by Bill McRae and 104 Squadron RAF on Palermo was just one of many in early 1943 in the elusive search to gain final victory over Axis forces in North Africa. In late-March and April 1943 the bombing raids on infrastructure, supply, Luftwaffe bases, Tunisian ports such as Sfax, Sousse, Bizerte and the capital Tunis, and those in Sicily and southern Italy, were being intensified.

Over the Tunisian battlefields DAF fighter-bombers were no less active. On 7 April No. 3 Squadron RAAF of 239 Wing RAF received orders to undertake bombing and strafing operations against extensive German troop convoys withdrawing towards Tunis along the road from Gafsa to Mezzouna. The convoys were believed to include 10th and 21st Panzer Divisions. Flying Officer Tom Russell and Flight Sergeant Rod McKenzie flew two of the squadron's Kittyhawk fighter-bombers on the second of their four missions that day.

We carried six 40lb anti-personnel bombs. Each had a stick about 18 inches long sticking out from the nose, so that they would explode above the ground. In the bombing run we encountered Breda 20mm anti-aircraft gun fire. We claimed four direct hits on vehicles and three near misses, but it was impossible to be sure whose bombs did the damage.

We then turned and came back on strafing runs against the convoys. On my fourth strafing run, just as I crossed the road, I received some strikes on my starboard wing, and some on the fuselage just behind the cockpit. I looked down and saw that the anti-aircraft fire was coming from a gun emplacement. After gaining some height I dived to attack and after a couple of bursts, the fire from the gun post stopped. My report shows that I claimed a gun post, and my log book that I also claimed a troop-carrier.[2]

Squadron Leader Brian Eaton led this mission of twelve Kittyhawk fighter-bombers, which also included Squadron Leader Bobby Gibbes. The squadron's operations record book shows:

Duty: Bombing M/T [motor transport] on road in Maharis area
Time Up: 1045
Time Down: 1150
Details of Sortie or Flight: A/C [aircraft] headed north, and flew over sea towards Maharis then turned in over land, where 40 M/T were seen on the main coast road, and bombed accurately at P/P. U6513 – 4 direct hits and 3 near misses were scored on the road. Slight Breda fire encountered. No E/A (enemy aircraft) were seen or reported.

One of the other missions that day was led by Squadron Leader Bobby Gibbes, and the squadron's Operations Record Book shows:

Duty: To bomb and strafe M/T [motor transport] on Maharis–Gafsa road
Time Up: 1515
Time Down: 1629
Details of Sortie or Flight: A fair concentration of 40+ M/T was bombed, getting one M/T flamer, then strafed with the resulting total strafing claim, 6 M/T destroyed, 16 damaged and 20+ bodies. Medium heavy accurate anti-aircraft and Breda fire was encountered.[3]

A total of twenty-seven pilots flew on the four missions that day, in forty-five individual sorties. No pilots were lost.

It is thought that Colonel Count von Stauffenberg, who drove up to be with the leading tanks and troops of 10th Panzer Division near Mezzouna, may have been wounded in these strafing attacks. He lost his left eye, his right hand, and two fingers on his left hand and, after evacuation, spent three months in hospital in Munich. Later, he was one of the leading members of the failed plot of 20 July 1944 to assassinate Hitler, for which he was executed.[4]

From 25 April the squadrons of 239 Wing of the DAF were thrown into a concentrated anti-shipping campaign, to prevent supplies reaching the beleaguered Axis forces in Tunisia. The Kittyhawks of 3 and 450 Squadrons RAAF would dive from up to 10,000 feet to release a 500lb bomb, sometimes as low as 1,000 feet depending upon the intensity of anti-aircraft fire. Between mid-April and 9 May 3 and 450 Squadrons made 840 sorties against Axis shipping.[5]

Because of the consequent massive destruction of seaborne supplies, by the end of March air-transport flights by the Luftwaffe had increased to around 150 per day between Sicily and Tunis. With a Junkers Ju52 transport able to carry two and a half tons and the giant, six-engined Messerschmitt Me323 more than ten tons, it was estimated they could provide up to a third of the Axis' daily supply needs. To choke off the enemy's last remaining lifeline, Operation FLAX was launched at the beginning of April.

Bombers from the North West Africa Strategic, Tactical and Desert Air Forces intensified their raids on the Axis air bases while fighters were thrown in to intercept transport aircraft on the air routes. On 10 and 11 April Operation FLAX began to pay huge dividends, when P-38 Lightnings of the US Twelfth Air Force claimed no fewer than fifty of the Ju52/3m tri-motor transports. Yet even worse losses for the Luftwaffe were to come.[6]

Over Cape Bon on 16 April Neville Duke was flying with two other Spitfires of 92 Squadron RAF when he sighted a formation of eighteen enemy transports flying near to sea level. They were the three-engined Savoia-Marchetti SM.82s. Duke called his leader and then turned into an attacking dive. Because of his speed Duke only managed a short burst on his first target aircraft. He closed on a second Savoia, slowing his speed so that his cannon shells raked the length of its fuselage.

After pulling his Spitfire narrowly over the top of the Savoia he saw it quickly plunge into the sea. Duke also claimed a second SM.82, to reach eight victories in North Africa. Once again Duke's flying skills were lethal, and he seemed to be indestructible. While five Savoia SM.82s were shot down in the encounter, luck ran out for Wing Commander 'Widge' Gleed of 244 Squadron who was lost.[7]

Two days later, on Palm Sunday, 18 April, the afternoon did seem to be drifting, like its name indicated into a day of relative peace and quiet. Following intelligence reports of German plans to airlift out some of their key staff of the Heeresgruppe Afrika and non-combat troops, on transports returning to Sicily, the USAAF 57th Fighter Group sent out successive patrols through the day to try and intercept any such flights. Pilots continually returned with nothing to report.

Late in the day, when the last patrol was organized, no contacts had been made with enemy aircraft. This final operation was a combination of 57th Group and 244 Wing RAF, whose Spitfires of 92 Squadron would provide top cover. At 1705 forty-eight Warhawks from all four of 57th Group's Fighter Squadrons, 64th, 65th, 66th, and 319th, began lifting off, led by Captain James 'Big Jim' Curl, the experienced flight leader of 66th.

Once they had met up with the Spitfires, Curl led the formation north-west over Cape Bon. Almost six miles out to sea dusk was gathering when Curl turned them back southwards to return home. He knew the light would not last much longer. Then he saw something, maybe 4,000 feet below them, close to the sea. At first he thought it might be a very large flight of migrating geese. The shapes became clearer under his gaze. He was looking at what he estimated to be about 100 of the Ju52/3m transports. They were all in a camouflage green colour, making them hard to pick out against the sea in the twilight, and were flying north in a giant 'V-of-Vs' formation. What came next was at first nicknamed by the American pilots as a 'goose shoot'.

While the Spitfires took on some escorting Bf109s, the forty-eight Warhawks descended onto the cumbersome Ju52s like falcons swooping on a flock of fat pigeons. In the mayhem Curl claimed two Ju52s and a 109. He described the engagement as chaotic, the sky filled with turning, wheeling aircraft. The Warhawks twisted around in the melee, firing at a mass of enemy aircraft that had no escape. Captain Roy Whittaker, flight leader in 65th Fighter Squadron, shot down two Ju52s and two 109s. His four victories took him up to a total of seven, which made him the highest scoring pilot in the 57th.

Lieutenant Richard O. Hunziker, of the 65th Fighter Squadron, on only his second combat operation, found himself in a baptism of fire. He was astounded at the number of enemy aircraft.

The enemy formation looked like a thousand black beetles crawling over the water. On our first pass I was so excited I started firing early. I could see the shots kicking up the water.

Hunziker went after a Ju52 near the front of the 'V' and saw his shots hammer along its tail and fuselage, and simultaneously realized he was being shot at by two Ju52s on either side of him.

It looked as though they were blinking red flashlights at me from the windows – Tommy-guns, probably. The ship I was firing at hit the water with a great sheet of spray and then exploded. As I pulled up I could see figures struggling away from what was left of the aeroplane.

Next Hunziker responded to a radio call for help against some Bf109s 5,000 feet above him. At first he struggled to latch on to the enemy fighters in the whirling dogfights. Taking evasive action he found himself crossing over land. Then, with his first burst of fire at one of the 109s, he blew its nose off, sending it into a steep dive to crash into the ground in flames.

The total losses and damage inflicted by 57th Fighter Group on the Luftwaffe transports and escort fighters were:

Squadron	Ju52/3m	Bf109	Bf110	Total
64th FS	0.5	6		6.5
65th FS	12.0	3	2	17.0
66th FS	23.5	3		26.5
314th FS	22	2		24.0
Total	58	14	2	74.0

Not surprisingly the media reported the one-sided air battle as the 'Palm Sunday Massacre'.[8]

However, the clashes between the fighters, the Warhawks and the Bf109s, were far from one-sided. The Bf109s were able to operate thousands of feet above the Warhawks, which were ineffective above 15,000 feet. This enabled the 109s to wait for an opportunity to mount a diving attack, ideally out of the sun on the American fighters. To counter the German fighters' advantage, 57th Group pilots, such as Lieutenant Mike McCarthy of 64th Fighter Squadron, knew that a 109 could not out-turn a properly flown P-40 War-hawk, 'We had to know where they were every moment, to time the 'break' call, and turn hard into them so we could bring our guns to bear and shoot.'[9]

On 22 April DAF Spitfires and Kittyhawks pounced upon some twenty Me323s which were flying a wide V formation. The main cargo of these six-engined giant transports was fuel. They were escorted by ten Bf109s and Macchi C.202s. Lieutenant 'Robbie' Robinson of 1 Squadron SAAF downed two 109s, which made him an ace. His fellow pilots sent six more of the 323s, engulfed in petrol-fed flames, plunging into the sea.[10]

Out of a fleet of around 250 of these huge workhorse planes, German records show that between 5 April and 12 May 1943, 166 aircraft and their cargoes of critical supplies were lost. Between 18 and 22 April Allied fighters claimed to have shot-down some 120 of the Luftwaffe's Ju52 and Me323 transport aircraft.[11] After 22 April the Luftwaffe was forced to fly air trans-ports only at night, and with continuing losses to Allied night-fighters, in ever reducing numbers.[12]

* * *

In contrast the Allies had no such supply shortages. On the ground they had more men, more guns, more tanks, and in the sky the decisive advantage – air superiority. Yet the Germans still held the vital passes through the hills surrounding Tunis, inflicting terrible losses as they withstood every Allied attack. In the southern and northern coastal corridors, it seemed impossible to concentrate sufficient forces to break through. The Medjerda Valley was blocked by German defences on Longstop Hill. After the Germans had defeated desperate Allied attacks on 25 December 1942 to retain Longstop, they had dug in extensive and formidable defences on what was for them, their *Weinachtshügel* (Christmas Hill).

At last, in the closing week of April the long-sought breakthrough came. Eighth Army captured Longstop Hill and other enemy strongpoints in the Medjerda Valley. Here was the opportunity to concentrate forces for a hope-fully decisive thrust at Tunis. The German generals knew a major offensive was coming, but not whether it would be Eighth Army from the south-east, First Army in the centre, or the Americans in the north-west.[13]

The final plan was for a spearhead attack in the centre in early May by First Army combined with elements transferred from Eighth Army. Battle-hardened British infantry battalions from the 1st Armoured, 4th and 78th Divisions would first break the German lines. Then 6th and 7th Armoured Divisions, after funnelling their way through the Allied-held strategic market town of Medjez el Bab, would smash their way down the Medjerda Valley through Massicault and St Cyprien to Tunis.[14]

However, in the redeployment and concentration lead up, there was great risk. The inherent weakness of the plan was that the tanks and their support vehicles transferred from Eighth Army in the south would have to move in open view through the hills north to Medjez el Bab. Then endless columns of tanks, infantry, and supplies would have to crawl across the one and only bridge over the Medjerda River at Medjez.

Only then could the attack concentrate across a narrow 3,000-yard front on the valley floor to drive towards Tunis. In the days of repositioning and con-centration, Allied forces would be glaringly susceptible to German recon-naissance, and consequent ground and air attack. Once again the question was: how could this be done without the Germans knowing, and countering with their own troop redeployments? Despite the huge losses imposed on the Luftwaffe, even late into April, with whatever aircraft they had left, the Germans had the capability to mount a desperate 'last throw' raid.

*   *   *

The Axis positions in the hills around Enfidaville were very strong, and from the air it was difficult to identify targets amongst the orchards, fields and plantations within the ridges and hilly terrain. It was very different from the desert and enemy vehicles were avoiding the use of roads during the day. In one operation the anti-tank Hurricanes of No. 6 Squadron, despite seeing the coloured smoke of Eighth Army positions, were unable to identify Axis forces hiding amongst olive groves. Rather than visible targets, pilots had to be briefed with designated areas on air photographs, which required a new approach and training.

From the sea north of Enfidaville Axis forces had established a defensive line through the hills north-west to Medjez el Bab in the Medjerda Valley, then north again through the mountains to the coast about twenty miles west of the port of Bizerte. The plain in front of Medjez in the Medjerda Valley was clearly the most favourable for an armoured attack to break through to Tunis. Alexander and Montgomery agreed that Eighth Army should restrict its efforts to maintaining pressure on the Enfidaville defences in a holding operation. On 18 April 1st Armoured Division and the King's Dragoon Guards, and later on 30 April the 7th Armoured and 4th Indian Divisions, 201 Guards Brigade and some artillery, moved across to join First Army near Medjez.

A joint planning conference determined that DAF would return to army/air close support to cover the armoured drive down the Medjerda valley to Tunis. The first moves of forces from Eighth Army began on 30 April. Because of DAF pilots not being experienced with the terrain of the battle area, and communications being channelled through both First Army and Eighth Army HQs, targets for DAF squadrons were drawn up and agreed in advance. A massive letter 'T' 150 yards long was marked out in white on the ground, as well as red and blue smoke, to assist the pilots' navigation.

The air support plan and timelines for an 'air blitz' on 6 May were:

0540: Eighty-four medium bombers of the Tactical Bomber Force (TBF) would bomb Axis ground positions directly in front of the Allied troops advance path.

0730–0800: 126 light bombers of DAF would attack their pre-selected targets further back.

0830–0930: Eighty-four medium bombers of TBF would bomb targets a further distance away.

0930–1200: Fighter-bombers of 242 Wing RAF would attack targets of opportunity in the battle area.

1200 onwards: 108 light bombers of DAF would be in readiness to hit enemy reserves, while DAF fighter-bombers would look for Axis force movements in roads and valleys.[15]

Contrary to some expectations, the initial move of the armoured divisions from the south to Medjez, protected by DAF's dominating air cover, was achieved without the knowledge of, or hindrance from, the enemy. It was a clear demonstration of how air superiority could enable ground forces to re-position without interference.

The armoured thrust for Tunis began with six divisions, and all their supplies, in a slow crawl across that single bridge at Medjez. Air power was tasked with imposing a protective screen, an umbrella over the valley route to make it impenetrable to any enemy reconnaissance or air attack. It seemed to scream out for one Stuka dive-bombing raid to hit that one and only bridge at Medjez, and cut the offensive in two.

On 6 May, day one of the advance through Medjez, Allied aircraft flew some 2,500 sorties, attacking Axis forces in their rear bases, and bombing and strafing their defences in the path of the Allied attack. By 0800 on 6 May the British infantry had cleared a path through German positions and their minefields, taken objectives such as Frendj, and dug in. In an example of the air-ground support, and in co-ordination with an artillery bombardment preceding the lead infantry and tanks, DAF light bombers and Kittyhawks hit Axis positions at Bordj Frendj and St Cyprien, halting a convoy of 100 enemy trucks.[16]

Then the armoured divisions burst through to take Massicault before nightfall. On 7 May the armour rolled into Tunis, taking many Axis forces by surprise. Some enemy troops even emerged from bars and restaurants, with stunned stares, and surrendered without a fight.[17] Allied air power had made the skies above Medjez and the Medjerda valley another no-fly zone.

It was the combination of an 'air blitz', air support, artillery and massed armour that, on 7 May, enabled the 7th Armoured Division to burst through to Tunis. In the north American forces took the port of Bizerte. Axis air forces were powerless to help their troops on the ground. On 8 May the front lines were advancing so rapidly that First Army only allowed specific requests for air support.

On 8 May the Luftwaffe could fly just sixty sorties, some from only two operational air bases they retained in the Cape Bon peninsula. On 9 May there were even fewer Luftwaffe sorties, and on 10 May there were none. The Germans had fled the Tunisian skies, evacuating what planes, equipment and personnel they could.[18]

Small boats attempting to evacuate Axis troops by sea were attacked by fighters. A large evacuation exercise on 9 May, when attacked by Tactical Bomber Force light bombers and DAF fighters, quickly surrendered. Large formations of Axis troops were surrendering, but some still moved towards the coast, despite no ships being able to leave. In the mountains north of Enfidaville on 10 May, the Italian First Army, including the German 10th Panzer, 90th Light and 164th Infantry Divisions, was still holding out. The 90th Light Division held the coast road, and was blocking First and Eighth Armies from joining up.

On 12 May a light bomber raid on 90th Light Division was planned. Allied troops were only 1,500 yards from the enemy, so an artillery bombardment of yellow smoke was laid on both north and south of 90th Light's positions. The bombings were spot on, and very quickly white flags were everywhere. It proved to be the last air attack on ground forces of the North African campaign.

The capture of Tunis brought the Axis surrender and 250,000 prisoners. It was on the same scale as the German defeat at Stalingrad, and hailed as the turning of the tide. And once again air power had been the decisive 'game-changer'.

The success in North Africa of DAF's support for the army was based upon gaining air superiority, which in turn rested upon winning the air war first. The integral foundation of winning the air war flowed from the RAF's strategic decision to purchase fighters rather than dive-bombers. And, of course, the superior performance of the Spitfire in aerial battles of fighter against fighter was a significant factor.

Perhaps most important were the army/air support control systems through the AASC groups, pioneered and improved between army and air force from 1941 to 1943. In the Tunisian campaign, in terrain so different from the desert, 'flash' messages from AASC at Army HQ to ALOs at DAF airfields were introduced. This much improved the ALOs' ability to communicate and explain new developments in the battle area to the pilots. DAF developed a platform in this area on which air superiority could be won and hopefully sustained in the planned Allied invasion of Italy.

*   *   *

While the Allied armies had over six months struggled for every inch of ground in Tunisia, not surprisingly the planning for the next offensive, the invasion of Sicily, or Operation HUSKY, had gone ahead in parallel. It was seen by some as poorly co-ordinated and riddled with disagreements. Although the strategic decision was taken in January 1943 by Churchill and Roosevelt at the Casablanca Conference, the Allies' military commanders such as General Montgomery were openly critical of the planning. Worse still, the Germans fully expected that the Allies would next attempt an invasion of Sicily, only 100 miles (160 kilometres) from Tunisia, and were preparing accordingly. Unbeknown to the battlefield commanders this problem had been foreseen for some time.

In the summer of 1942, in the midst of the planning and preparations for Operation TORCH, a small inter-Services security committee had begun to look ahead to what might follow. The Allies were under increasing pressure from the USSR to open a second front against the Third Reich in Europe. Once victory was achieved in North Africa the obvious next step would be Sicily, only some 100 miles from Tunis. The problem was that this would be obvious to the Germans too.

The Germans must be deceived into believing that Allied forces from North Africa would next invade Europe at somewhere other than Sicily. An idea was conceived whereby German intelligence would be provided with a dead body carrying false, secret documents. A dead body, with the uniform and rank of a senior staff officer, carrying supposedly secret documents, would be dumped at sea close to Huelva on the Spanish coast.

It seemed feasible that the officer would be thought to have died in an air crash at sea while en route to Algiers. The Spanish authorities, although neutral, favoured the Third Reich and could be expected to make the papers available to German agents. The documents would be created to convince German intelligence that an invasion would take place other than Sicily, such as Sardinia and Greece.

Although medical advice supported the feasibility of the plan, finding a suitable dead body of an acceptable age proved to be the first of many practical difficulties. After time-consuming enquiries a body of a deceased man in his early thirties, who had died of pneumonia arising from exposure, was obtained and medical opinion sought on its suitability. It was thought that, as the body would be kept in cold storage, and encased in dry ice leading up to the time of release into the sea, its subsequent decomposition would seem to be from drowning, and from immersion in the sea.[19]

In the face of some initial opposition, and debate at the highest levels, the plan codenamed Operation MINCEMEAT was eventually approved by Churchill with Eisenhower's endorsement on 15 April.[20] A letter was written by the Vice Chief of the Imperial General Staff, Sir Archibald Nye, to General Alexander in Tunis, to be carried on the body to give it the touch of authenticity. The dead body, in the guise of a senior officer, would also carry two similar fake letters from Lord Louis Mountbatten, one of which would be addressed to General Eisenhower.[21] It seemed that much now depended upon a dead man.

Or did it? For the DAF and the other Allied air forces, the invasion of Axis-occupied Sicily presented a challenge on a far greater scale than anything attempted before. It would clearly not be possible without Allied domination of the skies above Sicily, and the surrounding Mediterranean airspace. From the decisive triumphs of air power at El Alamein, Ksar Rhilane, El Hamma, and the capture of Tunis, the lessons learned must be applied to the largest amphibious landings ever attempted.

Notes
 1. Veteran's account, S/Ldr Bill McRae.
 2. Veteran's account, F/O Tom Russell.
 3. Ibid., and www.3squadron.org.au; No. 3 Squadron RAAF, Operations Record Book, Apr 1943.
 4. Veteran's account, F/O Tom Russell.
 5. Herington, *Air War against Germany & Italy 1939–43*, p. 407; Owen, op. cit., p. 173.
 6. Molesworth, *57th Fighter Group*, p. 41.
 7. Thomas, op. cit., pp. 33–5.
 8. Molesworth, op. cit., pp. 41–5.
 9. Ibid., pp. 24–5.
10. Thomas, op. cit., p. 35.

11. Herington, op. cit., p. 407.
12. Owen, op. cit., p. 173.
13. Evans, op. cit., p. 48.
14. Moorehead, *African Trilogy*, p. 593; Evans, op. cit., p. 48.
15. Smith, op. cit., pp. 49–55.
16. Owen, op. cit., p. 176–7.
17. Evans, op. cit., p. 49.
18. Owen, op. cit., pp. 176–7.
19. Montagu, *The Man Who Never Was*, pp. 15–37.
20. McIntyre, *Operation Mincemeat*, pp. 127–8.
21. Montagu, op. cit., pp. 38–50.

Chapter 8

Invasion of Sicily – another amphibious gamble?

Shortly after midday on 16 June Flying Officer D.T. Barnard DFM, of No. 459 Squadron RAAF, lifted his Hudson bomber into the air from the squadron's airfield at Lydda, Palestine. Barnard was a twenty-three-year-old Australian from Launceston, Tasmania. Before the war he had been a clerk in Melbourne, Victoria.

The Australian pilot's orders were to rendezvous and collaborate with an Allied naval force, which, as part of air interdiction operations against Axis shipping and naval vessels, prior to the invasion of Sicily, was searching for the U-boat U-97. The German submarine had sunk an Allied merchant ship near the port of Haifa. Despite good visibility and only scattered cloud, Barnard was unable to locate the naval ships. He decided to gain height and begin a search patrol on his own. He might be lucky and catch sight of the navy ships, or even the U-boat.

Two hours later Barnard and his crew spotted U-97. It was motoring slowly on the surface, north-westwards, perhaps making for its base in Greece, Sicily or mainland Italy. Some of the U-boat crew appeared to be relaxing, taking the sun on its narrow deck, and had clearly not seen the Hudson bomber. Barnard at once went into a dive while his crew readied the bomber's depth charges. At low level above the waves he began a run from dead astern of the U-boat.

Three depth charges were released. One fell directly onto the U-boat causing a massive 'dry-hit' explosion. Two other depth charges fell into the sea, and exploded alongside its hull.

The blast from the direct hit drove the Hudson bomber upwards for some 400 feet. Despite fighting for control of the plane, within five minutes Barnard saw the U-boat's bow rear up out of the sea, as U-97 sank stern first below the waves.

The Hudson had incurred serious damage to its wings, fuselage and rudder. Barnard turned the bomber in a homeward direction and, with the same skill shown in the depth-charging of U-97, nursed it safely back to Haifa.[1]

*   *   *

There were at least five major risks, or obstacles, to achieving a successful invasion and occupation of Sicily. The largest risk was the near certainty

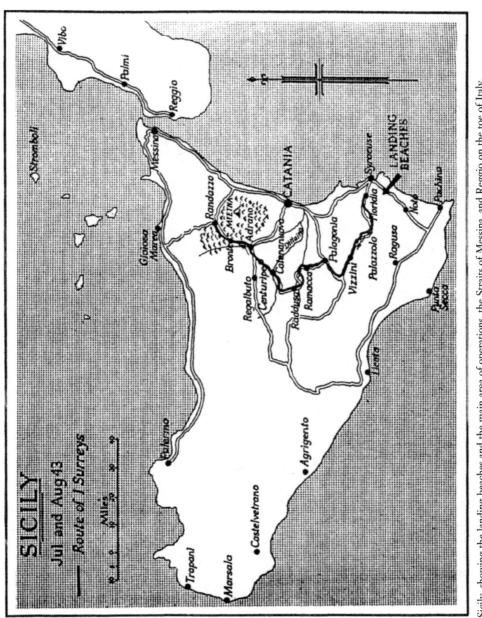

Sicily, showing the landing beaches and the main area of operations, the Straits of Messina, and Reggio on the toe of Italy.

that German intelligence services had learned of the Allies' planning for Operation HUSKY, the codename for the invasion of Sicily. From the Germans' perspective it was the Allies' obvious next step. From Tunisia the nearest and most logical place to land in Europe was Sicily.

Would the deception plan of Operation MINCEMEAT, using a dead man, allegedly Major Martin, and the fictitious plans placed in a bag with the body, lead the Germans into thinking Sicily was only a decoy invasion site? Only a few people at the Allies' highest levels knew of the deception and hoped that the Germans would be so fooled.[2]

The capability of the Axis to re-supply and reinforce Sicily's defences cried out for an interdiction strategy by the Allies. Axis supplies were brought from mainland Italy by sea across the narrow straits from Reggio di Calabria to Messina, the island's main port, in the far north-east corner of Sicily. These cargoes were out of range of Tunisian-based fighters and fighter-bombers. As a consequence, the landings in Sicily had to take place close to airfields which could be captured quickly. Allied aircraft operating from Sicilian airfields were essential to support the US Seventh and British Eighth Armies' advance through the island to Messina.

Once troops were well established ashore, locally based aircraft would give them that close support and cutting edge to move north. Besides support and protection of ground forces on Sicily, Allied use of local airfields would give aircraft the range to reach the Messina Straits and curtail Axis supplies. There was a further and related risk. How could Axis forces be prevented from withdrawing and escaping across the straits to Reggio on the Italian mainland?

In effect the campaign for Sicily, particularly for Allied air forces, began soon after the final victory in Tunisia. Air superiority over Sicily, and its extension over southern Italy, was an essential requirement for the invasion. Towards the end of May 1943 it was estimated that there were 2,374 Axis aircraft across the Mediterranean region. However, perhaps only 1,276 were serviceable and therefore operational. Such was the impact of the Allies' sea and air disruption of supply routes, and pounding of infrastructure and airfields, that the Italians could only put 698 into the air and the Luftwaffe 578.

To make matters worse, these reduced numbers of aircraft were being gradually pushed back by the Allied bombing raids to more northerly airfields spread across bases from southern France through mainland Italy and as far away as Greece.[3] In the lead up to the Sicily invasion there were constant air raids on major railway junctions, such as Catania and Messina in Sicily, and San Giovanni and Reggio in southern Italy.[4]

Perhaps equally important was the need for the Allies to achieve dominant air superiority so as to protect the open sea voyage and landings of a vast invasion fleet. The invasion would be larger and more concentrated than Operation TORCH in North Africa. A major concern was that the fleet would have to sail close to the Italian island of Pantelleria, which was a Malta-like threat to the invasion fleet. It was some fifty miles from the Tunisian coast, about halfway to Sicily.

* * *

The island fortress of Pantelleria was a major barrier which allowed Axis forces to dominate both the air and sea routes between Tunisia and Sicily. The island was around fourteen miles long and five wide, possessed an air-field with modern, underground aircraft hangars, a garrison of some 12,000 Italian and 600 German troops, a civilian population of about 10,000, and 112 fortified gun emplacements. Pantelleria was both a trip-wire that would give advance warning of the invasion fleet by Axis reconnaissance aircraft and a launching pad for damaging air strikes against the Allied ships. It was certainly a serious threat and had the potential to cause the invasion to be aborted.[5]

Besides the capability of mounting reconnaissance flights, some eighty or so Pantelleria-based aircraft could be rapidly increased by the Luftwaffe from Sicily and Italy. Axis aircraft known to be operating from Pantelleria included Italian Macchi C.202 fighters, Savoia Marchetti SM.79 torpedo bombers, and the German, twin-engined Messerschmitt Bf110 fighters and fighter-bombers. The slow-moving invasion fleet could be seriously damaged by well-planned Luftwaffe and Regia Aeronautica air raids flying out of Pantelleria.

The US planners in Washington were insistent that the threat of Pantel-leria must be eliminated prior to Operation HUSKY. As Supreme Allied Commander Mediterranean, General Eisenhower was less enthusiastic. He felt loathe to expend more men in what could be a costly operation to capture the island when the invasion forces for Sicily were being built up and trained for the landings. After taking advice from the UK's Professor Solly Zucker-man and his Operational Analysis Unit to advise on bomb tonnages needed, Eisenhower decided to attempt to bomb Pantelleria into submission.

The first phase of the bombing campaign, Operation CORKSCREW, was launched from 18 May to June 5. Nearly 1,000 aircraft were deployed: heavy bombers including B-17 Flying Fortresses dropping 1,000lb bombs; B-26, Wellington, Baltimore and Boston medium bombers; P-38 Lightning and Hurricane fighter-bombers; and Spitfire fighters. In the final week of bomb-ing raids between 6 and 11 June the Allies' Tactical Bomber and Strategic Air Forces in 3,712 sorties hammered Pantelleria's airfield runways, underground hangars, the island's gun positions, port facilities and town with 5,324 tons of explosive.[6]

Combined with naval shelling it was hoped that Pantelleria was being blasted into complete submission. As the Axis made a vain attempt to stem the onslaught, Luftwaffe aircraft from Sicily and Italy were confronted. Spitfires from a Free French squadron shot down a Junkers Ju88 bomber and a Focke-Wulf Fw190 fighter bomber. On 11 June a pilot from the US 64th Fighter

Squadron on only his ninth mission, William F. 'Bill' Nuding, came through a remarkable baptism of fire.

From the rear of a formation of sixteen P-40 Warhawks Nuding saw three Bf109s closing in on them. Even as he alerted his wing leader, he wrenched his Warhawk to port to hurtle head on towards the first 109. Nuding held his nerve and fired a burst which hit the enemy fighter's engine cowling and fuselage. After narrowly avoiding the damaged 109, he swung his P-40 around to starboard into the other two 109s. The next one in his view he raked with a burst of fire from its nose along its fuselage, smashing its cockpit cover.

It seemed to be within the same split second that Nuding saw the third 109 turning left and turned inside it. His first burst of fire hit the 109 on its port side, and when it went into a steep dive he followed it down near vertically. Another burst and he was watching it pouring out both brown and white smoke from its haemorrhaging engine coolant. Suddenly, Nuding realized that both he and the doomed 109 were heading straight into the sea. Some reflex instinct from his training saved him. Nuding made what he called later 'a maximum G-force pull out', to only just clear the clutching waves. That third victory in the swirling dogfights was observed and confirmed by pilots of some P-38s, who were escorting a US Naval Task Force. Unfortunately, it was the only one of the three with which Nuding was credited.[7]

In all twenty-three Axis aircraft were shot down or destroyed, as against fifteen Allied losses. In the three-week campaign around 6,600 tons of bombs were dropped on every possible target across the island to bludgeon the defenders into submission. When it came to landing troops, some of whom could face sheer cliffs rising out of the sea, the Allies did not wish to risk the loss of many men prior to the invasion of Sicily.

In the absence of any response to repeated calls upon the Axis forces to surrender, on 11 June British troops landed at Pantelleria's main harbour. There was no resistance. In widespread damage to buildings, gun positions and the airfields, telephone communications and the water supply had been put out of action. Just one Allied soldier was lost, knocked over by a maddened mule running out of control. At 1730 that day the Italian Admiral Pavesi signed a formal surrender in an underground aircraft hangar.

* * *

While Pantelleria was being blasted into surrender, DAF was re-locating its squadrons to Malta. Since January 1943 Malta's airfields and runways had been extended and improved to give it the capability to support around thirty squadrons. By 8 June more than half of 244 Wing's ground support, vehicles and equipment were in place. On 14/15 June aircraft of Nos 1 SAAF, 92, 145, 417 and 601 Squadrons RAF flew in. By the end of June there were three Spitfire wings, 244, 322 and 324 RAF, based on Malta.

Although DAF was now part of the Tactical Air Force (TAF), under the North West Africa Air Force (NWAAF) umbrella, its invaluable fighting experience, flexibility of roles and unique esprit de corps made it something special. In the planning for the invasion, Eighth Army's commanders wanted no other. The rock solid collaboration between Eighth Army and DAF, built upon personal contacts in the heat of battle, made DAF the leading exponents of close-knit air-army support.[8]

During the rest of June and into July the build-up of aerial forces on Malta gathered pace. One week before the Sicily invasion D Day operational strength based in Malta had increased to five squadrons of night-fighters, four reconnaissance flights, and twenty Spitfire squadrons. Ground crews were also in residence preparing for the arrival of three fighter-bomber wings. Having emerged from its long siege of 1940–42, Malta was now the equivalent of an unsinkable, giant-sized aircraft-carrier, strategically positioned to provide air support for the Sicily invasion.[9]

Yet towards the end of June the Axis air forces were still perceived as a serious threat. They had more than 800 operational aircraft within range of, or based on, Sicily. The Allies' invasion force would sail from Tunisian ports in some 3,000 ships and landing craft. Allied fighters based in Tunisia could not reach the landing beaches in south-east Sicily. Only those fighters based in Malta had the range to cover the first vital targets of the landing beaches at Licata, Gela and Syracuse.

In addition, even fighters based in Pantelleria and Malta would not have the range to support ground forces advancing into northern Sicily, or escort bombing raids over such as Catania and Messina. Air Vice Marshal Tedder, AOC-in-C Allied Air Forces in the Mediterranean, informed General Alexander that, immediately following the landings, the early capture of the Comiso-Gela air base was essential to maintain air superiority.[10]

From 15 June Allied heavy bombers, flying round the clock from North Africa, bombed the nineteen established Axis airfields and a dozen newly-constructed landing grounds in Sicily. Axis aircraft were forced to disperse to bases in the north of Sicily and to mainland Italy, which pushed Luftwaffe fighters back beyond effective range of the Allied landings.[11] Air interdiction operations were also intensified in the Mediterranean against Axis shipping, and to protect Allied convoys against U-boats.

*   *   *

As early as April 1943 the Allied planners decided that the invasion must take place on a date when the moon would be in its second quarter. They needed enough moonlight up to midnight for paratroopers and gliders to land, but from that time it had to be darker after moonset for the amphibious landings. The best date for these favourable conditions was agreed as 9/10 July.

In the final plan approved by Eisenhower the invasion forces would go ashore in the south-east of Sicily. Airborne troops would be dropped inland, followed by landings from the sea. The US Seventh Army would seize the port of Licata and Eighth Army the port of Syracuse to quickly take control of the airfields close by.

Asserting and sustaining air supremacy, however, and in effect fighting the Sicilian campaign before it was generally known it would occur, took its toll. As the bombing raids gradually reduced the number of operational Axis airfields in Sicily and southern Italy, Allied bombers suffered increasing losses from re-grouped and more concentrated anti-aircraft defences. Allied planners were allowing for the loss of around 10 per cent of the invasion fleet from Luftwaffe air strikes. They hoped that Allied air power could prevent any greater loss rate.

In the days and weeks leading up to the night of 9/10 July, tactical and strategic bombers hammered Sicilian airfields such as Sciacca and Milo in the west and Comiso and the Gerbini/Catania group in the east. In general, the USAAF were operating the bombers and transports while the RAF supplied fighters, coastal and sea patrol aircraft, and fighter-bombers. Two of the few exceptions were the two US 57th and 79th Fighter Groups which were also part of DAF. Allied air forces overall were able to call on some 4,000 aircraft.[12]

From the 64th Fighter Squadron of the 57th Fighter Group on 30 June, Second Lieutenant Bill Nuding was in an anti-shipping patrol, with Spitfires as escorts, over the Sicily coast near Malazzo. When the patrol took on a group of six Bf109s, Nuding cut out one of the enemy fighters that was intent on attacking his wingman. He got in several bursts of fire, before it went down in flames, crashing into the side of a mountain. It gave Nuding his second confirmed victory.[13]

In a typical bombing raid on 3 July Wing Commander Dundas led 324 Wing Spitfires as escort for fighter-bombers attacking the Biscari airfield in south-east Sicily. Soon after the completion of their raid they were attacked by more than twenty Macchi C.202s and Bf109s in a mixed formation. In the encounter Squadron Leader George Hill, already an experienced Spitfire ace of 111 Squadron, claimed his thirteenth victory. As the enemy aircraft broke off the dogfights, the Spitfires turned away back towards Malta.

It was then that Dundas noticed white smoke streaming from the engine cowlings of the Spitfire at his side, piloted by another ace, his No. 2, Flight Sergeant Frank Mellor. Dundas radioed Mellor, who told him that he had been hit in the air battle, and his engine temperature was rising dangerously. The pair had become isolated in the engagements, although still at 16,000 feet. Dundas turned them onto the most direct course for Malta and told Mellor that, by throttling back, he thought that they could nurse Mellor's Spitfire back to base.

With Malta in sight some fifteen miles away, Dundas received a radio call for help from Squadron Leader Hill who was circling around a downed pilot in a dinghy a few miles south of Cape Passaro, and under attack from six 109s. On top of this he only had twenty-five gallons of fuel left. Dundas radioed Malta to send out an air-sea rescue flight for the pilot in the dinghy, and told Mellor to fly on alone for Malta and if his engine temperature exceeded 125 degrees, he should bale out.

Dundas then turned back northwards for Cape Passaro. He remembered how the night before he and George Hill had argued heatedly about the wing's tactics. Hill thought Dundas was too cautious and should allow individual pilots more scope to make their own decisions. Dundas checked his fuel, and found that he too only had twenty-five gallons remaining. He told Hill that he would be there in a couple of minutes. Soon after, he saw Hill's Spitfire circling at around 500 feet, with the 109s a few hundred feet higher, also circling. They seemed to be taking it in turns to dive down and take on Hill.

Although the Spitfire could out-turn the 109, the German pilots would know Hill's Spitfire, having come on the raid from Malta, must soon run out of fuel. Dundas thought that both he and Hill, low on fuel and outnumbered, were done for. He radioed Hill that he had arrived and, gambling on his own fuel lasting, threw his Spitfire down into the ring of 109s. He fired a couple of bursts, then turned and climbed again to repeat the manoeuvre. Hill also climbed up to take on the 109s in a show of full fight.

Just maybe their pugnacious frenzy against the 109s, thought Dundas, might make the German pilots think that there were more Spitfires on the way. Perhaps it did just that. Suddenly the German fighters were gone. Together Dundas and Hill limped back to Malta, hardly daring to touch their throttles. Miraculously, they both landed under power, although by the time he had taxied to a stop Dundas could see his tank was empty.

Hill thanked Dundas for his rescue and they both knew that their previous disagreement was forgotten. Later they learned that Air-Sea Rescue found the pilot in the dinghy, not far from Sicily's coast. He turned out to be a German, and very ungrateful to be rescued by the Allies. Flight Sergeant Frank Mellor did not make it back to Malta, and was presumed lost at sea.[14]

On another bombing raid on 4 July, by B-17s on Catania, the New Zealander Squadron Leader Evan 'Rosie' Mackie, led No. 243 Squadron RAF as escort . Mackie was twenty-five years old, from a small dairy farm in the Golden Valley, near Waihi in the North Island of New Zealand. He had joined the RNZAF in January 1941 and, on completion of his training, was posted to the Spitfire-equipped No. 485 Squadron RNZAF, before transferring to 243 Squadron RAF. After completing the raid, as the Spitfire escorts turned for home, they too were set upon by six Bf109s. Mackie and his wingman, at 26,000 feet, were the first to be attacked.

Mackie turned into the 109 which was closing on him from starboard. He fired three sets of deflection bursts of both cannon and machine gun. Mackie's last burst of fire raked across both the 109's fuselage and cockpit. The enemy fighter exploded in flames to fall straight down, trailing black smoke. The very next day, on a similar operation, Mackie shot down another Bf109 for another victory. It made him the second highest scoring Spitfire ace, after Neville Duke, in North Africa and Italy.[15]

* * *

At the beginning of July Axis air forces were still estimated to have some 800 aircraft available for operations over Sicily; across the whole Mediterranean region they could call upon a maximum of around 1,900. Yet, because of German intelligence being uncertain of where the invasion forces might come ashore, the Luftwaffe's squadrons were spread across not only Sicily and mainland Italy, but also Sardinia and even southern France.

In Sicily itself there were only 460 mixed German and Italian fighters or fighter-bombers, and a meagre fifty Ju88 bombers. To make matters worse for the Axis, the incessant bombing raids on Sicilian airfields drove enemy aircraft progressively back to Italian mainland air bases. The decoy plans found on the body of Major Martin may well have influenced the Luftwaffe in their readiness to disperse their dwindling strength.[16]

A very specific threat to the invasion fleet was the Luftwaffe's Focke-Wulf Fw190 fighter-bomber. Both fast and resilient, the Fw190 could dive from 8,000 feet at a 50-degree angle, reaching a speed as high as 500mph. At 4,000 feet it would release a 1,100lb bomb at its shipping target. The Fw190 would then continue its steep dive and, as low as 150 feet above the waves, still be able to turn to escape.

However, the Allies' bombing campaign of Sicilian airfields forced the remaining serviceable Fw190s to relocate to Naples. From there they were 200 miles from the south-east of Sicily, which put them at the limit of their range. They then had little time to loiter looking for a suitable target, or take part in any aerial combat, before making their return within a 500 mile total for the sortie. The Luftwaffe's formidable Fw190 had been effectively neutralized.

* * *

For the Allied High Command the question was: had the prior weeks of the aerial bombardment across Sicily and southern Italy, against Axis infrastructure, supplies, airfields and the Luftwaffe done enough to safeguard the invasion? Conversely had the air campaign telegraphed that Sicily was the target?[17]

The Allies' invasion fleet of some 3,000 ships and landing craft in Operation HUSKY carried a combined force of around 160,000 men, three times the size of Operation TORCH. It was at the time the largest invasion fleet ever assembled anywhere. In the early hours of the night of 9/10 July, the US Seventh Army and the British Eighth Army began to land on the south-eastern corner of Sicily.[18]

At the same time as the amphibious assault, airlanding troops of the British 1st Airborne Division in 134 gliders approached the Ponte Grande bridge a little south of Syracuse. The bridge was crucial for the early capture of the east coast port. Weather, navigational errors, and friendly fire scattered or brought down a majority of gliders, so that only eighty-seven airborne soldiers reached the bridge.

Fortunately, Eighth Army's infantry landings farther south on the Gulf of Noto, on the eastern side of the Pachino peninsula, were more successful. Leading units were able quickly to reinforce the airborne troops and take the Ponte Grande bridge, but more than 600 casualties meant it had been a costly achievement. Then the coastal town of Cassibile and port of Syracuse were captured quickly.

By 12 July the British Eighth Army had advanced north of Syracuse and taken Augusta. West of the Pachino Peninsula in the Gulf of Gela, the US Seventh Army's landings encountered more difficult seas and stiffer resistance. In an uncanny parallel with Eighth Army an airborne operation turned into self-inflicted carnage. The 504th Parachute Infantry Regiment suffered 410 casualties, in possibly the worst friendly fire disaster of the war.[19] The Allies were ashore, but how soon and how strong would be the German counter-attack? Had the make-believe Major Martin played his part?

In the days following the landings, the lack of a cohesive plan to co-ordinate the advances of British Eighth Army and US Seventh Army came to a head. The two armies were breaking out from their beachheads and converging on the only road north to where the Axis forces were entrenched around Monte Etna. On 13 July Alexander met with Generals Patton and Montgomery to revise the plans and orders. Their agreement that day was not clear and unambiguous. Patton saw it as an opportunity and sent Seventh Army into a drive across Sicily to the north-west coast, and the capital Palermo. From there the US Seventh Army could advance along the north coast road to Messina, on Sicily's north-east tip.[20]

*   *   *

Allied aircraft were out in strength when the Sicilian invasion began in the early hours of 10 July. Allied planes flew 1,092 sorties protecting the ships and landings.[21] As it had in North Africa, DAF was right behind Eighth Army's front lines offering close air support. Two days after the landings, when Augusta north of Syracuse was taken by Eighth Army on 12 July, DAF's 244 Wing became the first Allied formation to commence operations on the ground in Sicily. First at Pachino, then at Cassibile, it was also the first on

European territory. Soon afterwards, 239 and 285 Wings, and the American 57th and 79th Fighter Groups, joined them.[22]

On 10 July the Luftwaffe could manage no more than 300 sorties by all aircraft. In the three days from 10 to 12 July DAF alone exceeded 3,000 sorties. Allied planners had allowed for a worst case of losing 300 ships from enemy air attack. In the event only twelve ships were lost.[23]

Another very practical illustration of the close co-ordination between Eighth Army and DAF was the operation of the sea ferries from Malta taking supplies and equipment to Sicily. Montgomery's chief of staff issued an order giving RAF/DAF transport requirements the number one priority. On 13 July it paid large dividends. Spitfires of 243 Squadron intercepted twelve Ju88s without fighter escorts. The result was predictable: five kills and damage to others were claimed. It proved to be the final attempt by the Luftwaffe at any significant challenge to the invasion by aerial bombardment.[24]

To try and counter the Luftwaffe's capability to mount night attacks against the invasion force, a group of Mosquito night-fighters was brought in. On 4 July Squadron Leader J.W. Allan DSO DFC had landed in Malta with a detachment of six Mosquitos from No. 256 Squadron RAF. Allan was twenty-years old, from Epping in Essex but of Scottish birth. His radar-navigator was Flight Lieutenant H.J. Davidson DFC, a thirty-year-old industrial chemist from Wingham, NSW, Australia.

On the night of 15 July the Luftwaffe sent a thirty-strong group of Ju88s and other bombers in a raid against Eighth Army at Syracuse. Allan and Davidson went to work, shooting down five bombers, four Ju88s and a three-engined Cant Z.1007. During the remaining four weeks of the battle for Sicily, this remarkable team of Allan and Davidson were to claim another nine Luftwaffe bombers. Several times their own aircraft was damaged, twice returning on only one engine, demonstrating both their own and the Mosquito's resilience.[25]

With freedom of the Sicilian skies, Allied aircraft bombed and strafed Axis road convoys, and hit ports and rail lines in Sicily and southern Italy, to curtail the enemy's supplies and communications. By the middle of July the Luftwaffe was restricted to only twenty-five aircraft based in Sicily. In comparison, on 30 July, the Allies were operating forty squadrons from twenty-one Sicilian airfields.[26]

*   *   *

Within a few days of their penetration north of Syracuse Eighth Army ran into German forces south of Catania. On 13/14 July glider-borne troops were unable to capture and hold the Primosole Bridge. Out of a 1,900 strong force only 200 landed near the bridge and were confronted by the German 3rd Parachute Regiment, who had dropped onto the bridge two days earlier.[27]

The ferocious Battle of Primosole Bridge raged over four days. When the bridge was finally in Eighth Army's possession on 17 July, and secured for crossing, it had cost around 4,000 casualties, including some 700 dead. The Germans had used those days to establish a defensive line along the Simeto river. Eighth Army's advance on Catania came to a standstill.[28]

Meanwhile, on the north-west coast of Sicily, the Americans had quickly taken Palermo and were commencing an advance eastwards towards Messina. However, the planned offensive drive by Eighth Army, using the narrow coastal route through Catania, and then between Monte Etna and the sea to Messina, presented a daunting bottleneck.

Eighth Army was stalled in the battle to take Catania, which guarded the narrow coastal strip between Monte Etna and the sea. It had become clear that the Germans meant to hold the important port of Catania and the north-east coast in strength, as part of a defensive line stretching westwards through the mountains to the important road junctions of Enna and Leonforte, and from there north to San Stefano on Sicily's north coast.

The east coast route to Messina was effectively blocked. So, as he had done in Tunisia, Montgomery reverted to his alternative tactic of a left hook offensive, this time through the mountains to the north-west. The 78th Division was to advance over the hills west of the Catania Plain, cross the Dittaino river, take Catenanuova, then assault Centuripe, Adrano and Randazzo. Montgomery aimed to split the final defensive line of the Germans around Monte Etna and force their retreat both on the north and east coasts to Messina.

On the night of 29 July 1st Canadian Division, supported by 5th Northamptons, crossed the Dittaino river for the attack on Catenanuova. Luftwaffe strikes in the morning destroyed the Northamptons' supplies and transport and inflicted significant casualties. It was another marked example of what the Luftwaffe could do if allowed. Despite this, enemy ground forces were overcome and, by sunset on 30 July, the Canadians had taken Catenanuova.

While Eighth Army's infantry fought in the mountains around Monte Etna to outflank the Axis lines, DAF fighters and fighter-bombers flew round-the-clock strikes, aimed at cutting off German supplies and communications north of Catania. The attempted air interdiction of Catania, to cut off all its communication routes, was probably the first air blockade on such a large scale against such a small target, a single city. They hit at any vehicles moving along the single coast road from Messina to Catania, as well as German positions in the hill towns around Monte Etna which were being assaulted by 78th Division. On 4 August DAF Kittyhawk fighter-bombers were lifting into the air every five minutes in close support operations.

In addition to the air interdiction operations, it took the capture on 2 August by 78th Division of the mountain town of Centuripe twenty miles away and, at about the same time Troina by the Americans, to sever the east-west route around Monte Etna to the north.[29] Hill towns around Etna, such as Randazzo, suffered from a combined and massive onslaught of the Allies' artillery bombardment and aerial bombing. Its population of some 10,000 either fled or were killed, as it was turned into rubble.

In the 1st East Surreys of 78th Division Lieutenant Woodhouse wrote to his parents on 11 August, describing what he saw on entering Randazzo:

> My dear Mum,
> I am on a hill with crowds of refugees sheltering nearby, they are half starved and ridden with disease. We have fed them out of stuff left over from our rations ... it brings home the true horror of war ... The devastation is absolutely staggering, the Luftwaffe is a child's toy compared with the Allied Air Forces out here.[30]

After the Allied breakthrough at Centuripe, when the Germans were forced to pull out from Catania, enemy forces withdrew right across the island, through the mountains around the slopes of Monte Etna, towards Messina. They also commenced a withdrawal across the Messina Straits of their heavy artillery, tanks, rear area staff, non-combatants, and any other unnecessary equipment. As Axis forces retreated to their Messina–Reggio escape route, they held up the Allies forces in bitterly fought rearguard actions.[31]

To prevent the Axis forces, particularly German troops and their equipment, making their retreat across the Messina Straits, Allied bombers targeted the ferries making the short sea crossing. The enemy, however, had learned a bitter lesson on the receiving end of Allied air power, especially the feared fighter-bomber. Lining either side of the Messina Straits were some 150 Italian anti-aircraft batteries, and an estimated 168 of the Germans' feared 88mm flak guns. Some estimates put the total number of anti-aircraft guns closer to 500, and some pilots claimed the intensity of the flak was worse than that confronted by Bomber Command in raids on Germany's Ruhr region.

Despite a maelstrom of flak, the Allied bombing raids persisted until the enemy's losses forced the Axis to confine their ferry crossings to the hours of darkness only. At the beginning of August it was recognized that only the high-flying heavy bombers of the Strategic Air Force could avoid the flak curtain around the Messina area. Because the Germans did not have their latest anti-aircraft 88mm Flak81 gun available they could not reach 25,000 feet, the operating height of the B-17s.[32]

As early as 3 August AVM Broadhurst, in a letter to Air Marshal Sir Arthur Coningham, Commander of NATAF, warned of the need for bombing raids by the B-17 Flying Fortresses to halt a German evacuation.

> I quite realize that we can do a lot with the air forces immediately available, but the exceptional flak on both sides of the Straits of Messina will need, I think, the use of Fortresses if we are to maintain continuous air action to defeat an attempt at evacuation.[33]

On 5 and 6 August a force of 121 B-17 heavy bombers, out of a total Strategic Air Force strength of 180, made the only heavy bombing attacks on Messina city and the road junctions leading into its centre. Two more, smaller, raids, by eleven B-25 medium bombers on 13 August, and twelve on 16 August, during the crucial evacuation days of 11 to 17 August, made insignificant impact. None of these bombing missions sank any Axis shipping, or much hindered their evacuation operations.

It was left to TAF and DAF to shoulder the major part of the attempt to stop the Axis evacuation. Some 89 per cent of all sorties flown were by tactical aircraft, in the main by light bombers at night by No. 205 Squadron RAF, and fighter-bombers in daylight at low level. Even so, only some 18 per cent of the 137 light bombers, and 721 fighters or fighter-bombers available, were committed to attacking Messina.[34]

On 11 August the Allied High Command decided to re-deploy the heavy bombing raids to a concentrated attack on German supply routes in mainland Italy. Meanwhile, to accelerate the extrication of their forces from Messina to Reggio, on 13 August the Axis began to operate daylight ferries across the Messina Straits. That very same day a maximum strength bombing group of 217 B-17, B-25 and B-26 bombers, with 140 P-38 fighter escorts, raided the railway marshalling yards at Rome.

It would be four days before the heavy bomber fleet could be regrouped and put back in the air. In that time the light- and fighter-bombers kept on trying to defy the flak, attempting to disrupt the evacuation. It was to no avail and, by 17 August, the round-the-clock daylight ferry service, transporting the Axis forces to Reggio, was completed.[35] In a Dunkirk-like escape across the Messina Straits the Germans had preserved a force upon which they would be able to build a ferocious defence of southern Italy.

Despite losing as many as possibly 100,000 Italians deserting or surrendering to become PoWs, the Germans were able to evacuate a substantial part of their force by ferry from Messina to Reggio. Around 60,000 troops, 10,000 vehicles, and nearly 150 guns were able safely to cross the strait.[36] A combination of mistaken strategic vision and poor co-operation between Allied commanders from Eisenhower down allowed the Axis forces to escape. Strategic bombing by the high-flying B-17s of the few approach roads to Messina and Reggio, either side of the Messina Straits, would almost certainly have prevented the 'Dunkirk-like' evacuation by the Axis. Unlike Dunkirk, however, a significant force with their vehicles, guns and equipment intact, had escaped. They would confront the Allies with renewed strength in mainland Italy.

Notes
1. Herington, op. cit., pp. 568–9.
2. Montagu, op. cit., pp. 51–85.

3. Brookes, *Air War over Italy*, p. 10.
4. Owen, op. cit., pp. 182–3.
5. Ibid., pp. 185–6.
6. Ibid; Belogi and Leoni, 'Pantelleria', in *After the Battle*, No. 127, 15 Feb 2005.
7. Molesworth, op. cit., pp. 61–3.
8. Owen, op. cit., pp. 182–3.
9. Ibid., p. 187.
10. Brookes, op. cit., p. 10.
11. Ibid., pp. 13–14.
12. Owen, op. cit., pp. 188–90.
13. Molesworth, op. cit., pp. 64–5.
14. Dundas, op. cit., pp. 121–3.
15. Thomas, op. cit., pp. 48–9.
16. Owen, op. cit., pp. 188–90.
17. Ibid., p. 192.
18. Atkinson, op. cit., p. 33; Evans, op. cit., p. 58.
19. Atkinson, op. cit., p. 90; Evans, op. cit., p. 60.
20. Evans, op. cit., pp. 56–72.
21. Brookes, op. cit., pp. 14–17.
22. Owen, op. cit., p. 194.
23. Brookes, op. cit., pp. 14–17.
24. Owen, op. cit., pp. 196–7.
25. Herington, op. cit., pp. 572–3.
26. Brookes, op. cit., pp. 14–17.
27. Carver, *The War in Italy 1943–1945*, p. 34.
28. Atkinson, op. cit., p. 127.
29. Owen, op. cit., pp. 196–7; Evans, op. cit., pp. 56–72.
30. Evans, op. cit., p. 69.
31. Owen, op. cit., p. 201.
32. Brookes, op. cit., pp. 17–18; Atkinson, op. cit., pp. 164–8.
33. D' Este, *Bitter Victory, the Battle for Sicily 1943*, p. 528.
34. Ibid., pp. 523–49; Atkinson, op. cit., pp. 164–8.
35. Brookes, op. cit., p. 18.
36. Ibid., p. 17.

Chapter 9

Salerno's near disaster: new enemies – rivers, mountains, cloud and rain

The Allies' occupation of Sicily in little more than a month, despite the Germans' successful withdrawal and evacuation, sent shock waves through the Axis powers.

Even before Allied forces reached Messina, Italy's King Victor Emmanuel set a trap for Mussolini and summoned him to his palace. He told Italy's Fascist Dictator that he was finished, and that Marshal Badoglio was taking over as head of the government. He then led a stunned, off-guard Mussolini outside to be arrested by the military police who were waiting, specifically prepared, for that purpose. The bloodless coup, deposing Mussolini, was welcomed by the Allies, but ironically it would lead to a stiffening of the Germans' resolve to fight for mainland Italy.[1]

When in mid-August the Germans withdrew from Sicily across the narrow Straits of Messina, they took most of their remaining vehicles, guns, tanks and equipment with them. They achieved more of a strategic withdrawal than a retreat. Together with the fall of Mussolini, it may have left some on the Allied side with a misplaced perception that the Germans had run away demoralized. Some over-optimistic thoughts that Rome could be taken by Christmas would soon evaporate.

On 3 September 1943 the first Allied invasion of mainland Europe proper began. General Montgomery's Eighth Army in Operation BAYTOWN was the first to go, landing uncontested at Reggio di Calabria on the toe of Italy. The main attack was planned for six days later. In a decision taken hastily after Mussolini's fall, General Mark Clark's Fifth Army, which included the British X Corps for about half of its strength, would land in the early hours of 9 September near Salerno, around thirty miles south of Naples.

For the crossing of the Messina Strait to Reggio on 3 September by Eighth Army, Operation BAYTOWN, and the landings at Salerno planned for a few days later, Operation AVALANCHE, the Air Plan included some 1,500 aircraft of all types. Allied air forces could count on 350 heavy bombers, 650 medium/light bombers, 160 fighter-bombers, 210 fighters, 32 night-fighters, and 110 carrier-borne Seafire fighters. Based on 75 per cent serviceability this would equate, in theory, to around 1,100 operational aircraft to protect the invasion forces.[2]

Italy including Sicily, showing the northern tip of Tunisia, and Slovenia, Croatia, Bosnia-Herzegovina etc. were Yugoslavia in 1943.

Eighth Army's crossing to Reggio was preceded by a combined bombardment, comprising aerial, naval and shore-based artillery in Sicily. As they landed and advanced inland, DAF fighters dominated the skies above. On the ground German forces had withdrawn, and there was only negligible resistance from a few Italian troops. After occupying Reggio with no opposition, 5th Division and 1st Canadian Division of Eighth Army's XIII Corps began to tackle Calabria's medieval roads and mountainous tracks. Ahead of them stretched the demolished sections of roads and hidden mines left by the retreating 29th Panzer Grenadier Division. All must be overcome before they could reach their first objective eighty miles away, the isthmus at Catanzaro on Italy's foot.

The Luftwaffe made little effort to counter Operation BAYTOWN, although one Ju88 and one Bf109 were shot down. It meant only one thing.

The Germans must be concentrating their air defences for the near certainty of the main invasion imminent at Salerno.[3] In the failed attempt to defend Sicily the Axis air forces had lost over 1,300 aircraft, in the air, destroyed or captured on their airfields. By 3 September the Luftwaffe's strength in the Mediterranean was down to some 880 aircraft, of which some 650 were estimated to be operational. The Allied air forces also suffered losses of a different kind. Substantial numbers of squadrons of both bombers and fighters were transferred to Britain for Operation OVERLORD, the planned invasion of north-west Europe.

This left the Allies with 800 fewer aircraft for the invasion of southern Italy than they had had for Sicily. However, compared with the more rapidly reducing numbers of the Luftwaffe, which had lost the Italians' all but disbanded Regia Aeronautica, the Allies had a total strength of 3,127 aircraft to call upon. The disparity was more than just numbers of aircraft. Because of the success of Allied air power both before and during the invasion of Sicily, Reichsmarschall Göring, commander of the Luftwaffe, ordered court martial proceedings on charges of cowardice against one in ten fighter pilots. This further undermined the morale of Luftwaffe aircrew.[4]

As well as the Luftwaffe possessing a lower number of aircraft, their serviceability level was only around 50 per cent, whereas the Allies were achieving as high as 75 per cent. Pilot attrition was another significant factor weighing against the Luftwaffe. Continual operations against the ascendant Allied air forces took its toll on the older surviving pilots, so that fewer and fewer of them were available to fill training roles. The result was that new younger pilots, both inexperienced and inadequately trained, were rushed into frontline squadrons, and more quickly paid the price.

The Allies' capture of the islands of Pantelleria and Lampedusa had done away with any hope which the Axis may have harboured, for those islands' airfields to provide either early warning of, or to harass, Allied bomber raids or the invasion fleet. In contrast, the surrender of Pantelleria and its garrison forces, solely by the massive saturation bombing, reinforced the established view of AVM Tedder (Acting Air Marshal) and other Allied commanders. Simply put, to win the war on the ground, the war in the air must be won first.[5]

For Allied air forces mounting air interdiction operations the Italian mainland presented a far larger challenge than Sicily or Tunisia. Sea routes into Italy had been closed off by the Royal Navy, so for all practical purposes nearly 100 per cent of imports, including oil and coal, came through the northern land borders. The prime targets for Allied air raids were the railway marshalling yards at Vienna, Milan, Turin, Trieste, Fiume, and Rome. Vienna handled some 50 per cent through the Alpine Brenner Pass. Milan serviced the Simplon and St Gothard lines, and Turin the route from southern France. By way of Trieste and Fiume came around two thirds of

Italy's oil imports from the Balkans. For all these imports Rome was the focal point for distribution to southern Italy.[6]

With inflated hopes of early success, a campaign of long-range strategic bombing to disrupt and choke off Italy's arteries began. On 13 August there was a massive bombing raid on Rome's rail yards but, in order to sustain the strategy over a long period, there was one singular dependency. The Luftwaffe, already reeling from defeat in Tunisia and Sicily, must be driven from the skies and its airfields south of Rome.

On 25 August 135 B-17 Flying Fortress bombers and 140 P-38 Lightning fighters raided the extensive cluster of Luftwaffe airfields at Foggia, which were about sixty miles inland from the Adriatic port of Bari. Besides the need to destroy the Luftwaffe, the Foggia airfields were an attractive target to be captured as soon as possible in the invasion of Italy. The runways were long enough to support the Allies' strategic bombers and the airfields could be supplied through Bari's deep-water port.

The raid on Foggia on 25 August was not easy. A crescendo of flak and rockets, and sixty enemy fighters, tore into the high-flying waves of Allied bombers. However, the steady deluge of bombing destruction from the B-17s could not be stopped. The next day, 26 August, the airfields around the other major port in southern Italy, Naples, were similarly pounded. Hangars, workshops and other maintenance facilities were flattened, and runways cratered, at every airfield except one. The Monte Corvino air base close to Salerno was spared. It must have seemed a very meaningful omission to the German High Command.

For the Luftwaffe, however, the devastation of rail transport was strangling the supply of replacement parts, aviation fuel and other supplies. And now their operations bases and runways were being destroyed. The remaining serviceable Luftwaffe bombers were sent north to more distant airfields. As it had been prior to the final battles at El Alamein and Tunis, Allied air power was eliminating any significant enemy threat from the skies.[7]

While the Strategic Air Force pounded Axis infrastructure from on high, DAF also hammered towns and transport across the toe and foot of Italy. Light and fighter-bombers struck against road, rail, bridges and enemy convoys. At the end of August 1943, only days before the planned Allied invasion of mainland Italy, air reconnaissance showed that Axis communication routes were severely disrupted across southern Italy. Many lines were blocked and transport was at a standstill, including routes to Salerno and Foggia.

Compared with Catania, where transport into the city had been restricted but not halted, interdiction through Allied air power had been stepped up several notches. Main line rail routes had been cut or reduced to slower flows. It was obvious to both German and Allied high commands that the Allied landings must come soon, before the disruptions were overcome, road and rail infrastructure repaired, and Axis reinforcements and supplies began flowing through again.[8]

In addition to the indications of invasion planning to be inferred by the Germans from the Allied air campaigns, there was another obvious reason why the landings must be imminent. The narrow gap between Messina and Reggio on the toe of Italy, was only some six miles or so wide. The Reggio di Calabria promontory and its rocky terrain with near medieval cart tracks could be easily cut off by Allied air power, and made indefensible by the enemy. The Germans must clearly discern that, under the umbrella of DAF air superiority, Allied troops would be able to cross the Straits of Messina whenever they chose.

At the same time, Naples the nearest major port south of Rome, beckoned the Allies' planners. It was within range of Allied fighters based in Sicily, and the Bay of Salerno south of the Amalfi coast offered some twenty miles of beaches suitable for landings. Behind the beaches was a flat plain stretching up to eight miles inland to the surrounding mountains.

Although the mountains would favour a defender, it was thought that rapid landings might enable the Allies to reach them first. For DAF and other Allied air forces, the airfield at Monte Corvino, only three miles from the beaches, was the clinching argument for selecting the Bay of Salerno. During August, however, the Germans, clearly anticipating the Allies' plans, held defensive exercises at Salerno under the direction of Rommel. It should have set some alarm bells ringing in the minds of Allied generals.[9]

The surrender of the Italian Government on the eve of the Salerno landings grounded the Regia Aeronautica. This left the Luftwaffe to muster whatever it could across its more northerly airfields in Italy and Sardinia. At the time Allied air reconnaissance estimated the Luftwaffe's remaining strength to be around 510 aircraft. Later figures suggested 270 bombers and 266 fighters and fighter-bombers but, at a lower serviceability rate of only 50 per cent, it meant perhaps only some 250 enemy aircraft could be anticipated to be operational.[10]

When Axis aircraft made a token attack on Eighth Army in Reggio Calabria on 4 September, DAF Spitfires quickly snuffed it out, claiming six Macchi C.200s and one Fw190. More ominously, another dangerous and implacable enemy began to appear. Some low cloud signalled the coming of autumn, and the rain, ice and snow of a European winter.

Italy's Apennine mountain spine meant that weather conditions could be completely different on one side of the country from the other, with unpredictable rain and fog even in summer. Outside of the summer months the weather was not unlike Britain's, variable rain and snow, sometimes worse over the higher mountains, closing down airfields very quickly. Unlike North Africa and Sicily, temporary air strips on hard ground were unavailable, and rolled-out tarmac runways would be essential for most of the year.[11]

By using airfields in Sicily the Allies planned to protect the Salerno land-ings with close air support over the beaches. Yet, despite the Luftwaffe's depleted strength, it was still capable of disrupting the invasion preparations. On 17 August ninety bombers raided Bizerte's harbour, which was full of ships of the invasion fleet. A similar raid on 24 August, possibly around fifty Ju88s and Dornier Do217s, hit the Palermo port.

Although DAF was to continue to support Eighth Army in Calabria and in its push up the Adriatic Coast, the TBF would contribute to the US 12th Air Support Command by sending A-36 Apache dive-bombers (a specialized version of the P-51 Mustang), Spitfires, Beaufighters and P-38 Lightnings into the skies above Salerno. Together with an added 100 Seafires from Royal Navy carriers, it would mean nearly 700 Allied aircraft being available to provide a protective umbrella for Operation AVALANCHE.

On the other hand, when ranges, fuel capacity, and flight times were calcu-lated, it meant that the average number of aircraft at any time over Salerno in daylight, would be only fifty-four. Air planning staff had cause for concern. Somehow, the threat of a major Luftwaffe attack on the Salerno beach-head had to be kept at bay.[12] Following more bombing on 6 September of Axis airfields, with the continued avoidance of the air base at Monte Corvino near Salerno, the Fortresses and Wellingtons returned to interdiction targets, raiding road and rail routes and marshalling yards.

*   *   *

On the night of 8/9 September the Allied fleet carrying Fifth Army in Opera-tion AVALANCHE, sailed past the Amalfi coast to its north, and approached the Bay of Salerno. The Allies were taking a great risk. An initial force of only 55,000 men heading for Salerno, compared unfavourably with the 160,000 in the Sicily landings. Yet it began well. In its approach to the Salerno beaches overnight on 8/9 September, the invasion fleet lost one ship to a seaborne torpedo attack, but not one from an air attack. The Luftwaffe did attempt a night attack, only to lose seven aircraft to RAF Beaufighters. During the day on D Day, 9 September, four more enemy planes were shot down for the loss of two Allied aircraft.[13]

The night before the Salerno landings, 8 September 1943, Eisenhower announced on radio the surrender to the Allies by the new Italian Govern-ment led by Marshal Badoglio and the King. Hitler was furious at losing his major ally, and fearful that similar revolts could spread to other Axis countries, such as Hungary and Rumania. The Italians moved Mussolini from place to place, such as the islands of Ponza and La Maddalena, to keep his whereabouts secret. They feared that the Germans might attempt to rescue him and re-instate him as Italy's dictator.

Meanwhile, for the Allied troops sailing through the night towards the Salerno beaches, news of Italy's surrender lulled some into a misconceived

top view of Spitfire
k VB No. R6923, QJ-S of
. 92 Squadron RAF in
41, similar to the Spitfire
wn by 92 Squadron's
ght Lieutenant Neville
ke in 1942 in North
rica.

6 November 1941 a
hall formation of
ellington bombers based
Malta raided Naples,
m where supplies were
ing shipped to the Axis
nzerarmee in North
rica. (*www.ww2today.com*)

A Vickers Wellington Mk II of No. 104 Squadron, Bomber Command, in April 1941. This aircraft moved to the Mediterranean in April 1942, where it was deployed until February 1945.

Ground crew of No. 274 Squadron RAF overhaul Hawker Hurricane Mk 1, V7780, AB-M, at Landing Ground 10/Gerawala, during the defence of Tobruk. This illustrates the ordeals of a burning sun, heat and dust faced by aircraft ground crews in the North African desert.

rmourers work on a P-40 Tomahawk of No. 3 Squadron RAAF in North Africa, December 1941.

Lockheed Hudson Mk V bomber of No. 48 Squadron RAF in 1942.

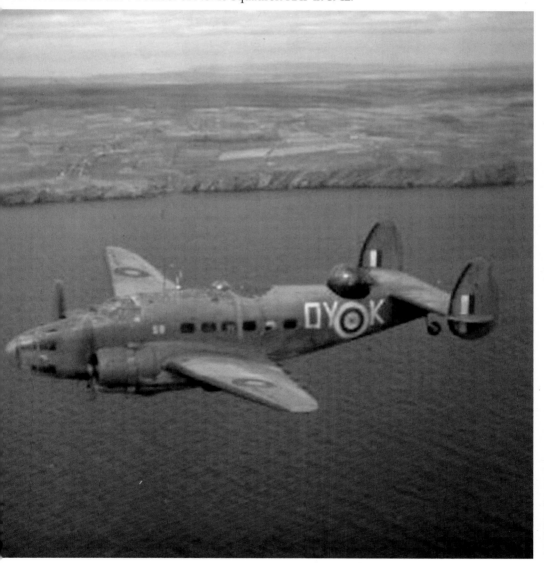

A Curtiss P-40 Kittyhawk Mk III of No. 112 Squadron RAF in 1943, with the red-painted propeller spinner of the Desert Air Force, taxies through the scrub at Medenine, Tunisia. The ground crewman sitting on the wing is directing the pilot, whose view ahead is hindered by the aircraft's nose. In mid-1941 No. 112 Squadron was the first of the Allies' squadrons to use the 'shark mouth' marking on the Kittyhawk.

A Spitfire Vc/Vb, ER338 QJ-S, of Flight Lieutenant Neville Duke, No. 92 Squadron RAF, flying over El Nogra, Libya in December 1942. (*www.forums.ubi.com*)

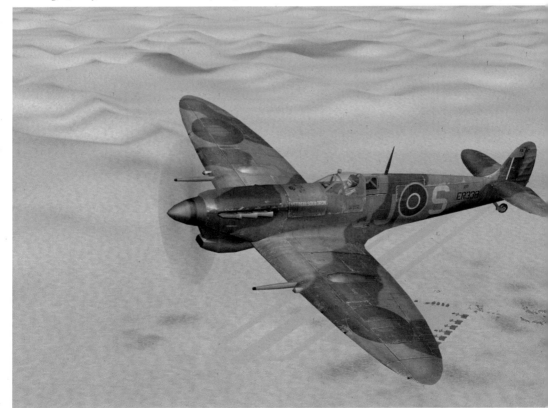

April 1943 Bristol Beaufighter V8318, F-Freddie, of No. 252 Squadron RAF, creates a cloud of dust as it moves out from its landing ground at Magrun, eighty miles south of Benghazi, in Cyrenaica (eastern Libya).

Three Curtiss P-40 Warhawks in line abreast, as used by the 57th Fighter Group USAAF in North Africa 1942–43.

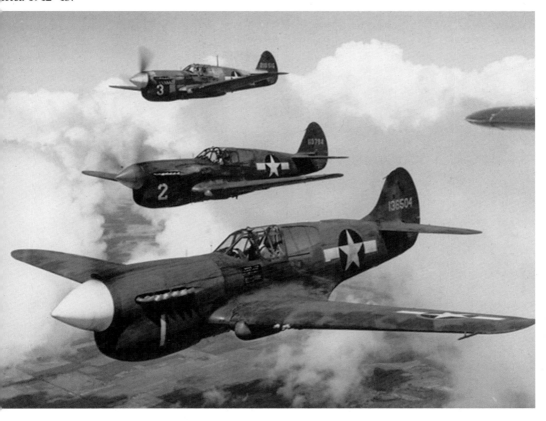

A Hawker Hurricane Mk IV (No. KZ321) in desert camouflage, including a red-painted nose spinner, typically used by fighters of the Desert Air Force.

A Republic P-47D Thunderbolt fighter of the Brazilian Air Force serving with the US XXII Tactical Air Command in Italy.

de Havilland Mosquito B Mk IV, DK336, before delivery to No. 105 Squadron RAF. The night-fighter variant, the NF XIII, was deployed in the Italian campaign.

Hawker Hurricane Mk IV of No. 6 Squadron RAF being serviced at Foggia, Italy, in July 1944 prior to a sortie over the Adriatic. It is being fitted with a 40-gallon long-range fuel tank under the port wing and four 3-inch rocket projectiles under the starboard wing while a Type G45 camera gun is being serviced by the airman standing second from the right.

The Royal Palace at Caserta was used as the HQ for Allied Forces in the Mediterranean but there were also rest centres in Caserta and the surrounding area that were used by personnel of the Dese Air Force.

light Lieutenant Neville Duke standing with
is Spitfire Mk V of No. 92 Squadron RAF at
iggin Hill in 1941. By August 1941 Duke had
aimed two victories of Bf109s. In October he
as posted to No. 112 Squadron RAF flying
ie Curtiss P-40 Tomahawk. He was shot
own twice in November and December, but
irvived and, by February 1942, his tally had
icreased to eight kills, and he was awarded
ie DFC. In November 1942 Duke rejoined
Io. 92 Squadron RAF in Egypt.
ww.thewowa.com)

n the left of the photograph is Squadron
eader Lloyd Wiggins. During the Battle of
l Alamein on 26 October 1942, Flight
ieutenant Wiggins of No. 38 Squadron RAF,
•d a formation of three Wellington torpedo-
ombers, which sank the Axis oil tanker
ergestea off Tobruk harbour. The *Tergestea*
as Rommel's last hope of receiving sorely
eeded fuel for his tanks and vehicles, and
ie sinking of the tanker condemned his
anzerarmee to the only remaining option,
efeat by Eighth Army and his retreat to the
est. (*Lloyd Wiggins*)

During the Battle of El Alamein on 26 October 1942, the Italian oil tanker *Tergestea* was torpedoed and sunk outside Tobruk harbour, by a formation of three Wellington torpedo-bombers led by Flight Lieutenant Lloyd Wiggins of No. 38 Squadron RAF. (*Lloyd Wiggins*)

Sergeant Alec Richardson, a Kittyhawk fighter pilot of No. 3 Squadron RAAF, who made a forced landing during the Battle of El Alamein, and was taken prisoner. (*Alec Richardson*)

Members of the 64th Fighter Squadron of the 57th Fighter Group, standing in front of one of their Curtiss P-40 Warhawk fighters in Tunisia. Pilots of 57 FG took part in the 'Palm Sunday massacre' over the Sicilian Straits on 18 April 1943, in which seventy-four enemy aircraft were shot down. (*US Library of Congress*)

Squadron Leader H.S.L. 'Cocky' Dundas, commanding officer of No. 5 Squadron RAF, photographed on 2 February 1942 at RAF Duxford. On 3 February 1943 Hugh Dundas DFC, still only twenty-two years old, yet a decorated veteran Spitfire pilot of the Battle of Britain, arrived in Tunisia to be Wing Commander of the Spitfire squadrons of No. 324 Wing RAF.

Captain James 'Big Jim' Curl, pictured with his P-40 Warhawk in Tunisia. A flight leader of the 66th Fighter Squadron, he led a formation from 57th Fighter Group USAAF on 18 April 1943, which claimed seventy-four enemy aircraft destroyed in the 'Palm Sunday massacre'.

CM Sir Arthur Tedder in December 1943 on the Italian coast. He had been appointed the temporary rank of Air Chief Marshal in July 1942. Later that month he returned to the UK, to take up his appointment of Deputy Commander of the Allied Expeditionary Forces, which were being assembled for Operation OVERLORD, the cross-channel invasion planned for early June 1944.

(*left*) Squadron Leader Bill McRae flew the latest Mk VIII Wellington torpedo-bomber from the UK across the Mediterranean to Cairo, on his first operation after completing his training. Bill celebrated his 100th birthday in January 2012 in Sydney Australia. (*Bill McRae*)

(*Right*) Brigadier General Michael C. McCarthy USAF (Rtd), who as a lieutenant in the 64th Fighter Squadron of the 57th Fighter Group of USAAF, was a pilot of P-40 Warhawks and P-47 Thunderbolts in North Africa and Italy. (*www.af.mil/AboutUs/Biographies*)

USAAF P-47D Thunderbolts of the 345th Fighter Squadron over northern Italy on 6 April 1945. The Thunderbolts were en route to attack targets in the Po valley. (*US Official*)

FROM: MAIN EIGHTH ARMY   031130 B

TO. DAF

COS 148 (.) PERSONAL FOR AIR VICE MARSHAL FOSTER FROM GENERAL McCREERY (.)

IN THIS THE HOUR OF OUR COMPLETE VICTORY I FEEL MY FIRST DUTY IS TO CONVEY
TO YOU AND TO ALL THE OFFICERS AND MEN UNDER YOUR COMMAND MY HEARTFELT
GRATITUDE FOR THE MAGNIFICENT SUPPORT THAT THE DESERT AIR FORCE HAS
RENDERED TO THE EIGHTH ARMY THROUGHOUT OUR LONG ASSOCIATION (.) THIS LAST
GREAT BATTLE HAS BEEN WON AS A RESULT OF COMPLETE CONFIDENCE AND
CO-OPERATION BETWEEN THE EIGHTH ARMY AND THE DESERT AIR FORCE (.) OUR AIM
WAS TO DESTROY THE ENEMY SOUTH OF THE RIVER PO, HOW COMPLETELY WE SUCCEEDED
IS PROVED BY THE VAST NUMBER OF ENEMY VEHICLES AND EQUIPMENTS DESTROYED
ON THE SOUTHERN BANK OF THE RIVER AS A RESULT OF YOUR ATTACK (.) THE
DESERT AIR FORCE HAS ACHIEVED A DEGREE OF EFFICIENCY IN CLOSE SUPPORT OF
THE GROUND FORCES THAT HAS NEVER BEEN EQUALLED IN ANY OTHER PARTNERSHIP (.)
THROUGHOUT THE LONG STRUGGLE THE GALLANTRY OF THE PILOTS OF THE DESERT
AIR FORCE HAS BEEN THE CONTINUAL ADMIRATION OF THE EIGHTH ARMY (.) THEIR
DASH AND COURAGE HAS NEVER BEEN MORE EVIDENT THAN IN THE GREAT BATTLE
THAT HAS BROUGHT ABOUT THE FINAL COLLAPSE OF THE ENEMY (.) THESE GREAT
RESULTS COULD NOT HAVE BEEN ACHIEVED WITHOUT THE MOST SKILLED LEADERSHIP
AND PLANNING, AND I SHOULD LIKE TO EXPRESS MY ADMIRATION AT THE MANNER
IN WHICH YOU AND YOUR STAFF HANDLED THE INTRICATE PROBLEMS THAT HAVE
FACED US (.) IN PARTICULAR I REFER TO THE PLANNING THAT WAS UNDERTAKEN
BY YOUR HEADQUARTERS WITH MATAF IN CONNECTION WITH THE HEAVY BOMBER
ATTACKS (.) THE RECORD NUMBER OF SORTIES THAT THE DESERT AIR FORCE HAVE
FLOWN IN A SINGLE DAY DURING THE RECENT WEEKS IS EVIDENCE OF THE UNSTINTED
LABOURS AND EFFICIENCY OF YOUR GROUND ORGANISATION (.) I WISH TO THANK
YOU PERSONALLY FOR ALL THE HELP AND CO-OPERATION YOU HAVE EXTENDED TO ME
WHILE WE HAVE WORKED TOGETHER TOWARDS THE ATTAINMENT OF OUR COMMON GOAL (.)
MY MOST EARNEST HOPE IS THAT THE COMRADESHIP AND TRUST THAT HAS BEEN BUILT
UP BETWEEN THE EIGHTH ARMY AND THE DESERT AIR FORCE WILL HAVE A LASTING
INFLUENCE ON THE RELATIONS BETWEEN OUR TWO SERVICES IN THE YEARS TO COME (.)
I AM CONFIDENT THAT THIS WILL BE THE CASE AND FEEL SURE THAT THE RESULTS
THAT HAVE BEEN ACHIEVED ON THE BATTLEFIELDS OF AFRICA AND ITALY WILL LONG
BE QUOTED AS A PERFECT EXAMPLE OF INTER SERVICE CO-OPERATION

IMMEDIATE

The personal message from General Sir Richard McCreery, commander of Eighth Army, to Air Vice
Marshal William Foster, AOC-in-C of the Desert Air Force, on the morning of 3 May 1945, following
the surrender of German forces in Italy on 2 May. (*Author's collection*)

to be of assistance to their less fortunate brothers on the ground. I can assure you that the support DAF has given to the Eighth Army is more than willingly offered.

With you, I too hope that the combined Eighth Army – Desert Air Force results in this campaign will provide an abiding foundation for Army – Air understanding wherever it is needed in the future.

I'd like finally to say that I think the Eighth Army is extremely fortunate in its Commander.

Yours sincerely,

R. M. Foster.

The personal handwritten letter from Air Vice Marshal William Foster, AOC-in-C of the Desert Air Force, on 3 May 1945 in reply to the personal message from General Sir Richard McCreery, commander of Eighth Army. (*Author's collection*) feeling that the invasion would be a walkover. In the early hours of 9 September, on the beaches south-east of Salerno, the British X Corps of Lieutenant General Richard McCreery went ashore to the left of the Sele river, with the aim of quickly heading up the road to Naples and Rome. On the beaches directly beneath Paestum, founded by the Greeks in the sixth century BC, the American VI Corps of Major General Dawley made landfall south of the river Sele.[14]

Field Marshal Kesselring had been appointed C-in-C South over all German forces in the Mediterranean. He saw the importance of fighting the Allies in southern Italy, to keep Allied bomber bases as far from striking range of northern Italy and Germany as possible.[15] Kesselring believed the Allies had to land where they had air cover, and close to the port of Naples. Because that made the beaches south of Salerno the most likely landing place, the 16th Panzer Division had been ordered to dig in on the coastal plain hemmed in by mountains either side of the Sele, to defend the whole Gulf of Salerno.

At first Clark's Fifth Army gained only small beachheads against 16th Panzer, before they came under ferocious counter-attack on 12 September from the Germans' Tenth Army under General Heinrich von Vietinghoff. Although Hitler had approved a strategy of gradual retreat to the Gustav Line south of Rome, von Vietinghoff was under orders to first try and throw the Allies back. Defying more than 6,000 sorties flown by Allied aircraft from North Africa, the Germans successfully brought in troops through the surrounding mountains from Naples and Calabria.

The British 46th and 56th Divisions, near Battipaglia and at Salerno beach itself, took the initial brunt of an attack by XIV Panzer Corps. In just the first two days Fifth Army suffered over 1,000 casualties, such was the strength of the German counter-attacks. Vietinghoff sent his Panzers in a concentrated surge down the valley of the river Sele to exploit the boundary between the British X Corps and the US VI Corps. The overall compression across the Allied salient from the German onslaught was such that Clark feared that the US VI Corps would be overrun.

The Monte Corvino airfield was captured on 10 September but German shelling from the surrounding hills made it unusable. Engineers began work on landing strips in safer areas, and the carrier-borne Seafires, with their close proximity to the landing beachheads, had to continue their patrols.[16] In response to the German counter-attack on 13 September against the Allies' beachhead, TAF flew some 700 sorties, while the Luftwaffe could only manage close to 100. The strategic bombers of NWAAF returned to interdiction missions with a vengeance. To cut off the Germans' lifelines for re-supply and reinforcements, roads north and south of Salerno were blocked, as Wellingtons raided Battipaglia, and in the south Mitchells, Marauders and Bostons hit Auletta and Controne.[17]

With no effective support from the Luftwaffe, the German Army could only rely on anti-aircraft fire against the air raids. To halt the German counter-attack Allied air power was called upon to completely shut down the enemy's communication and supply lines to the battlefield – to save the day. DAF fighters not only patrolled over the Salerno beaches, others in fighter-bomber roles bombed and strafed German troop convoys on the way to the front. Meanwhile, for DAF to support Eighth Army on the eastern Adriatic coast, personnel from No. 239 Wing RAF began the move to an airfield on Italian soil at Grottoglie near Taranto on 13 September. Following its principle of aiming to relocate and still operate on the same day, on 15 September Kittyhawks of 239 Wing flew from Grottoglie across Italy's toe to add to the desperate air strikes on German forces at Salerno.[18]

So as to avoid a long break in operations, which would result if the whole of 239 Wing were shipped by sea to Taranto and then by road Grottoglie, it was decided to send by air enough key men and supplies to get two squadrons flying at once – one of these was No. 3 Squadron RAAF. Once bombs, ammunition, fuel, oil, equipment, food and other supplies were loaded aboard the transport aircraft, selected fitters, riggers, armourers, cooks and other essential ground crew and support staff went on board. The squadron's Kittyhawks escorted the cargo planes north west from Sicily.

Once the transport planes were unloaded in Grottoglie, they flew back to Sicily for more supplies. The Kittyhawks were then checked, guns re-armed, bombs reloaded, refuelled, and stood ready for the first take-off from the Italian mainland. It is claimed that every one of the squadron's fighter-bombers was ready in half-an-hour. The first urgent operation that day was to bomb and strafe German armour and vehicles leading down to the beaches of Salerno.

Squadron Leader Brian Eaton of No. 3 Squadron RAAF, on their return from the operation, reported that some 700 vehicles nose to tail presented 'beautiful targets'. He thought it obvious that the Germans were unaware that the fighter-bombers had moved from Sicily, and had been caught by surprise in daylight in the open. In four operations over three days, 3 Squadron RAAF claimed twenty-five vehicles totally destroyed, eighteen set on fire, eighty-four damaged, one goods train strafed, four motorcycles and riders hit, and many enemy troops killed or wounded.[19]

* * *

Because of fighters from Sicily being 175 miles from Salerno, their time over the beachhead was limited. To increase fighter support over the landing force the Royal Engineers had quickly prepared two temporary landing strips, only a few hundred yards from the confused and chaotic front lines. For support of the Salerno landings DAF's 324 Wing was put under the command of Brigadier General Hawkins of the US Army Air Forces. In response to

Hawkins' orders to use the landing strips between patrols to refuel, the CO of 93 Squadron, Ken Macdonald, made the first such landing, only to be shot down and killed by Allied anti-aircraft fire. Despite the loss of his close friend, Wing Commander Dundas led another squadron to land on one of the beach-head runways.

Dundas dropped down onto the short strip only about a mile from the sea, as slowly as he could to pull up in time. From an olive grove lining the runway he was startled by flashes and explosions which drowned out his engine noise. From pilots of the preceding squadron and troops on the landing strip, he learned that there was a British artillery battery behind the olive trees that was firing across the runway. Dundas found a jeep and drove off to see if he could put a stop to a very dangerous situation.

Although he met with a Royal Artillery lieutenant colonel Dundas was unable to negotiate any change to the firing of shells across the flightpaths of the Spitfires. The battle for the beachhead was too precariously poised. Over the next few days Dundas was amazed that no more Spitfires were hit by shells from their own artillery. Some German shelling from a battery of 88mm guns also landed nearby, but again remarkably did not damage an aircraft.

Dundas thought that it was probably the only occasion in the war when Allied fighters operated from landing strips in front of their own artillery. In retrospect, he could only admire and respect the risky decision taken by General Hawkins, with typical American determination to win the battle at all costs.[20]

*   *   *

A retreat from Salerno was too horrendous for the Allies to contemplate. Naval staff plainly stated that the troops could not be re-embarked. The landing craft had not been designed for embarking troops from beaches, and any attempt to do so would result in a killing ground. It would isolate Montgomery's Eighth Army in Calabria, and put them at serious risk of being driven back to Reggio. Stalin's demand for a second front in Europe would be unmet, and the planning for OVERLORD, the Normandy invasion, would be deferred. As Alexander had insisted, Fifth Army just had to prevail in the Salerno bridgehead.

A naval bombardment by every ship, notably by the battleships HMS *Warspite* and HMS *Valiant*, and the cruisers USS *Philadelphia* and USS *Boise*, was mounted. Waves of bombing sorties by B-17s, carrier-borne aircraft and supporting Spitfires of the Desert Air Force from Sicily, were thrown at the German counter-attacks to avert disaster. The Luftwaffe fought back too, sinking the cruiser USS *Savannah* and crippling HMS *Warspite*, with the first radio-controlled bombs.[21]

Spitfire pilots of 81 Squadron were above *Warspite* at the time but did not observe the Fritz-X and Hs293 radio-guided bombs. At first they assumed that it had been a torpedo attack, although no torpedo-bombers had been seen. However, seeing three Dornier Do217s fleeing northwards they gave chase after the probable culprits for the *Warspite* attack. With a couple of other Spitfires, Pilot Officer Peart, a New Zealander, caught up with a 217 and, with his first burst of fire, hit its port wing. On his second burst a large part of the aeroplane broke off, hitting his own Spitfire.

Peart watched the Dornier crash into a hillside and wondered if the German crew had survived. Perhaps their daring was deserving of their luck holding. A second Do217 was also shot down by a pilot from another section of 81 Squadron. Peart was worried about what damage his plane may have suffered, as well as all three of his section's planes being in danger of running out of fuel. He took them down onto a rough landing strip within the beachhead, rather than risking the return flight to Sicily. It was Peart's final victory in the Mediterranean, before 81 Squadron transferred to Burma. There he claimed a victory over a Japanese aircraft to become an ace, and one of very few fighter pilots to do so in the war in the East on the back of victories against Italian and German aircraft. (In No. 152 Squadron RAF, which was also transferred from Italy to Burma in December 1943, was Flight Lieutenant Ron Paterson from Melbourne, Australia. He would shoot down a Japanese Zero fighter at 30,000 feet, which at that time was a record high altitude kill.)[22]

Despite Allied dominance in the air, on 16 September an estimated dozen Fw190s were threatening the beachhead – the Luftwaffe somehow still remained a potential threat. Flight Lieutenant Horbaczewski, a revered Spitfire ace known as 'Dziubek' and previously of the Polish Fighting Team in 145 Squadron, was in a patrol from 43 Squadron that sighted the Fw190s. Turning on the power, the Spitfire patrol took about three minutes to catch up with the enemy fighter-bombers.

Dziubek closed on a Fw190 at a height of only 300 feet, and at 200 yards fired his first burst. After his second burst the 190 turned over, then fell like a stone to crash a few miles south-east of Campagna. He then chased two more Fw190s, at tree-top height, before firing on the one on his port side, hitting its engine and cockpit. Dziubek's two victories increased his total tally to eleven.[23]

By the morning of 16 September the Germans had made no more gains, and showed signs of redeployment into defensive positions. Besides suffering the curtailment of supplies due to the interdiction strikes of Allied air raids, German commanders faced a growing risk of losing access to withdrawal routes, which were being increasingly threatened by the growing presence of Allied fighters and fighter-bombers.[24]

On the Salerno battlefield the combined effect of pouring in the reinforcements, the naval shelling, continual aerial bombardment, and with the threat of Eighth Army support from the south increasing by the day, forced the

German Tenth Army to pull back north to the Viktor Line on 17 September. This line ran along the river Volturno north of Naples in the west, and the river Biferno to the east, which the Germans planned to hold until at least 15 October, to give time for the Gustav Line south of Rome to be completed before winter.

Allied casualties had grown to around 9,000 against the Germans' 3,500, but the Salerno bridgehead had survived. The landings were secured but, as the Royal Navy's Admiral Cunningham said, 'The assault had come very near to failure, and for a time the situation was precarious.'[25] It was an early sign of the bitter struggle for Italy that lay ahead.

The Germans' tactical withdrawal soon became a full retreat. Fortunately for their snaking columns heading north, an onset of early autumnal cloud and rains came to their aid, hiding their vehicle convoys. Night operations by Allied aircraft, and many during daylight were cancelled. Though German forces made good a forced withdrawal, by 1 October Fifth Army had liberated Naples.[26]

* * *

While Eighth Army had diverted some forces to help at Salerno, their main body was expanding its offensive eastwards. Because of the Italian surrender the British 1st Airborne Division was able to land by ship on 9 September, unopposed near the top of the instep of Italy's heel at Taranto. The paratroopers quickly secured the local airfield before their first contact with German forces on 11 September.

Further up the Adriatic coast Brindisi and Bari were taken quickly, and a combination of elements from 56th Reconnaissance Regiment, The Royals, 17th Field Regiment, and 1st Airborne pushed on towards the Foggia airfields. Despite firefights with residual units of the German 1st Parachute Division, on 25 September B Squadron and Tactical HQ of 56 Recce reached the Foggia airfields.[27] Able to take heavy bombers, these airfields were seen as the highest priority for the Allied air forces. Washington and London rated them of immense strategic value, as they would allow the Allies' strategic bombers to mount strikes on industry and infrastructure targets in northern Italy and southern Germany.

It was planned for DAF to move up to the Foggia airfields, before once more accompanying Eighth Army northwards up Italy's Adriatic coast. DAF would then hand over the Foggia airfields to the Strategic Air Force. From Foggia heavy bombers could reach the Balkans, oil installations in Rumania, industrial cities across northern Italy and southern Europe, and even those in Czechoslovakia and southern Germany. The daylight raids into Germany by the US Eighth Air Force from bases in England were suffering heavy losses, and it was thought that strategic bombing raids from the south might draw off some of the Luftwaffe's fighters from northern Germany.

The Foggia airfields occupied a treeless, windswept plain west of the deep-water port of Bari. The featureless flat land was ideal for growing corn and, like eastern England, also well suited for heavy bomber bases. Supplies and bombs could be easily transported from ships in Bari's harbour, which was the only other alternative major port to Naples in the west.[28]

Following the German withdrawal from Salerno, and oblivious to Hitler's dilemma over the deposed Mussolini, Eighth Army quickened its advance through Taranto, which it was using as a base for moving up the Adriatic coast. Between 19 and 29 September most of 78th Division landed at Taranto.

Once 78th Division was in possession of motor transport, 11 Brigade set off north past Bari, towards their first objective 150 miles away on the Adriatic coast, Termoli. Its early capture by 78th Division was intended to provide cover for the seaborne landing of the Battleaxe Division's other two brigades. Although the plan was to occupy Termoli before the Germans could consolidate their line of defence, early winter rain threatened to slow things down.

German troops were withdrawing in a co-ordinated, tactical manner to major defensive positions on the Viktor Line along the Biferno river. It was also the route of one of the few east-west roads. The Battleaxe Division was tasked with crossing the Biferno and taking Termoli, which was the lynchpin to the eastern side of the Viktor Line. Its capture would outflank the Germans and force them to withdraw again to their next line of defence.

On 2 October leading troops of 78th Division were within a few miles of the Biferno river, a little to the south of the port of Termoli. The 2nd Lancashire Fusiliers headed north-east towards Termoli, and waded across the Biferno river. Also on 3 October at 0200, a Commando Brigade, made up of 3 (Army) and 40 (Royal Marine) Commandos, and the Special Raiding Squadron, landed north of the Biferno's mouth close to Termoli's port. By 0800 the commandos had secured the harbour, penetrated the town, and in places pushed out beyond its perimeter, seeking to make contact with the Lancashire Fusiliers. They were followed up in the evening by another sea-borne landing of 36 Brigade, who bulldozed shallow fords to drive vehicles across the Biferno.

On 3 October, it began to rain. For eighteen hours it rained, bogging down the division's supply vehicles. In addition, and contrary to their briefings that Termoli contained few enemy troops, it held the small *Kampfgruppe* Rau garrison force, and some accounts indicate that in addition the German forces in and around Termoli included elements of the 1st Parachute, 29th Panzer Grenadier and 26th Panzer Divisions. Hopes of an early occupation began to fade. By nightfall on 3 October some Panzers had probed into parts of Termoli town, in places pressing to within a few hundred yards of the commandos' bridgehead.

Allied intelligence also knew that 16th Panzer Division was on the move towards Termoli. As soon as Kesselring had heard of the Allies' attack on Termoli he ordered 16th Panzer to move from the Volturno on the western side of Italy, to counter-attack 78th Division from the north and west of Termoli.

Montgomery was taking an uncharacteristic gamble to capture Termoli and break the Viktor Line. He had only part of the battle-hardened 78th Division in position across the Biferno river. So, although the counter-attack by 16th Panzer was anticipated, when it came in force, despite a slow build-up by the Germans, its strength and ferocity was a shock.

On 4 October the 8th Argylls and 6th Royal West Kents advanced north some five miles from Termoli along the coast road, Highway 16, aiming to capture the village of San Giacomo, when they ran into forward units of 16th Panzer. Only four infantry battalions, two commandos and some Special Forces were across the Biferno river. To try to stop the Panzers they had only one field regiment of artillery and a few anti-tank guns. The infantry were on their own, cut off on the north side of the river.

A torrid unequal battle, tanks versus exposed infantry, had commenced for Termoli. Devoid of armoured support, lacking anti-tank artillery and any reinforcements, the 78th Division infantrymen were being systematically killed and pushed back all around the Termoli perimeter. A bulldozed ford over the Biferno did enable six Sherman tanks to cross, before it became a morass from the rain and flooding river. It achieved little as four of the Shermans were quickly destroyed by the Germans' Mark IV Panzers.

During 5 October the Germans forced the defensive lines back to within a half mile of the town. On the edge of Termoli itself, the infantry made a brave but futile stand at the brickworks site to try and stem the German offensive, before they were forced to withdraw. To save the troops in the bridgehead across the Biferno, and have any chance of turning back 16th Panzer, the river had to be bridged so that tanks could cross to support the infantry.

The fresh troops of the Irish Brigade had to come ashore as planned that night into Termoli harbour. Another day without tanks and German Panzers could be rolling into Termoli town. This would prevent any further reinforcements from the sea. Another day could see 78th Division forced back into a bloody retreat south across the Biferno river. It would mean a strategic defeat for Eighth Army and the Allies.[29] As the battle for Termoli reached a critical tipping point, and 78th Division hung on grimly against German armour, DAF made some telling strikes to help force the Germans to pull back.

Spitfires dived into an attack by a group of ten Fw190s, prompting them to jettison their bomb-loads and flee into cloud cover. In all, some 500 sorties by DAF Kittyhawks and Warhawks in fighter-bomber roles swooped onto German columns, claiming nearly 200 vehicles either destroyed or damaged.[30]

The loss of two Kittyhawks and one Spitfire was deemed a small price when set against Eighth Army's looming disaster on the ground. Once again the DAF close support for Eighth Army was doing its work, and once again it was largely unseen by the troops on the ground. But would it be enough to buy time to allow the Irish Brigade to land that night? If not, another bad day could see 78th Division forced back into a bloody retreat south across the Biferno river. It would mean a strategic defeat for Eighth Army and the Allies.

Notes

1. Annussek, '*Hitler's Raid to Save Mussolini*', pp. 1–7.
2. Owen, op. cit., p. 213; Brookes, op. cit., pp. 26–7.
3. Owen, op. cit., pp. 213–15.
4. Brookes, op. cit., pp. 20–1.
5. Ibid., pp. 21–2.
6. Owen, op. cit., pp. 207–8.
7. Ibid., p. 209
8. Ibid., pp. 209–10.
9. Ibid., pp. 210–11.
10. Ibid., p. 213; Brookes, op. cit., p. 267.
11. Owen, op. cit., pp. 216–17.
12. Brookes, op. cit., p. 27.
13. Owen, op. cit., p. 218.
14. Evans, op. cit., p. 74.
15. Brookes, op. cit., pp. 19–20.
16. Owen, op. cit., p. 219.
17. Ibid., p. 220.
18. Ibid., p. 221–2.
19. RAAF, Australian War Memorial, *RAAF Saga – The RAAF at War*, pp. 73–4.
20. Dundas, op. cit., pp. 131–4.
21. Evans, op. cit., pp. 76–7.
22. Veteran's Account – Flight Lieutenant Ron Paterson
23. Thomas, op. cit., p. 59.
24. Owen, op. cit., pp. 220–1.
25. Cunningham, *A Sailor's Odyssey*, p. 571.
26. Owen, op. cit., p. 225.
27. Doherty, *Eighth Army in Italy – The Long Hard Slog*, pp. 12–13.
28. Owen, op. cit., p. 225.
29. Evans, op. cit., pp. 83–88.
30. Owen, op. cit., p. 229.

Chapter 10

Termoli to the Sangro River – flying against the rain

As Eighth Army's battle for Termoli teetered at a tipping point, DAF struggled against the weather to provide close support, counter Luftwaffe raids, and attack enemy ground forces. Although in the poor visibility of rain and cloud DAF's numerical superiority was partly nullified, it was able to count on a new advantage – the first deployment of the new Spitfire Mk VIII.

On 4 October Flight Lieutenant Bert Houle, a Canadian, was leading a patrol of Spitfire Mark VIIIs of No. 417 Squadron RAF. When they came across Fw190s bombing Eighth Army positions at Termoli, Houle was the first to jettison his long-range fuel tank and turn against them. He fastened onto an Fw190, which had begun to flee westwards above him.

Despite having to climb, Houle's Spitfire caught up with the Luftwaffe's feared fighter-bomber and, from about 250 yards, he got in two bursts of fire. There was an explosion on the 190's tail, before it fell straight down into a cloud layer. Houle also damaged another 190, and then chased away a third at tree-top height up the Sangro valley.

The encounter proved the claims that a Spitfire VIII had the power even in a climb to catch an Fw190. Houle later stated that he thought the Spitfire Mk VIII the best of all fighters he had flown. With its clipped wings and quick roll, he found it could easily turn inside any Luftwaffe fighter he faced.[1]

On the ground at Termoli, despite the persistent rain and mud a Bailey bridge over the Biferno river was finally completed during the afternoon of 5 October, after which some tanks from 4 Armoured Brigade were able to move across. The armour pushed out with support from the 5th Buffs, and strikes by DAF fighters, to link up with 2nd Lancashire Fusiliers. In two operations No. 3 Squadron RAAF of No. 239 Wing RAF struck at both supply traffic and German forces.

In the first operation against a convoy of petrol tankers, three RAAF Kittyhawk fighter-bombers claimed twenty-five flamers, three smokers, and twenty-five damaged, as well as destroying two other motor vehicles and three petrol dumps. The tally broke the squadron's own record for one operation. In the second operation 239's Wing Commander Brian Eaton led an operation to bomb German troops, who were advancing to attack less than a mile from 78th Division troops. Two weeks earlier Eaton had broken his left hand,

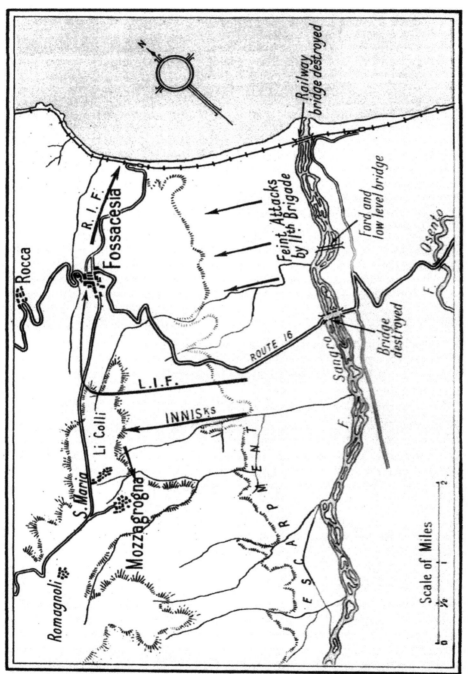

The Sangro Battle area showing the main road running north-south across the Sangro river valley.

and now flew with his hand and forearm encased in plaster, with a modified cockpit for his constrained hand movements.

It seemed that Eaton was little handicapped, as he claimed a tank set ablaze, an armoured car and two other motor vehicles destroyed. This second operation also hit a road convoy bringing reinforcement and supplies to the German front-line forces. The Germans' attack was stopped and Eighth Army sent a message to Eaton thanking the squadron for its effort, which largely prevented the advance. The two operations were typical demonstrations of how fighter-bomber interventions in close support of the army could affect the momentum of a battle.[2]

The next day, 6 October, was decisive. An attack by 16th Panzer came to a climax, with support from Panzergrenadiers, who broke through the lines in a number of places. In a desperate and chaotic battle to hold them back, the Lancashire Fusiliers and the Argylls resorted to bayonet charges.

Yet a 78th Division counter-attack was coming. The fresh troops of the Irish Brigade, who had come ashore during the night, were feeding through to the front lines, and made an immediate difference. Approaching midday the Irish battalions' counter-attacks, with the support of artillery and some eighty Canadian tanks, forced the Panzers to pull back. Next day, 7 October, 16th Panzer were in full retreat to the north. The insertion of the Irish Brigade's battalions had turned the battle at the eleventh hour.

In the skies above Termoli, largely unseen and unacknowledged, DAF had imposed its domination of the Luftwaffe once again in at least three ways. First, it had prevented any significant attack by the Luftwaffe on Eighth Army front-line troops. Second, when the weather allowed, DAF fighter-bombers had struck at German positions and their attacking Panzers, as well as inflicting significant damage on German supplies to their battlefield front lines. Third, its air superiority had allowed Eighth Army troop movements in rear areas, and the Irish Brigade to disembark in Termoli harbour, without any fear of air attack by the Luftwaffe.

*   *   *

The spine of the southern Italian Apennines separated Eighth Army from General Clark's Fifth Army on the west coast. There were very few east-west roads, and in any case they became nearly impassable in the rain, mud, ice and snow of winter. From here on the Germans would stand and fight on every one of the innumerable rivers and lateral dorsals, which led down to the Mediterranean and Adriatic coastlines. All the way to the Alps the terrain was perfect for defenders.[3]

Although after Termoli German forces had withdrawn northwards to the Trigno river, for two weeks Montgomery insisted on building up Eighth Army's reinforcements. The fragmented approach of the offensive at Termoli that had led nearly to a defeat was not to be repeated. It was obvious that the

Germans would be entrenched and waiting, some fifteen miles up the coast on the north side of the Trigno river.

Preparations for Eighth Army to move north and cross the Trigno river were also held up by the Germans' now persistent friend, the worsening autumn or, more accurately, the early winter weather. Some days all flying was grounded, such as on 27 October. Only twelve aircraft were able to take to the air that day, of which two did not return.

From the Foggia air fields the Strategic Air Force bombing raids were the main weapon of interdiction strikes on road, rail, town and city centres, while DAF was increasing both its size and reach in support of Eighth Army. In their longer range operations the strategic heavy bombers, Liberators and Fortresses, would sometimes be seen passing high overhead, escorted by Lightning fighters en route to targets in northern Italy and southern Germany.

In contrast, DAF Spitfires would fly up the Adriatic coast escorting DAF fighter-bombers and light bombers, as far north as Ancona. In close support operations for Eighth Army they would bomb and strafe ports, bridges, vehicle convoys, and German gun positions. In contrast Luftwaffe activity had a negligible impact, and DAF night-intruder operations over German lines rarely met much resistance.[4]

On Italy's west coast, between Salerno and Naples, Fw190s and Dornier bombers continued to make bombing raids. On 11 October Squadron Leader 'Rosie' Mackie, leading a Spitfire patrol from No. 249 Squadron RAF, caught sight of a Dornier Do217 3,000 feet above him at around 16,000 feet, and gave chase. The Dornier was heading north on a return flight from its intrusion over Allied lines. When its pilot saw Mackie's Spitfire in pursuit, he dived to escape.

Mackie followed, closing on the Do217 bomber in and out of cloud, and ignoring fire from its rear gunner. After several bursts at the Dornier, he saw parts of the fuselage fall off, before the stricken bomber spiralled into a death-dive and crashed. Mackie had chalked up his fourteenth confirmed kill.[5]

Of course the DAF fighter squadrons were unable to intercept and stop every Luftwaffe bomber attack. On the evening of 21 October Naples suffered a major enemy bomber raid. In the air defence of Naples that night was 25 Heavy Anti-Aircraft (HAA) Battery, of 9th (Londonderry) HAA Regiment RA (SR). Like many other ground roles, the crucial contribution of anti-aircraft formations in the air war is not well understood and appreciated. Ninth (Londonderry) HAA Regiment had an outstanding record. They had defended Alexandria harbour, including the Royal Navy's shore-bases HMS *Nile* and HMS *Grebe*, Tripoli harbour, and Port Sudan, the important shipping port for the delivery of new aircraft. In those critical air defences 25 HAA Battery could proudly claim that only one bomb fell on a ship, and that was in the final enemy bomber raid on Tripoli.

Gunner J.J. Ormsby was serving with 25 HAA Battery that night when, in addition to the city's bombardment, the Allies' anti-aircraft defences came in for particular attention from the Luftwaffe's bombers:

High above the bay and city of Naples at the N11 gunsite, A Troop/ 25 Battery received a direct hit from a Ju88 that dive-bombed the site. Fifteen men were killed, including all ten members of A Troop, 25 Battery and two of my fellow fire control operators. Ginger Evans died in my arms. [6]

It was a chilling reminder, that despite the Allies' dominance in the air war, the Luftwaffe was still capable of striking back, and must be continually targeted.

* * *

Early on 23 October some infantry units of the Irish Brigade and Lancashire Fusiliers waded across the Trigno's upper reaches. The river was wide but not much more than ankle deep. They picked their way through the heavily-mined valley floor and hurried to dig in near some woods. North of the wooded and undulating plain lay the San Salvo ridge and Vineyard Hill close to the town of Cupello. From this high point between the Trigno and Sangro rivers, the Germans shelled the probing infantry.[7]

Yet again, following their pull back from Termoli to avoid heavy losses, 16th Panzer Division was occupying that high ground. They were in front of San Salvo, and in well-prepared defensive positions. From there the Germans scanned the marshy and heavily-mined valley below and directed their artillery at any movements by Eighth Army.[8]

To push forward Eighth Army must overcome increasingly icy rain, mud, flooding rivers, hilly terrain and the enemy, before the full force of winter bore down. On the night of 27/28 October the Irish Brigade launched an attack to take San Salvo. A preceding artillery barrage was countered by German shelling and mortar fire, with fatal accuracy against the advancing Irish. As they were to begin their climb up the San Salvo ridge, 1st Royal Irish Fusiliers lost their CO, Lieutenant Colonel Beauchamp Butler, and two company commanders, all killed. If that was not bad enough all the fusiliers' platoon commanders were either killed or wounded. The London Irish Rifles also lost several officers. Despite digging in, the Irish battalions were forced to withdraw at first light. For a week, while more reinforcements were brought up, Eighth Army had to resort to night patrols and hold on.

In the first week of November the weather improved to allow Eighth Army to make its main crossing of the Trigno river. In better visibility DAF flew over 300 sorties against prior specified German positions.[9] While 78th Division expanded the bridgehead, forcing the German forces back towards Vasto, further upstream 8th Indian Division made another crossing of the Trigno.

The two divisions now concentrated their assaults to take Vasto and other towns and villages. The pressure built up so that there was no choice but for 16th Panzer to retreat.[10] But again it was more of a controlled withdrawal.

* * *

During the battles to cross the Trigno and Sangro rivers DAF enjoyed unrivalled air superiority, which enabled it to introduce a new refinement of close support. It was initiated by Group Captain David Heysham, a South African in command of DAF Operations, although it had its origins in the operation at El Hamma in Tunisia.

In what became known as 'Rover David Cab-rank', RAF officers travelled in armoured cars close behind the front lines, and were in radio communication with Eighth Army's AASC units. They also had VHF radio communication with fighter-bomber pilots. Sections of fighter-bombers patrolled above the Rover Control area. Pilots and all those involved on the ground, carried identical large-scale maps with numbered and lettered grids, and, whenever possible, aerial photographs.

Targets could then be requested, and agreed by reference to the squares on the grids, along the following lines:

> Pilot (Fighter Section Leader): Hello Rover David. Diamond leader calling. Over.
> Rover Control: Hello Diamond leader. Receiving you in the clear. Are you set for business? Over.
> Pilot: All set, Rover David.
> Rover Control: Your target today is a fortified farmhouse on map B, square C9. Understood?
> Pilot: Understood. Standby.

The pilot would then find the required map in his jacket, boot or somewhere in his cramped cockpit. This could be quite a struggle while he simultaneously flew the aeroplane. Then he had to identify the landmarks on the ground, while flying at around 10,000 feet, so that he could lead his section to the target. Once the pilot was comfortable with the map and his directions, he would contact Rover David again:

> Pilot: Hello Rover David. I have map B, square C9. Over.
> Rover Control: Ok, Diamond Leader, do you see the bend in the river, with the farmhouse on its southern bank?
> Pilot: Yes, I do, Rover David. Over.
> Rover Control: That is your target. Over.
> Pilot: Thank you, Rover David. Over and out.

The Rover David Cab-rank, as outlined in the above illustration, gained much more effective results, and could bring fighter-bomber support to ground forces sometimes within ten minutes. Not surprisingly, it also brought an immeasurable morale boost to Eighth Army troops, to see close air support attacks brought in so quickly when they were needed.[11]

Again it was also an indication of how DAF's fighters imposed and sustained a dominating air superiority, to allow fighter-bombers the time and clear air space to operate the Rover David Cab-rank system.

* * *

From the Trigno river and its valley Eighth Army drove on northwards in pursuit of the Germans, who were withdrawing to the Sangro river. Innumerable high ridges were crossed, and two more rivers were forded, the Sinello and the Osento, both uncontested. On 8 November some infantry battalions, such as 1st East Surreys, reached the hill town of Paglieta, where they looked down into the wide Sangro river valley. It was already a case of déjà vu. Both of the main bridges, on the railway line near the coast and on Highway 16 further inland were destroyed. The last of the German rearguards and demolition parties were in full view, leisurely crossing to the river's north bank to take up their next defensive positions.

A fearful battle loomed. On the Sangro's far side the estuary plain, in some places two miles in width, stretched away to the escarpment that hid the next German defences. Farther back there rose up snow-capped mountains, the real goal of the retreating Germans. The rain fell continually, river levels rose and flooded the valleys, and mud was everywhere. In places the Sangro was around six feet deep and 100 yards wide. The cold bit deeper. As the freezing rain seeped from sodden clothes into the men's bones, so did the real meaning of Kesselring's Winter Line.[12]

The Winter Line was actually a series of lines, or defensive positions, that stretched across Italy at its narrowest width of eighty-five miles, from along the Garigliano river through Cassino in the west, over the central Apennine mountains, and then along the Sangro river to the Adriatic Sea. The Germans' defensive strategy was favoured by the winter weather and terrain, and their ability to draw upon another fourteen divisions north of Rome for reinforcements, to supplement the nine which faced the Allies' fourteen divisions on the front lines.[13]

Overall the German Army could call upon a significantly greater number of divisions based in Italy to confront the Allies. However, air superiority was providing the Allies with an ever more powerful edge. Air interdiction operations had brought German supplies by rail to a standstill. Only road transport, particularly by night, maintained the German Army's tactical capability. Allied bombing of, and damage to, Luftwaffe airfields, not least their main supply depot at Cancello, forced a rethink by their General von Richthofen. The Luftwaffe commander was compelled to comply with Tedder's strategic goal, and pull back his aircraft and resources to bases in northern Italy.[14]

The Winter Line had been built by forced labour, and in places was up to twenty miles in depth. In some stretches as here with the Sangro, it only began some way north from the river. The Germans were in possession of concrete pillboxes, machine-gun pits, reinforced farmhouses, and countless miles of barbed wire, hills, mountains and rivers. General Kesselring's orders from Hitler were to bring the Allies to a shuddering halt here at the Winter Line.

On the escarpment the Germans watched and waited. The plain was heavily mined and the Germans could direct their fire at any movement. The Allies still harboured a vague hope of taking Rome before Christmas, for which the Winter Line had to be breached. The goal was Pescara, from where Eighth Army could move west to support Fifth Army in an offensive on Rome. Montgomery ordered that the crossing of the Sangro had to be made close to the coast so as to exploit Highway 16.[15]

Despite the Sangro being in flood, Eighth Army troops got across to establish a bridgehead, which was supplied by amphibious trucks (DUKWs). German positions were targeted by a combination of artillery, two destroyers of the Royal Navy, and medium bombers from DAF.

More troops were gradually brought across the river into the bridgehead. Yet repeated thrusts at the German lines were thrown back. Then the rain eased, the river level began to fall, so that on 27 November more armour was able to begin using the Bailey bridge again to cross over the Sangro. The build-up accelerated. A massive bombardment was launched with artillery, air strikes and naval guns off the coast until, on 29 November, 38 Irish Brigade with tanks in support broke through to take the villages of Santa Maria and Fossacessia.[16]

*   *   *

Winter was descending, hobbling the armies of both sides. Only when the skies were clear could Allied air power continue to punish the enemy. Even as far south as the Foggia airfields, on 1 December, snowflakes were in the air. Incessant rain and layers of cloud up to 20,000 feet, bringing poor visibility, were frequent daily conditions, rendering fighter-bomber operations impossible. The absence of guidance equipment either on the airfields or in aircraft also endangered safe return of aircraft.[17]

On 2 December the weather relented, and TAF mounted some 1,200 sorties, which was a single day record at the time for Tunisia and Italy. DAF Spitfires, Kittyhawks and Warhawks flew 340 sorties, hitting targets identified by Eighth Army. In addition, DAF Warhawks took off in another seventy sorties in support of the Partisan Resistance forces in Yugoslavia. Interdiction operations went on continuously against supply routes to the German lines on the north side of the Sangro. In four raids waves of ten Mitchell bombers at a time attacked a bridge on the Pescara river. Then, on 5 December, the new American P-47 Thunderbolt fighters of DAF's 79th Fighter Group, escorted Mitchell bombers in a raid on the Yugoslavian city of Split.[18]

The first four Thunderbolts received by the 57th Fighter Group (FG) were flown on 28 November from Tunis to Amendola in Italy by Lieutenant Bill Nuding and three other pilots of 64th Fighter Squadron. Its air-cooled and turbo-charged radial engine gave 2,000hp and, with its rugged construction, made the Thunderbolt very resilient in taking fire. It was designed for high altitude operation up to a service ceiling of 42,000 feet, and had a top speed of 435mph. Nuding and 57th FG pilots soon found the Thunderbolt's performance excellent, the plane easy to fly, and very fast to dive and roll.[19]

The impact of the cold and wet autumn, with the approaching winter, exacerbated the razor-edged tension of flying operations to take another toll on pilots in many ways. Wing Commander Hugh Dundas of 324 Wing felt depressed, increasingly exhausted and miserable, and flying seemed to require an ever increasing effort. Each evening he could be found drinking in the mess of a different squadron. Alcohol was an escape but also, he hoped, a way to rejuvenate his spirit.

The recurring operations for his wing's fighters, weather permitting, in those months leading up to the year's end, were twofold. Bombers were escorted in interdiction raids, while patrols looked to intercept Luftwaffe intruders, or strafe enemy road traffic. At only twenty-three years of age Dundas was in command of five squadrons, but at the same time he was aware of his inexperience compared to others of the same rank, in everything except flying a Spitfire fighter. He was tired and wished the war would end. Drink seemed to be the only recourse.

In December Dundas collapsed and, thought at first to have malaria, was confined to bed. His new CO, Group Captain W.G.G. Duncan Smith, promoted from wing commander in 244 Wing, told him that he must recommend him for a rest from operations. Dundas got up for a day or two, then collapsed again. He was taken to hospital, where he was diagnosed with a mild attack of jaundice. Told that he was to stay in bed until the end of December, he felt totally dejected. While in hospital he was told that he had been selected to attend a staff college course at Haifa starting in January. He thought of the college comforts and warmer weather, and in his weak physical condition, and mentally depressed, the thought of staying alive in a staff appointment suddenly seemed very attractive.[20]

When the weather allowed, other Spitfire pilots pursued their relentless campaign to maintain the dominance of Allied air power. High above the Sangro on 3 December, Flight Lieutenant Houle with a group of Spitfires of his 92 Squadron took on a group of Bf109s. He dived at the first German fighter, firing a deflection shot, and saw it fall away in flames. Closing in on another 109, he gave it a burst from about 250 yards astern. Part of the 109's tail blew off, causing it to roll before it dropped spinning away in flames. On the same day over the Sangro valley, Squadron Leader Mackie led more Spitfires of 92 Squadron against more 109s, claiming another kill, and on 5 December yet another victory.[21]

The momentum then built so that by the end of December's first week the Allies were well established on the north side of the Sangro. Montgomery wrote in his report to London:

> In spite of continuous rain and acres of mud I managed to get a good bridgehead over the Sangro; the trouble was to get my tanks and supporting weapons over, as the river was in flood and low level bridges merely disappeared. I took a good few risks. Twice I was pushed back to the river – once on my right, and once on my left. But we came again and refused to admit it couldn't be done. The troops were quite magnificent, and in the most foul conditions you can ever imagine; the Sangro normally is about 80 feet wide, and it became swollen to 300 feet and rose several feet; the water was icy cold as heavy snow fell in the mountains where the river rises. Many were drowned. Eventually we succeeded.[22]

The Winter Line had been pierced, but not broken. The next German fortresses were Orsogna in the mountains, and Ortona on the Adriatic coast. December brought even more rain, the Sangro rose even higher, so that by 5 December all bridges were either washed away or under water. The New Zealand Division did manage to cross the next river, the Moro, entered Orsogna, and then had to withdraw because of lack of weapons and ammunition. The Canadians also crossed the Moro, and were drawn into an epic house-to-house battle for Ortona. Montgomery was forced to write, 'I am fighting a hell of a battle here. The right wing of my army on the Adriatic side consists of three Divisions. I am opposed there by three and a half divisions; this combined with the mud, makes it not too easy.'[23]

By 10 December rain brought all operations to a halt. A breakthrough to the Pescara river and port began to seem a distant dream. Montgomery's goal, of gaining control of the main east-west road from Pescara through Avezzano to Rome, was not going to be attainable. Yet the Allied front line had now edged forward and extended along the northern side of the Sangro river through the mountains and around Cassino, then along the south bank of the Garigliano river to the west coast.

The truth, however, was that, like a spider, Kesselring had drawn the Allies into a web of defensive lines, such as the Sangro, the Gustav, the Bernhardt, and the Adolf Hitler Lines, that exploited the mountains and rivers to enmesh both Allied armies. It was where the Germans meant to stand and throw them back. There were to be no more planned withdrawals. The orders from Hitler were to fight the Allies to the death in these positions, and bring their advance to a standstill.[24] Whilst the Allies had fourteen divisions, the Germans had nine, supported by additional armoured units in the front line, and another fourteen divisions farther back to draw on.

Knowing the Germans' depth of strength in ground forces, Allied commanders were always conscious of the potential threat of a major German counter-offensive. It was probably only the Allies' air superiority which prevented the enemy from mounting a major counter-attack. For Eighth Army and Fifth Army, it must have seemed that the sustained domination of the skies by DAF and other Allied air forces was always their ace card. Or was it? In early December the Allies suffered a major loss at the hands of a Luftwaffe bombing raid. Although not many knew of its real significance at the time, it would bring far-reaching and unforeseen consequences.

Notes

1. Thomas, op. cit., pp. 62–3.
2. RAAF War Memorial, op. cit., p. 74.
3. Ford, op. cit., p. 142.
4. Owen, op. cit., p. 231.
5. Thomas, op. cit., p. 63.
6. Ormsby, interview with Richard Doherty, 1993.
7. Ray, op. cit., pp. 94–5.
8. Ford, op. cit., pp. 146–9.
9. Owen, op. cit., p. 231.
10. Ford, op. cit., p. 157.
11. Owen, op. cit., pp. 232–5; Dundas, op. cit., pp. 141–2.
12. Evans, op. cit., pp. 96–7.
13. Neillands, *8th Army, From the Western Desert to the Alps, 1939–1945*, pp. 296–7.
14. Tedder, *With Prejudice*, p. 487.
15. Neillands, op. cit., p. 299.
16. Evans, op. cit., pp. 102–3.
17. McCarthy, *Air-to-Ground Battle for Italy*, p. 59.
18. Owen, op. cit., pp. 235–6.
19. Molesworth, op. cit., pp. 75–7.
20. Dundas, op. cit., pp. 130–7.
21. Thomas, op. cit., p. 64.
22. Hamilton, *Monty - The Battles of Field Marshal Bernard Montgomery*, p. 192.
23. Evans, op. cit., p. 103.
24. Neillands, op. cit., p. 299.

Chapter 11

A second 'Pearl Harbor' for the Allies at Bari

High in the sky at 23,000 feet the plane was a solitary speck. It would probably have been ignored by any anti-aircraft gunner who might have spotted it, although at that altitude any aircraft would have been very hard to identify. On the afternoon of 2 December 1943 First Lieutenant Werner Hahn was the pilot of that plane, a Messerschmitt Me210, cruising deep into the airspace over southern Italy. Hahn was flying a Luftwaffe reconnaissance sortie over the Allied-held port of Bari on Italy's south-east coast. And it was not routine reconnaissance.[1]

After he had completed his final pass over Bari, Hahn turned his Me210 north over the sea, parallel with the Adriatic coast. He stayed high, hoping to avoid any Allied fighters which may have been scrambled to intercept his intrusion. Then he noticed he was behind schedule. He must speed up, and arrive back at his Luftwaffe base in northern Italy at the planned time with his photographs of Bari harbour. Otherwise the proposed bombing raid on the Allies' ships at Bari could not get there before dusk.

Hahn pushed the trim tab forward, angling the nose of the Me210 down, and increased his air speed. He also turned back over land on to a more direct course northwards, crossing the coast due east of the Foggia airfields. A flash of light caught his eye, as if the sun had glinted on something. Hahn squinted, waiting to see if there was another flash. Nothing, and he dismissed the phenomenon. Then he saw the two black dots on his port side and further to the west, in the direction of Foggia. And they were growing larger.

Hahn opened the throttles to their maximum and once again turned back to try and escape over the sea. There was no doubt in his mind: two Allied fighters were on course to intercept him. To Hahn it seemed just a few seconds, but when he next looked over his shoulder at the two dots, they were large enough for him to make out that they each had twin tail booms and engines. They must be American P-38 Lightning twin-engined fighters, and they were closing in on him rapidly.

The Messerschmitt Me210 had a service ceiling of 35,000 feet, could climb to 19,000 feet in eleven and a half minutes, and had a maximum speed of 370mph. In comparison, the Lockheed P-38 Lightning outperformed the Me210 in every way. The Lightning fighter could reach a service ceiling of 44,000 feet, climb to 20,000 feet in seven minutes, and had a top speed of 414mph. Hahn was running out of options.

He knew that there was one last slim hope, and dived for the sea, levelling out only a few feet from the wave tops. Now it was too dangerous for the American fighter pilots to dive onto him. A scatter of small spouts sprang out of the sea either side of his aircraft, as the Lightnings tried to hit him from astern. Despite his proximity to the water Hahn threw his Me210 into constant twists and turns to evade the bursts of fire from his twin pursuers.

As the three aircraft hammered north parallel with the coast east of Vasto, the American fighters began to fall further behind. Then, perhaps running low on fuel, they turned and pulled away. Miraculously, Hahn realized they were gone and he had not suffered any discernible damage to his aircraft. There was, of course, the fear that new relieving fighters were being vectored onto him. He maintained his flat-out maximum speed, turned once again over the land and, skimming the tree tops, took the most direct course for his home base.[2]

* * *

Bari's old town had a medieval Norman fort, Castello Svevo, and occupied a promontory jutting into the Adriatic Sea. Farther inland wider roads and modern buildings supported a population of some 200,000 and its role as a major deep-water port for southern Italy. The photographs taken by Lieutenant Hahn on the afternoon of 2 December would have identified more than thirty Allied ships moored in Bari's harbour. Bari was the main supply port for Eighth Army, DAF and the US Fifteenth Air Force.

Because of the increasing losses of the US Eighth Air Force, based in England, encountered in daylight raids over Germany, the Fifteenth had been created only months earlier. Under the command of Major General James H. Doolittle, the Fifteenth's mission was to be long-range heavy bombing of targets in northern Italy, the Balkans and Germany. General Doolittle had arrived in Bari on the previous day, 1 December, to take command of the Fifteenth at its airfields seventy-five miles away inland at Foggia. The Fifteenth's main supply route was by ship through Bari's port, then overland by road to Foggia.[3]

The front lines of Eighth Army were much farther north across the Sangro river, behind which Allied air superiority was well established over southern Italy. On that same afternoon of 2 December Air Vice Marshal Sir Arthur Coningham, C-in-C Mediterranean Air Forces, stated at a press conference that there was no risk of a Luftwaffe attack on Bari: 'I would regard it as a personal affront and insult if the Luftwaffe should attempt any significant action in this area.[4]

An element of hubris had won the day. The unloading of supplies through the night at Bari's well-lit docks would continue.

Only a handful of people would have known that one American ship in Bari harbour, the SS *John Harvey*, carried a secret cargo. A Lieutenant Howard D.

Beckstrom and six men of the 701st Chemical Maintenance Company were also on board. The *John Harvey* was also filled with munitions, food and equipment. Even its Captain, Elwin F. Knowles, had not been informed of certain classified items on its manifest.

On his return to the base of Luftflotte II in northern Italy, Lieutenant Hahn reported on his successful reconnaissance flight, and with photographs showing that the Bari harbour was full of Allied ships. Field Marshal Wolfram von Richthofen, commanding Luftflotte II, had advised Kesselring that a raid on the port of Bari, and Allied shipping in its harbour, was the best option to slow the Allies' advance in Italy. Richthofen, who was a cousin of the 'Red Baron' fighter ace of the First World War, Manfred von Richthofen, was opposed to the alternative strategy of mounting a bombing raid on the Allies' airfields at Foggia. Richthofen could only pull together about 105 bombers, not enough to damage seriously the complex of dispersed Foggia air bases.

After Hahn's unopposed reconnaissance flight over Bari, despite his lucky escape on return from the American Lightning fighters, his report on the harbour full of ships clinched it. The planned bombing raid was approved: to attack that same night. On runways at Luftwaffe airfields across northern Italy, Ju88 twin-engined bombers sat waiting, bombs loaded and ready to go. To ensure the raid would have the advantage of surprise, a number of measures were taken.

The bombing run flight path would approach Bari's harbour from the east over the Adriatic Sea. The Allies' expectation, if at all, would be for any air attack to come from the north. During their approach the bombers would drop Window tinfoil (*Duppel*) to attempt to confuse the Allies' radar. Arrival time over Bari harbour was scheduled for 1930, and shortly before that time parachute flares would be dropped to guide the Ju88s and their bomb-aimers. The pilots would also make their bombing runs at low level, to evade the radar.[5]

However, as well as mustering Ju88 bombers from Luftwaffe wings still based across northern Italy, and from some bases in Yugoslavia, Richthofen could draw on some very capable and experienced bomber pilots. They included Lothar Lintow who, while flying with the Luftwaffe bomber pilot hero Robert Kowalski, had learnt the 'Swedish turnip' bombing tactic against shipping in the Mediterranean. Kowalski had used the tactic to sink two ships on a single sortie on three occasions, and overall was credited with sinking over 100,000 tons of Allied shipping. Now Lothar Lintow had passed on the technique to other pilots in northern Italy.

The 'Swedish turnip' tactic was based upon approaching the ship beam on, when it presented the best target for the bomb-aimer. It was particularly effective when employed at twilight, or on a night well lit by the stars and moon. The bomber must fly at 200mph and at a height of forty-five metres. The bomb must be released at 245 metres from the ship, since at the aircraft's speed of 200mph, the bomb would fall forty-five metres in an arc covering the 245 metre distance from release to the ship.

The low level approach for the bombing run should also enable the Ju88 bombers to get under any Allied radar screen. For the raid on Bari, Richthofen had the pilots and their crews trained to use the 'Swedish turnip' tactic, and well briefed for their flights.[6]

*   *   *

A number of poor decisions taken by the Allies in regard to air defence of Bari would play into the Luftwaffe's hands. The main early warning radar at Bari had been out of action for days. It was not thought important. Since mid-October there had been only eight raids by long-range Luftwaffe bombers on the Allies in southern Italy. Although Ultra codebreaking intercepts by British Intelligence of German communications had revealed that the Luft-waffe had been flying reconnaissance operations over Bari, the intelligence information was evidently dismissed as unimportant.

There was an impression that Allied fighters totally ruled the skies. Routine patrols of DAF fighters over Bari had landed as scheduled before dusk began to gather. Then, as the Ju88s approached Bari from the sea in the east, their dropping of Window tinfoil confused and effectively nullified the anti-aircraft radars.[7] In rear areas, such as at Bari, the rules for unseen engagement did not allow anti-aircraft batteries to engage against an unseen target, and the dropping of Window was not considered as hostile, unless it was followed by a hostile act such as the dropping of bombs.[8] It looked as though Richthofen's plan and the 'Swedish turnip' tactic were going to face little or no opposition.

The harbour was still fully lit for unloading cargo as First Lieutenant Gustav Teuber led in the first wave of bombers to begin their bombing run. With the pathfinding flares further illuminating the docks, some thirty ships moored or riding at anchor were easy targets. The first wave of bombs burst upon Bari city; then wave after wave began to hit the harbour and its ships. Within minutes carnage was everywhere.

First the SS *Joseph Wheeler* was hit, then the SS *John Motley*, then the SS *John Boscom*. Munitions cargoes exploded, sending balls of fire jumping into the sky, and clouds of smoke pouring upwards. Men in the water struggling to survive were covered in oil and fuel. Moored at Pier 29, the SS *John Harvey* did not receive a direct hit, but caught fire from the explosions nearby. Captain Knowles and his crew resisted the urge to flee to safety, and fought to save the ship. Perhaps they knew what made up that secret cargo?

Knowles and his men were fighting a losing battle. In a flash a gigantic fireball erupted from where the *John Harvey* had been moored. Parts of the ship, its cargo and doomed crew rocketed high into the sky. The blast caused other ships to keel over and right across the harbour its explosive power threw men to the ground, or into the oily water.[9] As the *John Harvey* burned it was as if an inverted cascade of jets of multi-coloured flames fountained more than 1,000 feet into the sky.[10] One bomb severed an oil pipeline on the quayside, sending burning fuel surging across the harbour waters.[11]

By 2000 the Luftwaffe's bombers had done their job and gone. In about twenty minutes they had delivered near total destruction to Bari, its harbour and the congested array of Allied shipping. Next day revealed a sky full of black smoke. Large parts of Bari and its port infrastructure were in bombed out ruins, and continuing to burn. The Allies lost seventeen ships filled with critical supplies, of which the highest number were five American, the *John Boscom*, the *Joseph Wheeler*, the *Samuel J. Tilder*, the *John Motley* and, worst of all, the *John Harvey*.

About 800 Allied servicemen were either dead or in hospital. It is thought that many more than 1,000 civilians were casualties, but it may have been well in excess of that figure. Not surprisingly it was called another 'Pearl Harbor'.[12]

Casualties of all kinds overwhelmed the hospitals. Many people lay for hours in clothes sodden from oil and gas, with swollen eyes and blistering skin. Some endured extreme swelling of the genitals and blindness. Increasing numbers died.

Suspecting that the German bombers had dropped chemical weapons of some kind, doctors sent a cable to the Deputy Surgeon General, Fred Blesse, at Allied HQ in Algiers. An expert on chemical warfare medicine, Lieutenant Colonel Stewart Francis Alexander, arrived in Bari.

From examinations of patients Alexander suspected exposure to mustard gas. Then the recovery from the harbour of a fragment of a US bomb designed to deliver mustard gas confirmed Alexander's preliminary diagnosis. When port authority officials admitted that they knew the *John Harvey* was carrying mustard-gas bombs Alexander sent his report to Eisenhower.

While the devastating raid on Bari itself was made public the explosions of the mustard-gas bombs in the *John Harvey* were kept secret. Churchill insisted that the truth would be a propaganda coup for the Germans. He even had the medical records of patients injured or dead from mustard-gas exposure changed to state merely 'Burns due to enemy action'. This no doubt prevented proper treatment of many casualties, particularly of the Italian civilian population. Because of the exodus of Bari civilians in flight from the city it is not known how many suffered or died from mustard gas. Out of some 800 Allied casualties, 628 suffered mustard gas injuries.[13]

The Allies' neglect in ensuring that there were adequate air defence measures in place for Bari and its port seems astonishing with the benefit of hindsight. It was a particularly bad day for the DAF, whose fighters should have been able to defend an important rear supplies area, which was critical for Eighth Army.

*   *   *

The Luftwaffe bombing raid on Bari caused the port to be closed completely for three weeks, making it a major strategic setback for the Allies. In addition to the loss of seventeen ships and their cargoes in the harbour, the impact of the total shutdown for three weeks on supply shortages was even greater. Supplies destined for Fifth and Eighth Armies, and the US Fifteenth Air Force, had been destroyed. The elapsed time on ordered supplies in the pipe-line could not be recovered. The only other deep-water port, Naples, in southern Italy, was working at full capacity, and roads from there north and east were tortuous. Furthermore, an exacerbated supply shortage was now added to the transport delays emanating from the depths of a severe winter.

To counter the growing strength of Luftwaffe fighters in Germany, the Fifteenth Air Force had been scheduled to participate with the Eighth Air Force, based in England, in a combined bomber offensive against manu-facturing targets in Germany. The Bari raid caused the Fifteenth's contri-bution to be cut back heavily and it would not reach full operability until March 1944. Bari was indeed a second 'Pearl Harbor', and the only poison-gas incident in the Second World War. A need for secrecy at the time no doubt made it worse for many victims, and in some cases resulted in avoidable death.[14]

The disaster at Bari had serious implications for Operation SHINGLE, the planned landings for January 1944 at Anzio. Because Fifth Amy would not be able to reach Anzio by that time, it was planned that reinforcement troops and supplies could be brought in via the port of Bari. They would then move north as soon as possible as required, as both Fifth and Eighth Armies struggled to break through the Gustav Line and join up with the Anzio landings. Churchill and Roosevelt met in Cairo on 3 December and, despite this being the day after the raid on Bari, they confirmed the go-ahead for the plans for Operation SHINGLE.[15]

The loss of seventeen ships and their cargoes was a major loss to the Allies' supply chain. It had an immediate impact on supplies for Fifth and Eighth Armies in Italy, and the new US Fifteenth Air Force at Foggia. There were also other far-reaching consequences outside Italy, which even affected the planned D Day landings for June 1944 in Normandy. The plans of the US Fifteenth Air Force were in disarray. If the Bari raid had not occurred, a com-bined strategic bombing campaign by the Fifteenth and the Eighth Air Forces against fighter production factories in Germany would have weakened the Luftwaffe's capability before the Normandy landings.

The Luftwaffe raid on Bari, after Pearl Harbor in Hawaii, resulted in the second largest Allied shipping loss of the Second World War.[16] The Luft-waffe's bombs had destroyed 38,000 tons of cargo, which included a very large consignment of medical supplies, and 10,000 tons of steel planking for airfield runways.[17]

The US and Royal Navies made a huge effort at salvaging operations to clean up the harbour, but were hampered by the mustard-gas contamination and the recovery of dead bodies. The harbour was continually sprayed to alleviate the stench and prevent burns to salvage workers from the mustard-gas residues. It took three weeks before any kind of normal operation of the docks in a small way could even begin.

During these three weeks no supplies whatsoever came through Bari. The British War Office issued changed destination arrangements for shipping diverted to other ports until the end of February 1944.[18] The only other major port in southern Italy, Naples on the west coast, was not an option to take up cargoes previously scheduled for Bari.

Although the Operation SHINGLE landings at Anzio, scheduled for 22 January, were going ahead, General Wilson, now Supreme Allied Commander Mediterranean, gave some prescient advice in a report to London and Washington. He warned of potential disaster at Anzio if the landings could not be effectively supplied with troop reinforcements and supplies through the port of Bari.[19]

The leading role for providing air support for the Anzio landings was the TBF, with the assistance of Fifteenth Air Force. The main objectives of the TBF and the Fifteenth were to bomb Luftwaffe airfields so as to eliminate Luftwaffe raids on the landing areas, to cut the supply routes between Rome and the north, and between Rome and the Cassino and Anzio battle areas. To undertake these operations, the TBF and the Fifteenth were dependent upon fuel, bombs, ammunition and other supplies which, until 2 December, had been coming mainly through Bari.

Not until 2 January 1944 was the TBF able to begin these operations with the aim of blocking the supply routes north and south of Rome, before the Anzio landings. On 10 January the TBF requested Fifteenth Air Force to assist in combined operations of this kind. However, Fifteenth Air Force did not manage to fly in a joint operation with the TBF until 16 January. Six days had been lost. The cutting off of routes for German reinforcements was not achieved. It has not been proved, but there is a respected view that this critical delay was because Fifteenth Air Force was not ready, due to the consequent shortages of fuel, bombs, ammunition, parts and other equipment, as a result of the closing of Bari harbour.[20] Port operations at Bari harbour did not resume fully until February 1944.[21]

If the Bari raid had not taken place, or been prevented by anti-aircraft defences, or through interception by DAF fighters, clearly the supply situation for the offensives at Anzio and on the Gustav Line would have been much improved. It is impossible to assess what might have been achieved without the supply shortages caused by the Bari raid, although it seems reasonable to speculate that breakthroughs at Anzio and Cassino may have come sooner. The inability of the air defences at Bari, either to detect the approaching

Luftwaffe bombers or to shoot down any enemy aircraft, poses unanswerable questions. What can be said is that the supply shortages after the Bari raid further handicapped the Allies in Italy, had unforeseen consequences elsewhere, and indirectly was the probable cause of increased casualties beyond the raid itself.

And no doubt it gave a huge morale boost to the enemy.

Notes

 1. Leckie, *The World War II Reader*, pp. 159–60.
 2. Infield, *Disaster at Bari*, pp. 44–7.
 3. Leckie, op. cit., pp. 159–61.
 4. Atkinson, op. cit., p. 271.
 5. Leckie, op. cit., pp. 161–6.
 6. Infield, op. cit., pp. 44–7.
 7. Atkinson, op. cit., pp. 271–3.
 8. *The History of HQ 12 AA Brigade, 1939–1945*, p. 12.
 9. Leckie, op. cit., pp. 161–6.
10. Infield, op. cit., p. 61.
11. Atkinson, op. cit., pp. 270–8.
12. Leckie, op. cit., p. 167.
13. Ibid., pp. 168–70.
14. Ibid.
15. Infield, op. cit., p. 111.
16. Ibid., p. 225.
17. Atkinson, op. cit., pp. 270–8.
18. NA, Kew, WO 204/7759, 'Explosion at Bari: Redeployment of shipping at ports in the rest of Italy (period December 1943 to February 1944)'.
19. Infield, op. cit., p. 225.
20. Infield, op. cit., pp. 232–3.
21. Atkinson, op. cit., pp. 270–8.

Chapter 12

Cassino and Anzio – Bombing the Winter Line

The devastating impact of the Luftwaffe's raid on the port of Bari, the deaths through mustard gas and the real implications of disrupted supplies were kept under wraps by the Allied authorities. No doubt many supply shortages would have been put down to the freezing weather for, as the new year of 1944 began, a severe winter tightened its grip to slow down all movement on the ground or in the air. Measures not even thought of in North Africa and Sicily became routine: aircraft air filters and carburettors had to be de-iced, oil diluted and snow cleared.[1]

The weather was at its worst in the Apennines where, midway between Rome and Naples, sits the town of Cassino. On its eastern side are the mountains and valleys of the wild Abruzzo region. Perched close by on the 1,700-foot-high peak of Monte Cassino, overlooking the five-mile-wide Liri Valley, is the ancient monastery of Saint Benedict. More mountains range westward to the Tyrrhenian Sea. In 1944 the only viable north-south road was Highway 6, which ran through the Liri Valley and Cassino town under the dominant gaze of Monte Cassino.[2]

Cassino was the lynchpin of the Germans' Winter Line, a system of defensive lines of which the Gustav Line through Cassino was the strongest. After four months of fighting through the countless river valleys and mountains from the foot of Italy and Salerno, both Fifth and Eighth Armies were brought to a standstill by the Winter Line. The eastern and western coastal routes were much too narrow for a breakthrough, while the Liri Valley and its Highway 6 were perfect for a defending army.

To try to outflank Cassino the Allies decided to mount another amphibious landing, Operation SHINGLE, at the fishing port of Anzio, north of Cassino and only about forty miles from Rome. A few days preceding the Anzio landings, on 22 January 1944, General Mark Clark's Fifth Army would make the first attempt to break the Gustav Line in what would become known as the First Battle for Cassino. In a double hammer blow, the Allies' plan was to trap German forces in a pincer movement, and force them to withdraw.[3]

At its Foggia HQ on that first day of the attack at Cassino, 12 January, DAF lost one of its finest. Wing Commander Lance Wade, a fighter ace with ten victories in Spitfires and twenty-four overall, was killed in a tragic non-

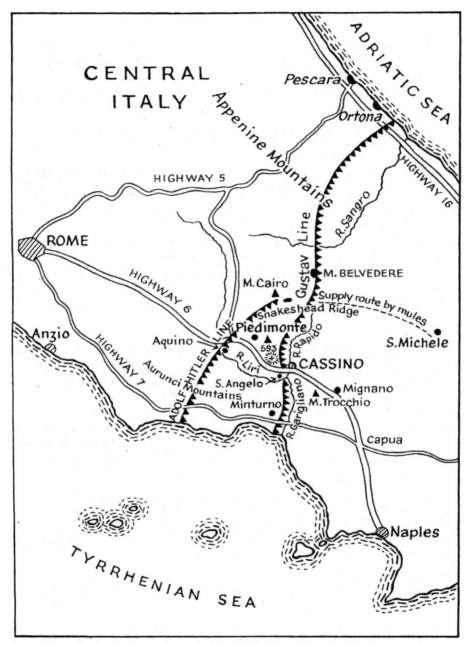

Central Italy, showing the Gustav Line, the Adolf Hitler Line, Cassino and Anzio

combat accident. It was perhaps an omen of the months of death and destruction to come at Cassino and Anzio.[4]

Some DAF formations, such as 244 Wing RAF from Madna and 79th Fighter Group USAAF from Termoli, moved from the Adriatic coast to come under US command in the west on the Volturno river. The Beaufighters of No. 600 (City of London) Squadron RAF also moved west to Marcianise, to provide a night-fighter/intruder role over the proposed beach landing area at Anzio-Nettuno. Since their introduction in June 1943 for the Sicily invasion, they had claimed 121 enemy aircraft kills for a loss of only eight of their own.[5]

Impressive as the victory tally of 600 Squadron was, such dry statistics are by their nature not descriptive of how the results were obtained. Despite the taut nerves and expectation of a defensive patrol, or a night intruder mission over enemy territory, many operations proved uneventful. Poor weather could often mean the sortie being aborted, with reduced visibility obscuring bombing targets. Fighters might make no contact with any enemy aircraft. Long periods of routine and boredom for the crews was a regular experience, but always with a nagging apprehension that the enemy and death lurked just seconds away. Then the wait would be broken and adrenaline would surge as a contact was made.

* * *

No. 600 (City of London) Squadron boasted a host of outstandingly successful crews from operations in North Africa and over the Mediterranean. Flying Officer A.B. Downing DFC DFM and his radar operator, Pilot Officer J. Lyons DFC DFM, are but one fine example. Not long after midnight on 1 May 1943, Downing and Lyons became aces in possibly the shortest time of the whole war. Around thirty miles south of Cagliari, they shot down five Ju52s in only ten minutes. On 1 February 1944 their fortune turned full circle, when they themselves were shot down and, after baling out over the sea, Lyons was lost.[6]

The victories of Downing and Lyons on 1 May were exceptional. The majority of night operations were undertaken in tortuous and patient stalking, combing the dark skies for suspected enemy intruders. In those relentless night-fighter patrols, two Australians in that same 600 Squadron, pilot Flight Lieutenant Jack Ingate and Flying Officer Truman, navigator/radio and radar operator, recorded their account of a Beaufighter defensive patrol:

> Above us a ceiling of twinkling stars vies with the blackness of a moonless night – a blackness so intense that we cannot distinguish the lines of our waiting Beaufighter, until we scramble into its tail. Even then we have to grope to find our way to the cockpit.
>
> Jack Ingate, my pilot, climbs up into the nose. While his mechanic straps him into his seat, I take a walk round the aircraft checking flaps, undercarriage locks and pitot head. Pilots look upon their Radio Officers

as handy-can-carriers when undercarts refuse to go up because the locks are still in after take-off, or if instruments don't register because the pitot head is still snuggling in its ground cover!

I clamber up my two-rung ladder, bump my head on the oxygen bottles as I have done regularly for the last six months, close the hatch, and turn on the dim light that illuminates my quarters in the Beau's belly.

Oxygen turned on, intercom tested, gun pressure checked. I take a look at the Very light cartridges to make sure that we have the correct colours of the day; the magazines that feed our four cannon are full to the brim; the armoured doors separating me from the pilot's cabin are secured. All is ready for the night's work.

Over the intercom I can hear Jack's breathing as he runs through his cockpit drill. I call him up to report that everything is under control in the back. He grunts 'OK' as he checks over instruments, pressures and voltages. In turn each of the engines hums to full throttle for a moment while revs are checked. Their roar dies away to a smooth ticking-over, and I can just see the waiting mechanics ducking under the wings to pull away the wheel chocks.

A clear voice from the control tower affably grants permission over the R/T for us to taxi out to the flarepath. Around us on the perimeter lamps flash red and green. In the distance the pinpricks of light illuminating the circuit for homecoming aircraft are almost indistinguishable from the stars. To the onlooker it probably all seems very pretty.

We reach the runway, line ourselves up between its two dead straight rows of gleaming lamps, and wait for the green flash that signifies permission to scramble. It glows for an instant from the airfield control pilots' hut, and almost simultaneously we start to take off.

As we gather speed, I can picture Jack shoving the stick hard forward to get the tail up while he steadily opens the throttles, playing one engine against the other to keep the aircraft straight. For him, this is the big moment in which every nerve must be at top line alertness, and each hand does the work of two. For me, sitting placidly in the back with my feet on the ammunition stowage, it is a passenger trip down the avenue of shimmering lights; my only concern is to attempt to assess the moment at which we leave the deck, in order that a laconic 'airborne' may be noted in the log.

The lights recede; the stars take their place. We are aloft in an infinity of darkness. I feel a slight bump as the undercarriage legs fold into their recesses, and I know that the business of take-off is completed.

The customary and desultory conversation over the intercom starts. We agree – Jack with some colourfully expressive feeling – it is the blackest night since the last moon, which rubs out the horizon. We check each other's tasks: 'Have you put the guns out?' 'Is the petrol OK?'

This business of airborne chatter is a strain on the conversational power. When night after night, the same two men find themselves alone a mile or two above the earth with little to do but attend routine affairs, talk is liable to flag for want of subject. Yet somehow a new topic usually emerges. Under such circumstances, the shortage of beer in the local pub becomes a matter of absorbing interest to be discussed at length and in detail.

We have been steering our easterly course. The smudgy coast appears below for a moment, to disappear rapidly behind us. A filmy cloud or two float up, and away to the north we notice wispy black clouds. They are drifting towards land, perhaps rain clouds building up, looking for all the world like witches' brooms wandering along.

I figure that we have reached our patrol line, and we turn onto a new vector. The monotonous up and down stooge known to all defensive fighters, whether they patrol land, sea or air, commences. So many minutes up, so many minutes down. Its regularity almost lulls us off to sleep.

The R/T comes to life. We prick up our ears, hopeful that business may be coming our way. It is the ground controller, vectoring homewards the crew which we have relieved. The dullness of perambulating the same piece of sky descends on us again; the night seems darker still.

We sing. Most crews sing on patrol, not from any particular joy of living, but because there's little else to do. Jack sings 'Yankee Doodle Dandy', and the Beau bucks as though in protest. I am bleating out the classical words of 'O'Reilly's Daughter', when I detect the click of the transmission switch. Jack, the treacherous swine has had me on the air, and for minutes the WAAF radio operators have been listening, and assailed with a story ill-suited for lady-like ears.

Once more the R/T surges. This time there is a message for us. The controller's voice is sharper than usual; we suspect activity. We are given a vector and instructions to increase speed. The Beau swings hard onto the new course and the engines scream a little more eagerly. Automatically we run over our combat gear. There must be something afoot.

'An unidentified aircraft is ten miles away from you, going west. Investigate.' The controller is talking to us again, wasting no words. I hear the click as Jack presses his transmitting switch long enough to acknowledge with an abrupt, 'OK'. The needle of the airspeed indicator has been stepped-up by a mile a minute. We are nearly all out to ensure a rapid interception of what may prove to be an enemy raider.

Our idle nattering has stopped, we speak only of essentials. Jack is already straining his eyes into the blanket of indigo before him. Suddenly I feel the aircraft banking into a hard, rate-three turn. Jack calls me to look out to starboard. He thinks he has seen a dim shape away to one side.

Even more speed – the Beaufighter is flat out. An occasional spark races back from the straining engines.

A yell from my pilot, 'There he is! Just ahead to starboard!' I jam my head up against the Perspex dome above me. Through a strip between the starboard engine and the fuselage, I detect a faint smudge flying steadily ahead of us. The smudge is growing bigger. We are gaining.

We belt after our quarry for all we are worth, peering into the cursed gloom that makes identification at any distance almost impossible. Suddenly our task is done for us. A glare of light momentarily illuminates the high tail of a Stirling bomber, and a Very rocket shoots into the sky. A vigilant gunner had seen us and wastes no time in assuring us of his aircraft's identity by firing the signal of the day.

So we have been chasing a 'friendly'. We relax and flash out a matey signal of recognition from our wing-tip lamps. The Stirling flashes in return, and we leave the giant bomber to pursue its homeward course. At a lessened speed we return to our patrol lane and renew our stooge.

Oh well, it was at least a break in the monotony. 'Wish it had been a ruddy Hun,' says Jack. We philosophize on the demerits of Stirlings that return by unorthodox routes. We decided that the bomber boys are entitled to come back any way they please after undertaking their hazardous tasks, even if it does mean that we have to chase after them to check up – and we resume 'O'Reilly's Daughter'.

Our time is nearly up. In a few minutes control calls up with directions to return to base. We turn happily westward and indulge wishful guesses as to the composition of the night-flying supper that awaits us.

The lights of base appear ahead. Over the R/T comes the fatherly voice of our controller, giving permission to land. Away to port a faint horizon appears. We have stayed away just long enough to see the beginning of daybreak.

The routine of landing is not prolonged. We orbit into a steep dive. I feel the wheels dump into place, sense the steadying of our aircraft as the flaps are lowered. We descend rapidly towards the welcoming rows of lights that pick out the runway.

A bump, a squeal from the brakes and we are down. Over towards the bay in which our Beaufighter lives, a torch shines out. The ground crew as always wait for us. Ready to guide their beloved aircraft to its standing, where they will refuel its tanks, and attend to any faults discerned during the flight.

We swing into position in the bay and the engines are silenced. A variety of mechanics await us as we climb from our cockpits. We answer their questions on the performance of our gear, and head for the crew room.

Dawn is breaking. The sky belongs once more to the day fighters, and the night fighters retire to bed and dream of home sweet home, Australia.[7]

* * *

As a decoy to the planned Anzio landings, farther north the only deep-water port close to Rome, Civitavecchia, was subjected to a diversionary bombing campaign. While the air offensives in the west targeted Civitavecchia, DAF squadrons from the Adriatic coast continued with attacks on Cassino and Anzio/Nettuno, close support operations for Eighth Army, and strikes to assist Partisan resistance forces in Yugoslavia.

Total Allied aircraft across Sardinia, Sicily and southern Italy exceeded 2,500, approximately split 45 per cent to the west and 55 per cent in the east. The wholly American Tactical Bomber Force (TBF) had now built up to six groups of Mitchell and Marauder bombers. Although under overall direction of TAF, its own HQ could respond directly to tactical bombing requests from ground forces. Meanwhile the Luftwaffe's numbers were down to what seemed a paltry level, approximately 200 Bf109s and thirty Fw190s. Further afield, scattered around Greece, Crete, southern France, and at Aviano and Villafranca in northern Italy near the Yugoslav border, there were a few torpedo-bombers and long-range Ju88s.

The Luftwaffe's Bf109s and Fw190s were in the main deployed in northern Italy, yet they had no respite. Massed bombing raids by Liberators and Fortresses and their fighter escorts pounded enemy air bases with fragmentation bombs, and hammered Italy's industrial cities. In contrast, Allied aircraft, enjoying the benefits of air superiority, could be parked in the open on airfields. At Naples 850 aircraft nestled up against each other like taxi ranks.[8]

However, the Bari raid on 2 December had severely constrained and weakened US Fifteenth Air Force at Foggia. Losses of equipment and a lack of trained personnel meant it did not have the resources, to seal off the Anzio beachhead by bombing raids on communication routes to the battle area.[9] If the Bari raid had been thwarted, would the Fifteenth Air Force have been able to close down the Germans' supply routes to Rome and Anzio? All that can be said is that the Germans did indeed quickly bring in reinforcements to mount a counter-attack at Anzio.

Over the Anzio landing beaches the Allies laid on air cover in ascending layers. At 20,000 to 25,000 feet four Spitfire patrols flew over the invasion fleet and beachhead. At 16,000 to 18,000 feet over the ships there were four patrols of Spitfires and eight of American Warhawks, while over the beachhead there were eight patrols of Spitfires and eight of Warhawks. Coordination of aircraft operations was handled by air controllers in Naples, a control ship in the fleet, and a control post on the beachhead itself. The latter had a particular emphasis on coordination of fighter-bombers for close army-air support.

With this level of air activity targeted at Anzio, would the element of surprise be quickly lost? To add to the uncertainty in the minds of the German High Command, as to whether the main landings might be closer to Rome, a naval bombardment also pounded Civitavecchia. In addition a bombing raid on Perugia, which destroyed Luftwaffe reconnaissance aircraft, aimed to further confuse the enemy's intelligence.[10]

*   *   *

In the feeble light soon after dawn on 22 January the Spitfires of 92 Squadron RAF, from their base at Marcianise near Naples, were patrolling above the Anzio-Nettuno beaches. The pilots looked down on a British infantry division disembarking five miles to the north-west of Anzio. To the south they could see American troops landing near Nettuno. Squadron Leader 'Rosie' Mackie felt honoured that 92 Squadron had been chosen once again, just as they had at the Sicily and Salerno invasions, to be the first fighter cover over the landing beaches. However, the patrol was uneventful, with no enemy aircraft sighted.

By this time 92 Squadron had racked up 295 victories, and Mackie knew his fellow pilots were eager to notch up the 300th before the month's end. On 8 January Flying Officer R.W. 'Curly', Henderson in a patrol over Ortona at 28,000 feet, had pursued some vapour trails, and his Spitfire quickly caught up with an Me210 twin-engined fighter. Only some 200 of these Me210s had been built, because they proved to be unstable and prone to stalling and spinning. A burst of fire by Henderson set its starboard engine on fire. Pieces of its port wing fell off from another burst, causing it to roll into a vertical dive, at the end of which it was confirmed as destroyed. On 10 January Flight Lieutenants J. Edwards and B. Garner of 92 Squadron had intercepted two Bf109s, which were making diving turns from 15,000 feet. Garner shot down one of them, to claim that 295th kill.

Despite a scarcity of engagements with the enemy, as experienced by 92 Squadron, the exacting demands and inherent risks of flying operations so essential to maintain air superiority, still levied a toll on the squadrons' pilots. On 4 January Warrant Officer K. Symes found his engine cut out on take-off. The crash fractured his skull and lacerated his scalp. On the Anzio D Day morning of 22 January, the first dawn patrol lifting off at 0710 suffered a similar casualty. The tenth Spitfire to take off, of Flying Officer G.J. Dibden, hit a tree and burst into flames. Dibden subsequently died from his injuries and burns.[11]

While on 22 January German ground forces were sparse, unsuspecting and not prepared in the Anzio-Nettuno landing areas, the Luftwaffe was able to respond quickly with some probing air raids. Early in the morning four Fw190s ventured an appearance. One was shot down and, faced with the greater number of Allied aircraft, the remaining three turned away. Later in the morning eight more Fw190s appeared briefly before being chased off. Around midday a Kittyhawk squadron claimed six kills, and two more probables.[12]

Also on 22 January Squadron Leader Houle of No. 417 Squadron RAF came upon some Fw190s at around 6,000 feet below his Spitfire patrol, dropping bombs on the newly-landed Allied troops. He at once jettisoned his long-range fuel tank, ordered his fellow Spitfire pilots to do the same, and dived towards the enemy fighter-bombers. The Fw190s were turning onto their return leg home as Houle closed on the nearest at the back of their formation.

He thought he was less than 150 yards away when he fired his first burst. From hits on the 190's fuselage, engine and cockpit, black smoke spewed out instantly, and oil sprayed on to the Spitfire's windscreen. To Houle it seemed like only split seconds, but before he could fire again, a cascade of machine-gun bullets jack-hammered into the armoured protection behind his seat.

He found his reflexes wrenching the Spitfire to starboard and surprisingly into a climb. The attacking Fw190 flew straight ahead and underneath him. Houle turned again in pursuit. His few bursts of fire were unable to make a kill, but sent the German fighter on its way.[13]

Flying Officer Leonard Brian 'Mac' McDermott of 92 Squadron was in a Spitfire patrol over the Anzio-Nettuno beaches on 22 January, and there again on 24 January. McDermott was a twenty-eight-year-old Australian from Albury in New South Wales. Even with five days in early January unfit for flying because of gales and snow, which demolished many of the men's tents, McDermott was on his twenty-first operation out of just nineteen days in the month available so far.

McDermott had joined the RAAF in 1940, then gained his wings in September 1942 in Australia flying Tiger Moths. He joined 92 Squadron in May 1943 in North Africa, when he made his first flight at the controls of a Spitfire. In a dawn patrol on 24 January after take-off at 0710, McDermott was flying one of ten Spitfires of 92 Squadron led by Flight Lieutenant J. Edwards.

Six Spitfires patrolled over a convoy bringing troops to the Anzio-Nettuno landings and four directly over the beaches. No enemy aircraft were seen by either group. Then after an hour and forty minutes, as the patrol was return-ing south to their Marcianise base, McDermott's aircraft suffered engine failure. He was then seen to bale out over the Gulf of Gaeta. The nine other Spitfires landed back at Marcianise at 0915.

Search patrols were immediately organized, with the first four Spitfires in the air by 0940. A ship and an air sea rescue launch were also alerted with the coordinates of where McDermott was seen baling out. For the rest of the day all the twenty remaining pilots in 92 Squadron, including Squadron Leader Mackie, went out in search patrols of either four or two Spitfires. For nearly seven hours the 92 Squadron search patrols departed in successive sorties, with departure times preceding the return of the previous patrol:

Depart	Return	Depart	Return
0940	1125	1405	1600
0955	1125	1510	1700
1100	1245	1530	1630
1215	1410		

When the last patrol returned at 1700, the dusk of a mid-winter evening would have been gathering. Although in his summary of the day's events Squadron Leader Mackie stated that seven aircraft patrolled over the Anzio-Nettuno beaches during the afternoon, remarkably the 92 Squadron operations record book shows that no other kind of sortie took place that afternoon other than search patrols for McDermott.

All search efforts failed to find McDermott. Just two weeks earlier on 8 January McDermott himself had escorted a B-25 bomber looking in vain for a pilot downed in the sea, who had been seen in a dinghy. His fellow pilots in 92 Squadron must have thought a lot of Flying Officer 'Mac' McDermott, and a distressed Squadron Leader Mackie wrote:

'MAC' joined us at the end of the North African 'show' and has proved himself a most reliable and steady pilot – our hope is that he may have been picked up by a ship before our aircraft and the ASR launch began their search.

To this day McDermott's record merely shows '24 January 1944, missing believed killed, baled out over the Gulf of Gaeta, cause unknown'.[14]

By the end of January, despite the bad weather totally grounding aircraft on six days, and severely limiting flying operations on a number of others, 92 Squadron had flown 775 hours and 35 minutes in 540 operational sorties. It was their highest operational total since the invasion of Sicily in July 1943.

*   *   *

Elsewhere, in interdiction operations, DAF Baltimore bombers hit road junctions at Popli, trying to block 26th Panzer Division from reaching the Anzio beachhead. Together with naval bombardments, air support and interdiction sought to delay the German counter-attack.

With a numerical advantage in their aircraft aloft of around five to one over the Luftwaffe, by 1 February the Allies claimed to have shot down some thirty enemy aircraft, and possibly damaged or destroyed another forty. Whereas an equivalent number of Allied aircraft lost or put out of action could be easily replaced, the Luftwaffe's losses out of a total strength of perhaps 300 at that time were very significant. In the short term at least they were effectively irreplaceable.

Even so it was not all one-way traffic. The Luftwaffe attacked the invasion fleet with their new radio-controlled bombs. By 19 February their raids had sunk the cruiser HMS *Spartan*, two destroyers and a hospital ship. Three more destroyers and a number of merchant ships were damaged. These losses, caused by relatively few successful raids, did indicate the scale of the damage which the Allies' air power was inflicting on the Germans, by much heavier and more intensive air strikes.[15]

Nevertheless the Luftwaffe continued to sustain fighter-bomber forays against the Anzio beachhead, and all fighter squadrons were heavily engaged to nullify the threat to Allied troops. The Bf109 was also deployed in a fighter-bomber role and, on 27 January, Squadron Leader Houle claimed one to add to his tally.

The same day Flight Sergeant James Andrew from Yorkshire and 93 Squadron RAF, notched up his fifth victory to become a fighter ace in heroic circumstances. Andrew broke up six Bf109s as they were approaching the Allies' naval force at Anzio. He shot down two 109s before his engine failed. To emphasize it was his day, Andrew managed to make a crash landing just behind Allied lines, getting away with only a superficial injury, and later being awarded the DFM.[16]

At night, from DAF's eastern airfields, Bostons crossed the Apennines to bomb vehicle convoys by picking out their dimmed headlights on the Frosinone to Rome road. With the Germans curtailing movement during the day around Cassino, fighter-bomber attacks against enemy positions dug into the mountains and underground were proving of limited effect.

On 7 February on a mountain road at Sora, near Cassino, a German vehicle convoy carrying supplies for their Gustav Line defences became stuck in snow in daylight. DAF patrols found them, marooned and defenceless like beached dolphins. Wave upon wave of Spitfires, Kittyhawks and Thunderbolts claimed forty-six vehicles destroyed, fifty damaged and no doubt many enemy troops and civilian casualties.[17]

Anzio proved to be a productive hunting ground for Squadron Leader Houle and his 417 Squadron. On 7 February he shot down another Bf109. Then, on 14 February, Houle and a fellow ace, Canadian Flying Officer Gareth Horricks, each claimed Bf109s. For both Spitfire aces they would be final victories, leaving Horricks with a total of seven claims, and Houle with eleven.[18]

On the ground in the wintry claws of the Gustav Line at Cassino, Fifth Army made little headway. At Anzio the landings came under serious threat of failure from a German counter-attack. At one stage ten German divisions were pitted against only four Allied divisions. Anzio was not going to make the Germans withdraw to the north. A second attempt to break through the Gustav Line at Cassino had to be made immediately.

While Eighth Army troops moved across the mountains to bolster Fifth Army, the second assault on Cassino on 15 February was led by II New Zealand Corps. It was preceded by an air raid of 254 bombers which blasted Monte Cassino's monastery to little more than rubble. When, on 18 February, however, without any tank or anti-tank support, the New Zealanders were driven back, the second battle for Cassino was called off.[19]

At midnight on 15 February, the same day as Allied bombers destroyed the Monte Cassino monastery, the Germans began a counter-attack at Anzio. To support their Panzers on the ground, the Luftwaffe somehow found long-range bombers, and on three days, 16 to 18 February, flew in the order of 100, 170 and 150 sorties respectively on each day. As well as the timing being uncannily coincidental with the Allied bombing of Monte Cassino monastery, the Germans were attacking American troops who had just relieved a British division, and who were unacquainted with the Anzio battlefield. The German armoured thrust, as it had at Salerno, was attempting to drive a wedge between the Allied forces all the way down to the landing beaches.

The Allied response was also similar to their reply to the German counter-attack at Salerno. On 17 February, in combined operations, DAF, Strategic and Tactical air forces dropped 952 tons of bombs onto German forces, the highest total of bombs in one day in the Mediterranean. From 18 February the Allies' other constant enemy, bad weather, intervened to prevent the intensity of the bombing raids being sustained. Then, on 2 March, more than 600 tons of bombs were dropped on enemy concentration areas.[20]

Both before and during the second battle for Cassino Eighth Army moved forces across the Apennines to the west to join up with Fifth Army. The Allies' main objective had now become Rome, for which the two armies must combine to break the Gustav Line. As the battalions crossed the mountains they were able to look down upon what was left of the bombed monastery atop Monte Cassino.

*   *   *

In January 1944, after his recovery from jaundice, Wing Commander Hugh Dundas had been appointed to a DAF staff position with AVM Broadhurst. With his own personal Spitfire, Dundas' role was to visit and monitor the performance of each squadron in Desert Air Force and report to Broadhurst each evening. The evening meeting was usually at the advanced HQs of Eighth Army and DAF, co-located at that time near Vasto on the Adriatic coast, in trailers and tents a few miles behind the front lines. Those present would typically include the DAF senior air staff officer, group captain operations and wing commander intelligence, and Eighth Army's brigadier general staff, G1 intelligence, G1 operations and G1 air, who would jointly plan and agree operations for the coming days and weeks.

The main DAF formations for which Dundas in his staff officer role was responsible in January 1944 were:

Formations		Main aircraft type
Wings:	244 RAF	Spitfire fighters
	324 RAF	Spitfire fighters
	7 SAAF	Spitfire fighter-bombers
	239 RAF	Kittyhawk fighter-bombers, and Mustang fighter-bombers
	57th Fighter Group (USAAF)	P-47 Thunderbolt fighters and fighter-bombers, and Mustang fighters
	79th Fighter Group (USAAF)	P-47 Thunderbolt fighters and fighter-bombers, and Mustang fighters
	3 SAAF	Medium bombers
	232 RAF	Medium bombers
Squadrons:	600 (City of London) Squadron RAF	Beaufighter night-fighters

Dundas believed that 239 Wing was the outstanding exponent of fighter-bombing at that time. Their commander was Colonel Wilmot of the SAAF and his deputy Wing Commander Brian Eaton of the RAAF. Their command of 239 typified the multi-national nature of DAF which included units of the British RAF, Australian RAAF, Canadian RCAF, South African SAAF, and the American United States Army Air Forces. Wilmot and Eaton were tough, respected and inspiring leaders. The Kittyhawks of 239 normally carried 500lb bombs, and the Mustangs 1,000lb bombs. On their own initiative, Wilmot and Eaton instigated modifications and trials so that these bombs were increased to 1,000lb for the Kittyhawk and 2,000lb for the Mustang. At first they limited the use of these high bomb loads to their own personal sorties, and a few other very experienced pilots.

In early March 1944 Dundas learnt that he was being considered as replacement for Wilmot who was being promoted to a more senior position in the SAAF. His dream of a quiet life at the Haifa staff college was long gone, and he was truly back in the real war.[21]

* * *

The 57th Fighter Group re-located in the first week in March from Amendola at Foggia to the Cercola base near Naples. From there they were tasked with flying interdiction missions against targets near Rome. Earlier in

January, after it was learned that their new P-47 Thunderbolts were badly designed for a fighter-bomber role, it was intended to transfer the group to the UK to undertake fighter escort duties on bombing raids on Germany. The bomb-release toggles of the P-47 had been installed on the cockpit floor, making it impossible for a pilot to pull them while flying the plane in a dive-bombing approach, and simultaneously aiming for the target.

Major Gil Wymond, commander of the 65th Fighter Squadron of the 57th FG, was averse to the proposed transfer. Despite the greater losses of fighter-bomber operations, he wanted to fulfil their air-to-ground missions in the Italian air war. At Wymond's directive his ground crew built and tested a modification within two days. A bar attachment with a cable to two release toggles on the instrument panel, allowed the pilot to activate easily the release of all three bombs, while still in full control of flying the plane. It was tempo-rary until a more permanent alteration by the manufacturer was delivered, but it worked.

In their interdiction missions during March 1944, 57th Group fought a number of engagements with Luftwaffe fighters, claiming four victories for the loss of the 64th Fighter Squadron's Flight Lieutenant Towner. Tragic-ally, on 24 March, they lost another pilot on a mission near Rome, when Flight Lieutenant Coughlin was shot down by friendly fire from a Spitfire. About this time they first encountered the Luftwaffe's renowned 'Yellownose' Squadron.

In a bid to strengthen its meagre numbers in the skies above Cassino and Anzio, prior to the next push by the Allies to break the stalemate, the Luft-waffe had re-located the 'Yellownose' Squadron of Fw190s from their base at Abbeville in France. The 'Yellownose' Squadron was comprised of very experienced pilots from countless dogfights with Allied fighters in the skies of France. In disciplined formations, the Yellownose pilots maintained a two-plane integrity, and climbed aggressively into an attack out of the sun. On one occasion, although Fw190 pilots normally tried to avoid a turning dogfight, Lieutenant Mike McCarthy of 64th Fighter Squadron found himself trying to outturn a Yellownose Fw190.

McCarthy and the German pilot were flat out in a very tight circle at a ninety-degree bank, whirling around with neither seeming to gain on the other. When McCarthy saw gun flashes from the Fw190, his instant thought was dismissive of being hit. But he was hit, one cannon shell below his wind-shield, and two more behind the cockpit. Such accurate firing required the maximum lead and a full ninety-degree deflection. McCarthy was soberly impressed. He survived the encounter to take on the 'Yellownoses' with more success in subsequent months.[22]

*   *   *

When the first rays of the dawn sun broke over the Monte Cassino peak on 15 March some sunlight was glimmering through the clouds and mountains which surrounded the Liri Valley and the Cassino battleground. The rain had finally stopped and later in the morning the air raid to signal the start of the third battle to break the Gustav Line pounded down on the German lines.

While DAF fighters and fighter-bombers patrolled the fringes of the Cassino battle area to ward off any Luftwaffe intruders, the strategic and tactical bombers began an onslaught to destroy the town of Cassino. In approximately fifteen-minute intervals from 0830 until noon, eleven groups of heavy bombers and five of medium bombers swept over the doomed town.[23]

> At eight o'clock in the morning the first wave of bombers was seen, flying high above Cassino. They circled the town, looking to the men below like lazy silver insects, and soon the ground itself seemed to shake with the fury of the bombardment. For over three hours the machines went over in waves – Fortresses and Liberators, in formations of eighteen and thirty-six.
>
> Over 1,000 aircraft took part; some 500 blasted Cassino with 1,100 tons of metal, while 300 fighter-bombers, with as many fighters as cover, attacked targets immediately nearby. There was no such opposition from either enemy aircraft or flak. No land forces in the war had yet seen such a massed attack on so small a target, and it seemed to those watching that at last we had found the key to success in attack, without the inevitable casualties of an infantry assault.[24]

It proved to be wishful thinking. At midday, as the last bombs fell, the New Zealanders attacked. They immediately ran into German troops who were supposed to be dead. German infantry and paratroopers emerged from the town's ruined buildings and many, it was later discovered, from reinforced cellars, even from deep underground tunnels, to put up an unexpectedly strong defence. Also unanticipated was the extent that the bombed buildings and craters obstructed the bringing up of tanks and artillery to support the infantry. To add to the misery, the rain began again. Because Cassino's underground culvert for the Rapido river had been smashed by the bombing, craters, ditches and any depression in the town flooded, and the mud was back.

At Cassino, by the evening of Sunday 19 March, the third Allied attempt to take the town and its Monastery was in serious trouble. Likewise the Anzio bridgehead was stuck in a battle of attrition, and had become another static killing ground reminiscent of the First World War. When the bombing was over, and the inferno of flames and smoke cleared, only unrecognizable ruins and rubble remained.[25] However, just as Stalingrad's wasteland had for the Russians, Cassino town's total destruction created a rabbit warren of defensive positions. German troops were able to first lie low in underground bunkers and tunnels, then emerge to defy Allied troops' attacks. Some alleged it was counter-productive and a misuse of Allied air power. It had certainly created new obstacles in the path of Allied armies on the ground.[26]

The air blitz and Allied air superiority had not provided a sufficient advantage to enable Fifth and Eighth Armies to break out from Cassino and Anzio. Air interdiction had not yet fully choked off German supplies. Perhaps the consequences of Bari on Allied supplies and operations still cast a shadow. The bombings of Monte Cassino monastery and Cassino town were controversial and their effects not yet clear. However, if it had been the Luftwaffe dominating the skies, there would have been no question as to the outcome on the ground.

Yet the strategic urgency was unremitting. Rome must be taken before the end of May so that German divisions were kept engaged in Italy, ideally destroyed, and prevented from being deployed back to north-west Europe. The planned Normandy invasion for early June, Operation OVERLORD, must be protected. It was feared that reinforcements transferred from Italy could feed into a German build-up to counter the Allied landings.

Notes
1. Owen, op. cit., p. 240.
2. Smith et al., *The Cassino Battles* (Queen's Royal Surreys' Association Museum), p. 1.
3. Ibid., pp. 1–3.
4. Thomas, op. cit., pp. 65–6.
5. Owen, op. cit., p. 241.
6. Bowyer, op. cit., pp. 212 & 224–6.
7. Veterans' accounts, F/Lt Jack Ingate; Truman, *Night Sortie*, 600 Squadron RAF.
8. Owen, op. cit., p. 242.
9. Infield, op. cit., pp. 232–3.
10. Owen, op. cit., pp. 243–4.
11. National Archives (NA), Kew, AIR/27/746; Avery, *Spitfire Leader*, p. 128; Crosby, *A Handbook of Fighter Aircraft*, p. 103.
12. Owen, op. cit., pp. 243–4.
13. Thomas, op. cit., p. 66.
14. NA, Kew, AIR/27/746; Avery, op. cit., p. 128; National Archives of Australia (www.naa.gov.au), barcode no. 5243743, F/O LB McDermott, No. 413011.
15. Owen, op. cit., pp. 244–5; Brookes, op. cit., pp. 53–4.
16. Thomas, op. cit., p. 66.
17. Owen, op. cit., pp. 245–6.
18. Thomas, op. cit., p. 67.
19. Smith et al., pp. 3–4.
20. Owen, op. cit., p. 247.
21. Dundas, op. cit., pp. 140–3.
22. Molesworth, op. cit., pp. 83–6; McCarthy, op. cit., pp. 69–70.
23. Owen, op. cit., p. 248.
24. Ray, op. cit., p. 114.
25. Evans, op. cit., p. 129.
26. Owen, op. cit., p. 248.

Chapter 13

Breakthroughs at Cassino and Anzio – but the Luftwaffe fights back

Despite the bombing and total destruction of Cassino town by the Strategic Air Forces, on the evening of 19 March the Allies were forced to called off their third attempt to break through the Gustav Line. In five days the New Zealand and Indian Divisions had lost nearly 5,000 men. All immediate offensive plans were shelved. What was achieved in return for a heavy loss of life and casualties? Three incursions made in the Gustav Line seemed a paltry reward. A small bridgehead across the downstream Garigliano had been established, about half of Cassino town and Castle Hill captured, and in the east the Americans and French at great cost had taken more mountains.[1]

While the end of the third battle for Cassino seemed to have little meaning, in the air the DAF continued its incessant fight to keep the Luftwaffe subjugated and to provide close support to Eighth Army. Towards the end of March 1944, DAF's AOC-in-C, AVM Broadhurst, who had led them from the deserts of North Africa to Italy's Apennine mountains, departed to be replaced by AVM Dickson. Exactly one year before, at El Hamma in Tunisia, Broadhurst had pioneered DAF's innovative use of fighter-bombers in close support of a decisive breakthrough on the ground. He also had ensured that, despite the massive growth of Allied air forces in diverse roles, DAF retained its powerful and unique identity.

At the time of DAF's operation at El Hamma in Tunisia, Dickson had been making an inspection visit of DAF with Air Marshal Leigh-Mallory, AOC-in-C Fighter Command. They returned to the UK armed with lessons learned from DAF's organization and tactics, which were put to good use in the air support planning for the Normandy invasion. Not least of these were the DAF operations using fighter-bombers. Modification of fighters for the fighter-bomber role had first been developed in the Western Desert in March 1942 when the Luftwaffe had some ascendancy over DAF.

In his Tunisian visit Dickson must have been impressed with what he saw and learned of DAF's close support tactics for Eighth Army, for on taking up his new command of DAF in late March 1944, Dickson ordered more and more conversions of fighters to this role. Into April and May in support of ground forces at Anzio and Cassino, Kittyhawks carried a 1,000lb bomb under the aircraft's belly, and two 500lb bombs under the wings. Mustangs and Thunderbolts also carried 1,000-pounders, and even Spitfires a 500-pounder in 'Spitbomber' mode.[2]

The Rover David Cab-rank system was intensified to bring even closer support on the battlefield. As well as the Mobile Operations Room Unit (MORU) named David, in recognition of its introduction by Group Captain David Haysom, five more MORU Rovers were established, Paddy, Jack, Joe, Tom and Frank. Each MORU would normally have an RAF officer in command, and preferably one who had some army experience. Around eighteen Eighth Army men in a MORU would include two officers, a sergeant, a radio operator, a cipher clerk, technicians, drivers, mechanics, a cook and guard troops. Their vehicles and equipment, typically comprising an armoured car and trailer, a light truck, and three jeeps with trailers, gave them a high degree of self-sufficiency.

Some fighter-bombers ranged farther afield in modified air interdiction operations. Rather than targeting infrastructure concentration points, strikes were re-focused against bridges and the movement of the enemy's road and rail traffic. To raid rail routes and traffic deep behind and to the north of the Germans' right flank at Anzio, on 31 March the 57th Fighter Group USAAF relocated its fighter squadrons of P-47 Thunderbolts to Alto near the port of Bastia on Corsica's east coast. Flying across the Tyrrhenian Sea, their priority targets would be railway locomotives, rolling stock and road traffic in northern Italy. The squadrons were set a target of forty-eight sorties a day, and within two weeks were averaging eighty a day.

While at Alto they began to be armed with eight- to eleven-second fuses for 500lb and 1,000lb high-explosive bombs. The delayed fuses led them to begin dropping their bombs from below 500 feet so as to achieve more direct hits on the railway tracks. This prompted their Major Dick Hunziker to form a flight of 'Tunnel Busters', led by Captain Lyle H. Duba. The tactic was to skip-bomb the railway tunnels, where it was thought trains used to hide out in daylight. Duba believed that he and three other pilots of the 'Tunnel Busters' Flight caught several locomotives and trains hiding out in the tunnels:

> We flew at least 20 of these hair-raising missions on the deck, strafing the target, dropping a single bomb and then immediately going into a high-G pull out to avoid the ridge the tunnel went through. On several occasions the bomb exited the other end of the tunnel before exploding, but most of the time it detonated inside.

Hunziker was of the view that, even if there was no train in the tunnel, the underground track and tunnel structure would have been severely damaged.[3]

In anticipation of the Allies' build-up for spring offensives at Anzio and Cassino, the Luftwaffe garnered its remaining numbers to try and blunt

Allied air attacks. However, air superiority and many more fighter squadrons gave DAF a lethal tactical advantage. Rather than being drawn into individual dog-fights, they were able to shift to an emphasis on formation group work.

While the resourcing of air forces in UK to support the Normandy landings attracted the latest types of aircraft, DAF was left to persist with many outdated models such as Baltimores, Bostons and Kittyhawks. This was only viable because of the Allied air forces' superiority over the Luftwaffe's meagre strength in Italy. Bari may have had far-reaching consequences for the Italian campaign but, day in day out, Allied air power still continued to dominate the skies.[4]

*   *   *

To achieve a decisive advantage on the ground, General Alexander planned a build-up with a number of deceptions. The vast bulk of Eighth Army was gradually moved at night time from the Adriatic coast to the Cassino front. False information on planning for another seaborne landing north-west of Rome at its port of Civitavecchia was leaked to the Germans. It must have had an effect, for Kesselring kept strong reserves north of Rome until a few days after the start of Eighth Army's Operation HONKER, the next attack on Cassino and the Gustav Line.

The Canadian Corps of two divisions was brought into Eighth Army reserve without announcement. At the same time fictitious information was issued which indicated that the Canadians were relocating to Naples to embark for the fake amphibious operation to land at Civitavecchia.

The Allies' overwhelming air superiority reduced reconnaissance by the Luftwaffe to a minimum, strengthening the cloak of secrecy. The concealment of forces was not just to give the benefit of surprise, it would hide the reserve capability to exploit the capture of Cassino and Monte Cassino, so as to surge forward up the Liri Valley in Operation DIADEM, to combine with an Anzio breakout – codenamed Operation BUFFALO.[5]

However, with the weather improving, and recognizing the inevitability that the Allies must be rebuilding for a new offensive, the Germans began to throw their remaining air power into some large air battles.

Despite the priorities of the war in north-west Europe, some newer model aircraft did keep feeding through to DAF. In mid-March Squadron Leader Neville Duke, the leading Spitfire ace in the Mediterranean, returned from his sojourn as a training instructor, and took over as commander of No. 145 Squadron RAF. Soon after his arrival he was delighted to take possession of a new Spitfire Mk VIII. In this new Spitfire, on 24 March, Duke led two patrol operations of 145 Squadron. On one patrol they engaged in a battle with more than thirty Luftwaffe fighters. The result was five more victories to take 145 Squadron's overall score above 200.

Duke had brought with him to 145 Squadron Australian Flight Lieutenant Rod McKenzie, who for a period had been a fellow training instructor in Egypt. On one of those training days Duke had asked McKenzie to fly with him. He accepted only on condition that he could fly a Spitfire, and if Duke promised to get him a transfer to a Spitfire squadron.[6] In a fateful decision Duke found a way to fulfil his promise

Ensuring that experienced pilots spent time away from operations on training instruction duties, was a further strength of the Allied air forces. The Luftwaffe's loss rates were too high for them to effectively allocate sufficient experienced pilots to training. The result was that new pilots in Luftwaffe squadrons were thrown into combat without experienced pilots to pass on their knowledge and guide them. It seriously shortened their survival rates, but on both sides a victory could be quickly followed by a defeat and death.

On 27 March Canadian Bill Downer of No. 93 Squadron RAF shot down two Fw190s to become an ace. A couple of weeks later, in a patrol off Anzio, Downer misjudged his height, crashed into the sea and was killed. His fellow pilot, Australian Warrant Officer Bobby Bunting, who had shot down two Fw190s on 29 February over Cisterna for his first victories, had a lucky escape. Outnumbered in a dogfight over Cassino, his Spitfire was hit. Wounded in the right leg, Bunting somehow got away to return safely to base.[7]

Another Australian, Squadron Leader Bobby Gibbes of No. 3 Squadron RAAF, one of Australia's most distinguished fighter aces and leaders, spoke of his innermost feelings in air fighting:

In that one minute the air is full of twisting, turning, frantic aeroplanes, and the next minute not a single enemy machine can be seen. The enemy has completely disappeared. You then collect the remnants of your squadron, count them hastily, then the fires burning below. The feeling is a strange one. Some of those fires down below contain the mutilated bodies of your friends. But as you look down, you have no real feeling other than, I hate to confess, probably terrific relief that it is them and not you.

It must be the animal in us really I suppose, and the strong spirit of self-survival which has become uppermost. Man becomes animal when he thinks he is about to die. As you fly back to your base, now safe at last, a feeling of light-hearted exuberance comes over you. It is wonderful to be still alive and it is, I think, merely the after-effect of violent, terrible fear. I am not afraid to confess to being frightened. I was almost always terrified.

On landing back, you look for your squadron aeroplanes at the dispersal sites, and if your friends' aeroplanes are there, your heart fills with gladness for you have become a caring human being again.

He thought it often seemed to be an interminable wait for other missing aircraft. Then when the elapsed time appeared to be too long, an aircraft approached and touched down, 'You look eagerly for its identifying letters, hoping against hope that it is one of the missing, returning'.[8]

Engagements were often very brief, and always violent, but could be interspersed with interludes of uneventful operations. The dogfights and victories were statistics which belied the massive number of sorties flown. Many operations were completed without any engagement with enemy aircraft, or only a fleeting contact, with no claimed kills. On 29 March, over Anzio, Pilot Officer Doyle of No. 417 Squadron RAF claimed his first victory, a Bf109. Despite then being attacked, wounded and his Spitfire catching fire, he probably also downed an Fw190. Doyle managed amazingly to crash-land in the Nettuno beachhead and survive. His first victory had come on his 185th sortie.[9]

*   *   *

In early March Group Captain Hugh Dundas was awarded the DSO, and informed by AVM Broadhurst in confidence that, if he wanted to get back into operations, he was to be appointed commander of the renowned No. 239 Wing RAF. At the same time as feeling very flattered, Dundas was very apprehensive. The battle-hardened 239 Wing included the formidable Nos 3 and 450 Squadrons RAAF. It was the largest wing in the Mediterranean theatre, and was looked upon by nearly everyone as the best formation operating in the fighter-bomber role. Dundas himself, just twenty-three years old, thought it a staggering promotion, and also daunting:

> It was the question which I had been both dreading and hoping for. The old struggle was raging within me – the struggle between the knowledge that I should fight on and the desire to call it a day and stay alive.

Furthermore, Dundas knew really nothing about the skills of flying fighter-bomber roles and dropping bombs. He knew he would have to learn new flying techniques, and regularly lead the wing on operations. Whereas in fighter dog-fights you pitted your plane and ability in one-on-one contests, as a fighter-bomber you had to dive into heavy flak, and a random but increased risk of being shot down. Dundas told Broadhurst that he would take the job.

It was soon after this meeting that Broadhurst was transferred back to the UK, to command the air forces for the D Day invasion, before Dundas' promotion was approved. The new AVM Dickson chose the Australian Brian Eaton, commander of No. 3 Squadron RAAF, to be commander of 239 Wing. Dundas had great respect for Eaton and, despite missing out on promotion, still found himself wanting to get back into operations. At the beginning of May he persuaded Dickson to let him join No. 244 Wing RAF as a wing leader of their Spitfires, under his old friend Wing Commander Brian Kingcombe.[10]

While Dundas waited for the paperwork to be processed for his promotion and transfer, the overall build-up to a spring offensive increased.

* * *

In late March and early April 1943 the weather improved. The intensity of air attacks forced most German road traffic to move only at night. The Boston bombers of No. 3 Wing SAAF, in their night-intruder role became the most favoured strike aircraft to try to plug the night-time gap in interdiction operations. The Bostons, nick-named the 'Pippos', short for 'Pipistrello', the Italian word for a bat, exemplified how DAF had resisted becoming composed solely of fighter squadrons. Once again DAF had demonstrated that its retention of bombers made it unique in its make-up, and highly adaptable to ever-changing circumstances.

During April the command of the Tactical Air Force (TAF) raised the tempo of the air war, with the instigation of Operation STRANGLE. The objectives were the interdiction of Rome, the battlefields at Anzio, Cassino, and the enemy's communication routes leading to the Gustav and Adolf Hitler Lines. Just as it had at El Alamein and for the invasion of Sicily, the massive air superiority of the Allies also created a No Fly Zone. This allowed Eighth Army to move west with impunity over the Apennines to join Fifth Army for the major offensives at Cassino.

The air interdiction strategy of Operation STRANGLE was the idea of General John K., 'Uncle Joe', Cannon, commander of MATAF, to break the stalemates at Cassino and Anzio. It aimed to do what its name suggests, to cut off all rail, road and river routes across Italy, and prevent supplies reaching the German armies. An unforeseen and beneficial outcome was the near paralysis of any tactical mobility of the enemy forces.[11]

DAF Kittyhawks, Mustangs, Baltimores and Spitbombers struck at rail-tracks, overpasses, tunnels and bridges, in central and eastern areas along the Teni-Perugia and Terni-Sulmona-Pescara lines. Trains were being hit or halted as far as 120 miles from Rome.[12] Of course, Operation STRANGLE was not without its consequences. To counter the growing air-to-ground onslaught, which clearly preceded another major offensive by Allied armies, the Germans took their ground-to-air defences to another level. More intensive anti-aircraft fire of various types imposed greater losses on Allied air forces, particularly the fighter-bombers in their low level dive-bombing runs.

Although low level attack was the essence of fighter-bomber operations, tactics varied in different ways, according to the type of aircraft, and from squadron to squadron. In a typical Kittyhawk air-to-ground attack for instance, the pilot would dive at around a sixty-degree incline, and at up to about 400mph. Groups of four 88mm shells could be the first anti-aircraft fire encountered. Set to explode at a specified height, bursts of orange balls of fire, intermingled with puffs of black smoke, would usually seek out the fighter-bombers before they were close enough to begin a descent. The 88mm fire would then follow the Kittyhawk's dive down to around 4,000 feet.

A near miss from an 88mm shell could seriously damage an aircraft, while a direct hit would destroy it. Below 4,000 feet a mass of small puffs of brown smoke from 40mm cannon shell explosions could be expected. This was a rapid-fire barrage which would bring down many an aircraft. At 2,000 feet 20mm cannon fire would commence, very probably in heavy concentrations. A direct hit at this altitude was perhaps the most lethal as, even if the aircraft was still flying, the pilot had no time to try and regain height.

As the pilot dived closer to the ground, to release his bombs within 1,500 feet of the target, he would be met with small-arms fire from the enemy troops. As the pilot pulled out of the dive, the G-force tightened and distorted his face into a grotesque mask. And in a desperate climb away to safety, pilots were still being hunted by the anti-aircraft fire. All they could depend upon to successfully complete the mission was their own ability to fly the aircraft with skill, speed, and manoeuvrability – and of course some luck.[13]

Although from late March, because of the massive disruption caused by Operation STRANGLE, no major through traffic was reaching the Italian capital,[14] air interdiction could not cut off all the enemy's transport lifelines. It could not entirely prevent the flow of some supplies, and the movement of some reinforcements. What it did do was to severely weaken German defences, and undermine their capability for sustaining indefinite resistance. And at the same time Allied air superiority prevented the Luftwaffe from having any material impact on Allied ground forces. This meant that some Allied anti-aircraft units, with little or nothing to do, were converted to supplement the army's artillery. Allied air power also ensured that the German army stayed on the defensive. As Air Chief Marshal (ACM) Slessor said, 'if there had been no air force on either side, the German Army could have made the invasion of Italy impossible ...'[15]

From the beginning of April in the lead-up to Operation DIADEM, No. 40 Squadron SAAF flew every day from first light to nightfall in low-level recon-naissance. They photographed every German gun position and, as spotters, they were in radio contact with the HQ of 6th Army Group Royal Artillery (6 AGRA), for updating artillery target information. Using large-scale maps and aerial photographs with numbered grids from prior reconnaissance, pilots had direct communication with HQ 6 AGRA while they were in the air, to pass on coordinates of enemy guns which they had spotted.

They also communicated with 239 Wing via the Rover David Cab-rank, to send fighter-bombers against identified targets. Observation posts on Monte Trocchio, staffed in a mix of RAF and Eighth Army Air Control officers, directed Kittyhawks and Mustangs, such as on 15 May against communications centres, and then on the next day to hit German mortar positions at Cassino.[16]

In the days before the fourth battle to break through the Gustav Line at Cassino and, a little farther north, its fallback, the Adolf Hitler Line, the stalemate appeared to be entrenched. A new observer of the Liri Valley from the distance of the surrounding mountains would have been misled. The occasional gunfire, bomb-blast or shell-burst would have seemed desultory, almost languid in the late Italian spring.

> Flowers caressing the roadside half hid the coils of telephone wire; the song of innumerable birds, which had grown used to the fighting, only served to emphasise the fevered stillness of anticipation. The peeling pink plaster of a roofless house, the twisted balcony rails, shimmered like an artificial eighteenth century ruin in the liquid sun.[17]

In reality the Allies' tactical air forces were at work around the clock, bombing raids hitting the German front lines and blocking all rail lines to the north.

On 7 May DAF struck a most remarkable blow against the Luftwaffe's attempts to make some kind of threat against the coming offensive. Squadron Leader 'Duke' Arthur was leading a Spitfire patrol of No. 72 Squadron RAF over Lake Bracciano when they intercepted a formation of eighteen Bf109s of I./JG 4. Arthur shot down one, and his fellow pilots claimed another eight victories as they racked up a total of nine kills of the eighteen Bf109s.[18]

*   *   *

In the hours of darkness over Cassino, Anzio and the Germans' winter lines, the Beaufighter night-fighters of No. 600 Squadron RAF continued to take their toll of any Luftwaffe night intruders. No. 600 Squadron, the City of London's Auxiliary Air Force squadron, was one of the first to be equipped with AI radar for night-fighter operations.

Throughout the war the Beaufighter was the RAF's heaviest armed fighter. In addition to four 20mm Hispano cannon under the forward fuselage, it could carry three Browning machine guns in each wing. Its two Bristol Hercules radial engines also enabled it to carry under its wings long-range fuel tanks, bombs, torpedoes or rockets. The Beaufighter was capable of deployment to a greater variety of use than any other aircraft, until the arrival of the Mosquito, the original multi-role combat aircraft.

The Beaufighter Mk VIF night-fighter had a top speed of some 330mph, and a range of around 1,500 miles. The plane's design and construction strength allowed it to shrug off remarkable amounts of enemy fire, and permitted its two-man crew to survive a crash-landing which normally could be fatal. Despite being heavy and unwieldy to manoeuvre, once pilots were experienced in their characteristics they were devoted to the Beaufighter.[19]

During May 1944, as Allied armies surged north from Cassino and Anzio, Lieutenant Jack Ingate and his fellow pilots of 600 Squadron scoured the night skies for intruding enemy aircraft. Every night their Beaufighters, sometimes as many as nine aircraft, were out on defensive patrols seeking a radar contact with an enemy 'bandit' or 'bogey'. Finding and closing in on a radar contact, unsure whether it was friend or foe, demanded painstaking and disciplined work by the two-man crew.

The Beaufighter's navigator/radio/radar operator was confronted by radio/radar jamming by German ground defences, and 'Window' tinfoil dropped by enemy aircraft, which would snow the reception of the aircraft's radar equipment. Patrol durations, depending upon contacts and other circumstances of operational activity, could last even beyond five hours. On the night of 14/15 May 1944 a typical eight Beaufighters took off on defensive patrols, in staggered departures from 2015 to 0405 from their base at Marcianise.

14/15 May 1944, No. 600 Squadron RAF Operations Record Book (summarized extracts):

> At 0020 on 15 May in a Beaufighter Mk VIII AI, Flight Lieutenant G.B.S. Coleman DFC and Australian Flying Officer N.R. Frumar took off from their Marcianise air base in a defensive patrol. It was a clear night with flak and explosions seen some 20 miles out to sea, and the lights of Allied Army motor transport convoys visible, as they pushed out many miles into enemy territory. At 0400 Coleman and Frumar were vectored by ground control onto a bogey.
>
> Within a few minutes they obtained contact with the target over mountainous terrain. It was at a two-mile range, and slightly above their altitude. Despite the bandit jinking violently to evade the Beaufighter's pursuit, they held onto the contact. Coleman closed up to about 1,000 feet from the target, and visually identified the aircraft as a Ju87B Stuka dive-bomber.
>
> At 0415 Coleman opened fire. Simultaneously the Stuka hurtled into a steep dive down amongst the mountain peaks, which prevented observation of any damage to the Ju87B. Because the Beaufighter was already low on fuel, Coleman was unable to pursue. When they arrived back at Marcianise at 0515, Coleman and Frumar had clocked up a flight time of 4.55 hours.
>
> Some two hours after Coleman and Frumar's departure, at 0230, Australian Flying Officer S.F. Rees and Flying Officer D.C. Bartlett lifted off their Beaufighter Mk VIF AI (No. V6574) from Marcianise. North of the River Tiber sometime after 0400 they made contact with a bogey and gave chase. When close enough they identified a Ju88. This time there was no escape for the German intruder, and at 0441 Rees shot down the German bomber. Rees and Bartlett returned to Marcianise at 0520.

Frequently after being vectored onto a suspected bogey and contact acquired, it could be lost not only through enemy radar jamming, and 'Window' interference, but also by the target outrunning the Beaufighter or escaping into cloud. In many instances Beaufighters would intercept a vectored bogey, only to find it was another Allied aircraft.

29/30 May 1944, No. 600 Squadron RAF Operations Record Book (summarized extracts):

On 29 May from 0200, on a defensive patrol from Marcionise, Flying Officer A.M. Davidson and Warrant Officer J.A. Telford were flying their Beaufighter Mk VIF AI (No. MM905). On three occasions, 0320, 0350, and 0450, they were vectored and obtained contacts on bogeys coming from the north. All three contacts were identified as Allied Boston bombers.

In the evening of 29 May at 2225 Warrant Officer D. Kerr and Warrant Officer G.H. Wheeler lifted their Beaufighter Mk VIF AI (No. ND148) into the night sky from Marcianise. At 2225 in the vicinity of Anzio they were vectored on to a slow-flying aircraft. Twelve miles north-east of Anzio they obtained contact. After a six-minute chase they had closed to about 500 feet of the target, when the suspected bandit dived and contact was lost. Another contact, possibly the same target, was picked up immediately.

Kerr closed up to minimum range but then overshot. Kerr carried out the overshoot procedure, and again closed up to the minimum range from target. In a brief visual identification Kerr and Wheeler identified the contact as a Ju87 Stuka, moments before it flew into a bank of mist. Before Kerr could line up his guns on the German dive-bomber, it dived and radar contact was lost in ground return interference. During the rest of the patrol Kerr and Wheeler obtained and chased three more contacts where, through the targets' evasive action, their pursuit proved fruitless. After a flight time of 4.05 hours they safely landed their Beaufighter back at Marcianise at 0230 on 30 May.[20]

The night-fighters of 600 Squadron were waging an unremitting air war of attrition, often tedious, exasperating, energy sapping and at the same time nerve-racking, yet unspectacular, unseen and little recognized. But the cloak of the night must not allow the Luftwaffe to make a resurgence.

* * *

The next attack on Cassino and the Gustav Line, Operation DIADEM, was planned for early May by the combined forces of Fifth and Eighth Armies. The timing was significant. Together with the simultaneous break-out from Anzio, Operation BUFFALO, there would be less than a month before the planned D Day landings in Normandy. The hope was that the offensives would draw German attention and their forces to Italy, and away from Normandy and north-west Europe. At the same time Operations DIADEM and BUFFALO in themselves must succeed. Any further stalemate or defeats in Italy could be catastrophic, and allow the Germans to divert divisions to Normandy. A strategic loss in Italy would be a huge psychological blow to the Allies in all theatres.

The night of 11 May 1944 was set for the fourth battle to begin, the hoped for final battle for Cassino and the Monte Cassino Monastery. With the bulk of Eighth Army now added to Fifth Army, the Allies planned to throw over-whelming force at the mountain bastion. In a concentration of numbers, firepower and a massive artillery bombardment, they intended to smash their way through the Gustav Line and north onto Highway 6.[21] It was not just a pincer movement of ground forces. While Allied movements had little or no fear from Luftwaffe air raids, the German Army found in retreat that they were under constant attack from Allied air forces.

In one instance on May 14, 239 Wing targeted some 200 or so vehicles trying to withdraw at Subiaco. By the day's end there were an estimated 120 destroyed or damaged. In the last six days of May Allied fighters and fighter-bombers claimed 1,148 vehicles of all types destroyed and 766 damaged. This may have even been under-stated. Between Cori and Artena on the Adolf Hitler Line, Fifth Army counted 211 vehicles wrecked clearly by air strikes, whereas air force claims had only estimated 173.[22] With the waning of the Luftwaffe's attempted offensive, and its inability to stem the Allied armies' offensive, DAF operations became predominantly fighter-bomber attacks against the retreating columns of enemy troops.

During this time, while DAF once more was asserting its air superiority, Wing Commander Hugh Dundas could only watch from the sidelines. He was not able to join 244 Wing RAF until his appointment came through at the end of May. The Spitfire fighters of 244 Wing had built an enviable record through the North African desert war, Alamein, Tunisia, Sicily and southern Italy. As the Allies broke out of the Gustav Line and Anzio, Dundas must have looked on with heightened interest, as 244 Wing added to their exploits in the air battles of May.

In a desperate attempt to make an impact, the Luftwaffe threw all its remaining fighters and fighter-bombers into the fray. The air battles once again included Squadron Leader Neville Duke, recently returned from a period in training duties, to lead No. 145 Squadron RAF in 244 Wing. Over Arezzo, close to Florence, on 13 May Duke led a patrol of six Spitfires into an engagement with six Bf109s. Duke expressed his relish to be back in an aerial battle with the Luftwaffe, showing his typical confidence in himself and his aircraft:

> Great things at last! We met up with six Me109s ... and we had a good dice. I got a burst at one and saw strikes under its belly before he rolled down and off. Stayed up and dodged and turned for a bit, finally fixing

onto one up above, whom I climbed and turned with, easily climbing and out-turning him.

As the 109 tried violent evasive action, Duke stayed with him and saw his fire strike its fuselage and engine. Parts fell off the enemy fighter as it plunged into a death spin. Soon after he saw the explosion where the 109 crashed, for his first confirmed victory in Italy.[23]

When Dundas took up his appointment as commander on 31 May and arrived at 244 Wing, he found a massive celebration underway at an abandoned farmhouse. Each of the wing's five squadrons had set up a bar, and were in competition to serve the strongest alcoholic drink. He learnt that the party was to mark 244 Wing's 400th victory of the war. Between 13 and 31 May, when the Luftwaffe found a way to launch a significant challenge in the air, 244 Wing shot down twenty-three enemy aircraft, three probable, and another twenty badly damaged.[24]

Although Allied air power confronted and killed off the Luftwaffe's desperate attempt at a counter-attack, the real questions were on the ground. Could Operation DIADEM, at last bursting through the Gustav Line, combine with the break-out from Anzio? Would Fifth and Eighth Armies in the Allies' pincer strategy, Operation BUFFALO, crush and destroy the German Tenth Army as if in a vice?

Notes
 1. Evans, op. cit., pp. 141–2.
 2. Owen, op. cit., p. 251.
 3. Molesworth, op. cit., pp. 88–9.
 4. Owen, op. cit., pp. 249–51.
 5. Smith et al., op. cit., pp. 6–7.
 6. Veterans' accounts, F/Lt Rod McKenzie.
 7. Thomas, op. cit., pp. 69–70.
 8. Gibbes, 3 Squadron RAAF (www.3squadron.org.au), *You Live But Once* (extract).
 9. Thomas, op. cit., pp. 69–70.
10. Dundas, op. cit., pp. 143–4.
11. Molesworth, op. cit., p. 87.
12. Owen, op. cit., p. 258.
13. Ayris, *Kittyhawk Pilots*, p. 87.
14. Owen, op. cit., p. 258.
15. Ibid., p. 255.
16. Ibid., p. 256.
17. Ibid., p. 257.
18. Thomas, op. cit., pp. 72–3.
19. Bowyer, op. cit., pp. 212 & 224–6.
20. NA Kew, AIR 27/2062, ORB, 600 Squadron RAF
21. Evans, op. cit., pp. 146–7.
22. Owen, op. cit., p. 258.
23. Thomas, op. cit., pp. 73–4.
24. Dundas, op. cit., p. 145.

Chapter 14

Rome to the Gothic Line – Allied fighters rule the skies

Operations Record Book, No. 145 Squadron RAF (summarized extract 21 May 1944):

> On 21 May 1944 near Anzio Squadron Leader Neville Duke led eight Spitfires of his 145 Squadron in an attack on more than twenty Fw190s. This forced the enemy fighter-bombers to jettison their bombs over their own lines. Duke shot down two Fw190s, and his fellow pilots another six, for a total of eight destroyed, one probable, and one damaged.[1]

But the day also belonged to Flying Officer J.S. 'Joe' Ekbery. The twenty-three-year-old Ekbery dived after three fleeing 190s. He caught up with his first 190 to give it a burst at 200 yards. As it spun out of control trailing black smoke, he closed in on another. Again Ekbery fired from about 200 yards, hitting its wing and fuselage, to force the pilot to bale out. He then pursued a third 190 first seen some six miles east of Rome. Ekbery caught up with the 190 from a quarter astern on its port side, and fired from only 150 yards. The 190 went straight down and crashed. Ekbery's three victories made him an ace.[2]

More important was that 145 Squadron claimed eight Fw190s in just one day to inflict a crushing blow on the Luftwaffe. A major enemy raid using its formidable Fw190 fighter-bombers was probably the largest the Luftwaffe in Italy could put together at that time. And it was as though it had been brushed aside with disdain. Flight Lieutenant Norman Brown, who wrote up the Operations Record Book of 145 Squadron, thought it was Duke's greatest victory in Italy.

*   *   *

The breakthrough at Cassino, Operation DIADEM, had come on the morning of 18 May 1944, when the last of the German defenders had fled from the rubble of Monte Cassino monastery. Four divisions of Eighth Army with more than 20,000 vehicles began to move north up the Liri Valley's Highway 6, in pursuit of the Germans' Tenth Army. In order to join up with Allied forces also breaking out from Anzio, it was urgent to follow up quickly on the breakout at Cassino and prevent the Germans re-establishing their

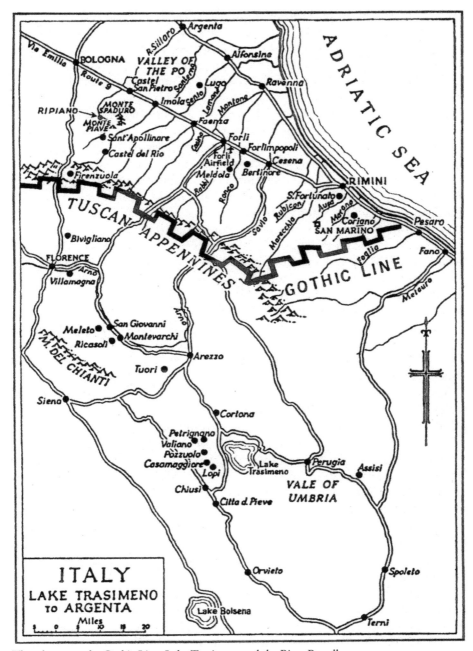

The advance to the Gothic Line, Lake Trasimeno and the River Po valley.

defences on the Adolf Hitler Line. Acting as a back-up defence to the Gustav Line, the Adolf Hitler Line stretched from the coast through Aquino and close to Piedimonte, to join the Gustav Line near Monte Cairo. For Operation DIADEM to succeed, and with it any hope of a quick liberation of Rome, Eighth Army must race north from Cassino, and immediately smash through the Adolf Hitler Line.

The Allied command in Italy lobbied London and Washington for additional forces in order to exploit the victories at Cassino and Anzio to liberate Rome, so as to then accelerate a drive into northern Italy. The underlying motive was to draw German forces away from north-west Europe, in particular Normandy, where the Operation OVERLORD landings were anticipated in early June. However, Eisenhower and the American Joint Chiefs of Staff believed that Operation ANVIL, a landing in the south of France, would draw even more German troops away from Operation OVERLORD.

The main attack on the Adolf Hitler Line, Operation CHESTERFIELD, began on 23 May, and was coordinated with a break-out from the Anzio bridgehead further north up the coast, Operation BUFFALO. The plan required Truscott's VI Corps, part of Clark's Fifth Army, to break out from Anzio and move from the coastal Route 7 inland to cut Route 6. Then, as Eighth Army pursued the German Tenth Army up the Liri Valley on Route 6, Truscott's VI Corps must block them at Valmontone. The trap was being closed when, on 25 May, Clark sent orders to Truscott to turn back with the bulk of his VI Corps and head north up Route 7 towards Rome.

As a consequence the German Tenth Army brushed aside the small, residual contingent of VI Corps troops and made its escape northwards. This left the question as to where the Germans would make a stand. Hitler feared that if Tenth Army sought to defend Rome, it could be enmeshed in another 'Stalingrad-like' defeat. He approved the retreat to continue past the Italian capital, and declared it an open city. Subsequently, on 4 June, Fifth Army entered Rome. Meanwhile German forces streamed northwards past Rome in retreat to regroup and fight on at a place and time more to their choosing. Two days later on 6 June, D-Day, the Allies in Operation OVERLORD landed in Normandy.

Despite the failure of Operation BUFFALO to trap and destroy the German Tenth Army, Allied forces pressed on in pursuit. At this time they had twenty-eight divisions and unchallenged air superiority against the badly mauled and retreating twenty-one divisions of the Germans. General Alexander still hoped to reach the River Po valley or even the Alps before winter set in. The theory was that from there he could plan to drive on to Vienna in the spring, or even into the Balkans to beat the Russian advance.

Any such vision was short-lived. The Americans' insistence on the priority for allocating force strength to Operation ANVIL, the invasion of southern

France, won the day. By early July eleven divisions had been transferred from Italy to ANVIL. The southern France invasion later came to be known as Operation DRAGOON, in recognition of the forces commandeered from Italy.

In the transfer were four divisions of the experienced French Expeditionary Corps, and their mountain troops. The loss of such specialist forces experienced in the Italian mountain ranges would be sorely felt. For ahead of Fifth and Eighth Armies between Rome and the River Po stretched the Tuscan Apennines, which swing across country from the west coast north of Florence to the east almost to the Adriatic shore. Farther south there was a more immediate barrier, the Albert Line, through Umbria's mountains around Lake Trasimene.

Kesselring had built the Albert Line from Grosseto on the west coast along the Ombrone river around the southern edge of Lake Trasimene and across to the east coast north of Pescara. It was meant to delay the Allies reaching the strategic ports of Livorno in the west and Ancona in the east. The Allies' first objective was to capture Florence on the River Arno. While Fifth Army nearer the west coast was making for Pisa, Eighth Army tackled the Albert Line and Umbrian hills heading for Florence. Could the Germans be caught before they reached the Tuscan Apennines, where for a year or more they had been preparing their Gothic Line defences.[3]

From the start of their retreat from Cassino and Anzio, the Germans had their eyes on making for the Gothic Line. They saw it as their final defensive line in Italy, using the Tuscan Apennines to guard the Po Valley, and Italy's industrial north. Even so it was still the Germans' usual practice to withdraw at night leaving booby-traps, mines and rearguards to provide covering fire during the next day, to obstruct and slow down the Allies' pursuit. For they knew that the months of stalemate at Cassino and Anzio, and every day they gained from here on, was enabling the Gothic Line to be built into their toughest defensive barrier.[4]

* * *

As the Allied armies pursued the Germans in their retreat, DAF moved its squadrons and HQ with them, from south of Rome at Castrocielo, and in step with Eighth Army. Allied bombing of Rome itself had concentrated on the rail marshalling yards, sparing most of the buildings of antiquity. At the same time DAF operations in support of the partisans in Yugoslavia continued in conjunction with the newly formed Balkan Air Force. At times when the weather curtailed operations in Italy there were better flying conditions on the other side of the Adriatic. However, in raids on Yugoslavian towns and cities heavy flak was bringing some heavy casualties.[5]

After Rome was liberated by the Allies on 4 June, enemy aircraft engagements began to be infrequent. The Luftwaffe and its recently formed Italian ally, the Aeronautica Nazionale Republiccana (ANR) of the puppet Italian Government in northern Italy, were being dominated in the skies by the Allies' air forces. It allowed many Spitfire squadrons to be converted to a fighter-bomber role for attacking enemy ground forces and interdiction missions. Ironically, this was thought to result in higher losses and casualties from the enemy's anti-aircraft fire. Compared with holding their fate in their own hands in dogfights with enemy fighters, many pilots felt that in the fighter-bomber role they were at the mercy of anti-aircraft fire, and at greater risk of being hit.

*   *   *

Neville Duke had enjoyed a very productive period with 145 Squadron in May, personally claiming five victories. Yet there was always a price to pay. On that day of 21 May, when Duke's section had claimed eight FW 190 victories in a single engagement, on returning to base he had found that his No. 2, Flying Officer Somers, was missing. For hours Duke hung around the squadron's dispersal area, longing to see Somers' Spitfire appear in the sky. He remained missing, with no-one knowing what had happened to him. Somers would be the only No. 2 pilot Duke lost in the war.

On 7 June Duke, with fellow pilots McKenzie, Milborrow and Anderson, took off on the squadron's first strafing operation. While in a low level attack on a convoy of enemy trucks in the Rieti region he became another victim of the air-to-ground war, when flak or even ricocheting friendly fire off the ground, hit his Spitfire. The engine began to vibrate immediately and burst into flames. Even as he strove to gain some height, Duke was engulfed with smoke and flames streamed either side of his cockpit. He rolled the aircraft onto its back and at the same time slid back the cockpit canopy. Then, as he attempted to fall backwards out of the Spitfire, Duke found he was jammed in by his parachute.

By kicking hard he fell free and pulled his ripcord handle. As the parachute billowed out, one of the shoulder straps snapped, causing Duke to hang precariously to the harness. Finally he came to earth, or rather fell into the nine-mile wide Lake Bracciano. In the water Duke must have felt that fate was against him. He could not free himself from one of the parachute's leg straps. The chute billowed in the wind, dragging and part submerging him across the lake. As he thought he was going to drown, Duke looked up at the sky, and thought he could see the rest of his section circling above him. One of those pilots, hoping against hope that Duke would survive, was his wingman and friend from Egypt, Australian Flight Lieutenant Rod McKenzie:[6]

> I stayed there circling alone, until a boat of Italians picked him up. I wrote in my log book, 'CO got a glycol leak and had to bail out. He landed in Lake Bracciano, and I covered him all the time. Never got a squirt.'[7]

Where Axis fighters did make an appearance they were both outnumbered and outclassed by such as the Spitfire. On 15 June Wing Commander Tony Lovell of 322 Wing, an experienced fighter ace, led a formation of Spitfires from 243 Squadron into an encounter south of Piacenza with a group of Italian ANR fighters. Lovell claimed a Fiat G.55 for his twenty-second victory, which would prove to be his last of the war.[8]

On 15 and 16 June Wing Commander Dundas' 244 Wing lost four Spitfires and their pilots to anti-aircraft fire. Because of the reduced numbers of enemy fighters to be confronted, the Spitfires were flying low-level air-to-ground strafing missions. Soon after, in late June, Dundas received orders to convert his squadrons to Spitbombers for the fighter-bomber role. They had one week to make the modifications and learn the new tactics for dropping bombs. Running the gauntlet of anti-aircraft fire was only going to get worse.

On 10 July Dundas was leading an interdiction operation from their base at Perugia to bomb a target close to Arezzo. There was a loud bang and thuds against his fuselage. Hot white smoke surged into his cockpit, telling him that an 88mm shell had exploded very close, its fragments rupturing the Spitfire's glycol tank. Dundas instantly banked into a dive, and pulled his cockpit canopy release lever, to be ready to bale out. However, instead of the canopy being dragged away from the aircraft by the slipstream, it slammed down onto his head.

Stunned, half-aware his face was cut and bleeding, Dundas managed to push the canopy out of his cockpit. Despite being befuddled and scared, he could see that he was down to only 5,000 feet, and his engine was running hotter and hotter. The hill country below prohibited a forced landing, and in his condition he could not face baling out. Dundas set the Spitfire in the direction he thought was towards Castiglione, but feared the aircraft would not hold up long enough to reach its airfield.

As he gradually lost height, the temperature of the Spitfire's engine surpassed 110 degrees. Then Dundas caught a glimpse ahead of Lake Castiglione about eight miles away. But did he have the height, and would the engine blow up before he reached the airfield? A few minutes later he found himself in line with the runway. As the temperature went beyond 125 degrees Dundas cut the engine, switched off the fuel and everything else, and dropped his wheels. He glided down, rolled to a stop, and pulled off his goggles and oxygen mask. His right hand then felt the warm blood from his split face; a cut from outside his eye had slashed across his cheek. Soon after he was in an ambulance. He had made it after all.[9]

Another Spitfire ace, Flight Lieutenant Turkington, was flying a reconnaissance Spitfire of No. 241 Squadron RAF on 19 July near Ancona, when he came upon two Bf109 fighters. Disregarding the aim of his tactical reconnaissance mission, he gave chase. Turkington caught up with one of the Bf109s, shot it down in flames, and saw the pilot bale out. In the days and weeks following the Allied armies' surge out from the static battlegrounds of Anzio and Cassino, DAF and other Allied fighters, particularly the Spitfire squadrons, confronted and defeated the Luftwaffe's last major challenge in Italy. Flight Lieutenant Turkington went on to claim three more 109s before the end of July.[10]

From Rome to the Gothic Line Allied ground forces made the most rapid rate of advance in Italy. It meant that DAF responded, to maintain their effectiveness of close air support for Eighth Army, by taking its principle of 'moving and operating simultaneously' to a new level. This was only made possible by the resilient morale and adaptability of DAF ground services, such as signals, maintenance, supply, medical services, and many others to keep moving from airfield to airfield, and delivering the services at the same time as relocating, to keep the squadrons continually in the air.

Trailers with mobile hot showers providing a thirty-second burst were part of continual efforts to maintain hygiene and combat sickness, including venereal disease and malaria. Mobile field hospitals, as they had in North Africa and now in the Apennines, carried out emergency surgery, X-rays and laboratory testing. Many airmen survived because of the clinical staff providing these services, and prominent among them were Princess Mary's Royal Air Force Nursing Service.[11]

By late July elements of Eighth Army had reached the banks of the River Arno, and in early August were pushing towards Florence. In the face of the Allies' offensive, in the first two weeks of August Kesselring began pulling his forces out of Florence. The German forces began a withdrawal to the north up to the Gothic Line in the Tuscan mountains. The Gothic Line stretched along the Tuscan Apennines from Spezia on the east coast, north-west of Florence, then south and due east across the breadth of Italy.[12]

For over a year the Germans had been using forced labour to construct the Gothic Line – a highly developed series of strongpoints stretching for about 200 miles across the Italian peninsula. It skirted the principality of San Marino, before reaching the Adriatic coast above Pesaro, and south of Rimini. In this Apennine mountain range, which barred access to the River Po Valley, and the industrial heartland of northern Italy, the Allies faced a ferocious struggle.

Nevertheless, on 19 July the Tactical Air Force and its HQ (NATAF) transferred to Corsica to support Operation DRAGOON, the invasion of southern France. It left DAF on its own in Italy to provide battlefield support for both Fifth and Eighth Armies. Operation DRAGOON, as well as the transfer of many divisions from the two armies, also led to the transfer of some DAF squadrons.[13]

The DAF principal strength and dispositions in August 1944 were:[14]

	Wings	Squadrons	Location
West Coast		Det Flt 92 Squadron	Rosignano
		HQ and Flt	
		600 Squadron	
	232		Cecina/Fano
Central Sector	7 (SAAF)		Florence
(OPS A, and		208 Squadron	Florence
MORU B)		12 (US) Squadron	Florence
	239		Jesi
East Coast	253		Falconara
		Det 255 Squadron	Falconara
		Flt 600 Squadron	Falconara
	3 (SAAF)		Pescara/Jesi
	244		Borghetto
	285		Mazzolaio/Piagiolino

To further strengthen air support for Operation DRAGOON, DAF's 322 and 324 Squadrons, and the 79th Fighter Group transferred temporarily across to Corsica. To compensate for this loss in Italy DAF increased its sorties to 340 per day, and on 15 August exceeded 500 sorties. The higher level of operational activity did not, however, stop DAF from holding a dance at its host hotel in Assissi. While the DAF Band played jive and blues, the invited single ladies of the town seemed distracted. Suffering with the rest of the civilian population from chronic food shortages, they were more intent on packing away as much of the buffet as they could into their handbags.[15]

When Eighth Army pierced the Gothic Line and advanced into eastern Emilia Romagna it was supported heavily by DAF fighter-bombers in ground attack roles. Casualties from enemy flak mounted, and death in many guises awaited pilots. On the west coast Flight Lieutenant Montgomerie of No. 92 Squadron RAF shot down a Bf109 on 25 August over the enemy's La Spezia naval base. The victory made him a Spitfire ace. Next day Montgomerie returned from pursuit of an Me410 reconnaissance intruder and when his engine failed on approach, possibly from flak damage, he crashed on landing. The next day he died from his injuries. Montgomerie proved to be the last Spitfire pilot to become an ace in the Mediterranean theatre.[16]

When on 26 August, Eighth Army launched its attack on Pesaro on the Adriatic coast it found the town to be fiercely defended by the Germans' 1st Parachute Division. It turned once again to DAF for support. The response was Operation CRUMPET, for which AVM Dickson called upon the Strategic Air Force for assistance. After listening to the needs expounded by Eighth Army, it was a judgement decision he had to make. This also meant that DAF had to suspend other operations to concentrate on Operation CRUMPET, one example being No. 7 Wing SAAF who flew 115 sorties bombing Pesaro. In the first two days 205 Group dropped near 600 tons of bombs on Pesaro, to force the German paratroopers to withdraw.[17]

As the campaign pushed into autumn DAF was pursuing three core strategies. Depending upon circumstances priority could change for any one of the three: interdiction to sever enemy supplies close to the battlefield; close support to Allied ground forces; and various support missions for the Yugoslav partisans. At the beginning of September, as if it had accepted that it was pointless to contest Italian airspace any further, the Luftwaffe transferred all of its remaining day fighter units to Germany.[18]

Only some Bf109 night-fighters remained in northern Italy. Near Ravenna on 3 September Squadron Leader Neville Duke went after some of those 109 night-fighters.

Operations Record Book, No. 145 Squadron RAF (summarized extract):

At first light the CO (Squadron Leader Neville Duke) lifted off leading an Anti-Reconnaissance patrol over the battle area. At 0645 control reported 2 Bogeys going north-west at 13,000 feet off Pesaro. The CO searched the area and saw two aircraft cross the coast going north west in the Cesenatico area about five miles away. Giving chase he caught them up, identified them as Me109s [Bf109s], and was getting in range when a third Me109 was seen lagging behind the other two. Pulling into this third enemy aircraft, the CO fired from 400–600 yards astern seeing strikes behind the cockpit.

He closed to 200–300 yards gaining further strikes, seeing the hood fly off, the pilot bale out, the Me109 burst into flames and crash. S/Ldr Duke then turned on the other two, and after a dive from 9,000 feet and a climb up to 15,000 feet, he closed rapidly on the No. 1 and fired from 200–300 yards astern, starting a fire behind the cockpit. The pilot baled out, and the Me109 went down in flames.[19]

These two victories took Duke's tally to twenty-seven, plus two shared, one probable and six damaged. At only twenty-two years old, and after 486 sorties and 712 hours in operations, he had become the top scoring Allied fighter pilot in the Mediterranean.[20]

On 13 September under Duke's leadership 145 Squadron completed the most sorties namely sixty, as 244 Wing recorded 251 sorties in one day. This beat their previous record of 247 in North Africa. Great credit as always was due to the ground crew, who maintained ten to twelve aircraft serviceability, when only twelve to thirteen were available.[21]

Duke completed his third operational tour on 23 September, was awarded a second Bar to his DFC, and was posted back to UK. Flight Lieutenant

Norman Brown wrote with feeling in the 145 Squadron's operations record book:

> It is hard to put into words the loss the squadron has sustained. Neville Duke has had a distinguished career which is unparalleled by any fighter pilot in the Mediterranean theatre of war. His leadership, keenness and personal charm are qualities which will never be forgotten.[22]

* * *

With the Germans having withdrawn to the Gothic Line, Alexander had agreed a plan for Eighth Army to move to the east, in order to launch an offensive towards Rimini on the Adriatic coast. It would be followed by a Fifth Army attack in the mountains in the centre of the Gothic Line. The plan for Eighth Army was to drive into Emilia-Romagna and the Po Valley. Three Divisions were to cross the Marecchia River ten miles south of Rimini, then to burst through the Rimini Line, which was part of the eastern Gothic Line. It began on 13 September; Canadian troops crossed the Marecchia River, and then reached Highway 9, the Via Emilia. The following day 4th Division attacked, crossing the Marano and Ausa rivers, and on 19 September were thrown into heavy hill fighting to assault San Fortunato at the end of the Coriano Ridge.

When in its advance towards Rimini Eighth Army was held up at the Fortunata Ridge, DAF received a request for close support. Once again like so many others the request was branded with the catchphrase 'like at El Hamma'. Sometimes such a request referred to as ' DAF's secret weapon'. So at 1000 in the midst of other operations that had begun at dawn, Operation TIMOTHY began a 40 minute blitz to force German troops to bury their heads in the ground.[23]

A bomb-line for the blitz was marked by the artillery with blobs of white smoke, about a mile apart and 3,000 yards in front of the forward troops. About every fifteen minutes the bomb-line moved forward, controlled by the Rover David system, which coordinated the attacking aircraft. For about two hours DAF fighter-bomber squadrons of 244 Wing strafed the forward side of Fortunata Ridge at ten-minute intervals, while 239 Wing squadrons dropped fragmentation bombs on enemy gun positions on the reverse slope.[24]

Although Canadian troops were delayed from advancing immediately behind the aerial attack, the Fortunata Ridge was taken next day and Rimini the day after. The eastern end of the Via Emilia and the Gothic Line were in Allied hands. Eighth Army's appreciation of DAF support can be seen, when because of its success, 'Operation TIMOTHY' became the new catch-word, requested by the army at every opportunity.

Around this time Wing Commander Dundas received orders for a squadron from his 244 Wing to bomb and destroy an important road bridge north of Rimini. Every day from dawn to dusk his Spitfire pilots were flying into the steep-sided valleys of the Tuscan Apennines, and into a terrifying blizzard of flak. They all knew that this bridge was one of the most intensely defended targets of all. Dundas also knew that once again he must lead this operation.

In the operation briefing, when he saw the fear on the pilots' faces, he fully understood why. On these air-to-ground missions it was only luck that decided who survived. A fighter-bomber pilot could not defend himself against the flak. Some of those who survived long enough would succumb to that fear. Dundas felt that no-one could be more scared than he himself, but it was his job to make sure that fear was kept in check.

For this raid it was a fine clear day and the squadron's approach would be seen well in advance. Dundas led the formation northwards parallel with the coast then, once they were north of Rimini, he turned in towards land. Even before they crossed the coast, as Dundas set their course for their bridge target, which was still some five miles distant, shell bursts of black smoke were peppering them.

> The temptation to swerve was almost overpowering. I felt naked and exposed, and was sure that I was going to be hit. The target passed under my wing and I rolled over into a dive. Down through the black bursts, down headlong into the carpet of white, where the 40mm shells came up in their myriads to meet me, down further into the streaking tracer of machine-gun fire.[25]

Dundas dropped his bomb unscathed but stayed low as he turned for home. In this intensity of flak he thought it the best bet. He radioed the rest of the squadron to employ the same tactics and each make their own way back to base. Then his aircraft convulsed in a violent explosion. A shell had burst clear through the middle of his port wing. Incredibly the Spitfire kept flying. Somehow he limped home but, on touching down, a damaged wheel gave way. The aircraft twisted around, amazingly without flipping over, and came to rest with one wing jammed against the ground.

When Dundas walked into the mess his wing commander, Brian King-combe, and another senior officer greeted him light-heartedly with a laugh about his forced landing. Dundas gave him a curt response and in so many words told him where to go. Once in his quarters he collapsed on his bunk and thought that he had reached the end of his tether.[26]

The pressures building up on commanders like Dundas, and all pilots, were not surprising. DAF operations were targeting enemy positions in the imme-diate path of Allied offensives, at a level of concentration and repetition never previously maintained. In a message to AVM Dickson, General McCreery said:

> Please convey to all ranks of the Desert Air Force the gratitude and appre-ciation of the 8th Army for their magnificent close support throughout

our recent operations. Our forward troops have entire confidence in the accuracy of close-support bombing and express the greatest admiration for the dash and gallantry of your pilots.[27]

Just as the Gothic Line was breached, the Allies' other enemy appeared upon the scene. Heavy autumn rains had begun early on 20 September. Streams quickly became fast-flowing rivers, rivers swelled into raging torrents, fields turned to swamps, and tracks to glutinous mud. Any ideas to immediately make a rapid armoured drive north-west towards Bologna and the Po Valley, were put on hold.

*   *   *

In October, across Allied airfields, whether at Foggia, Bari, Falconara, Fano, Cecina or many others, winter rain began seriously to curtail operations. For the heavy bombers returning from long-haul raids on Germany and northern Italy, they struggled increasingly to find their way in the conditions and particularly on the return leg southwards to reach their bases near Foggia and Bari. With radios out of order, engines feathered, their petrol short, with wounded and dead aboard, they put down on the first concrete runway they could find behind the Allied lines.[28]

Despite being a mere sixteen miles from Bologna as the crow flies, Fifth Army was held up by the lethal combination of fierce German defences, mountainous terrain and the increasingly severe early winter. Operation PANCAKE, a combined operation by strategic and tactical air forces similar to Operation TIMOTHY, reached a crescendo in mid-October. It was meant to blast a way through the mountain pass to Bologna. However, in their rocky clefts and ravines, German troops were too well dug-in to be dislodged.

Despite the poor visibility, which reduced the number of missions throughout October, DAF still found a way to continually cut rail and road routes, and destroy bridges and enemy traffic. For their next chosen line to make a defensive stand, the Germans were falling back to the River Savio. By 15 October DAF had broken apart all the Savio's bridges. Yet there were few clear days, and in the second half of October the average daily number of sorties fell, with five days recording less than 100. Despite the deteriorating elements, during the month air power destroyed fifty-seven locomotives, sank fifty-two boats or barges, and damaged another 166 vessels.

Into November DAF continued interdiction operations against supply routes in northern Italy and Yugoslavia, as well as close support in response to requests from ground forces. In Eighth Army's battle for Forlì, DAF was asked to hit targets in the path of a planned advance by V Corps. Two squadrons of Kittyhawks, and one of Thunderbolts firing rockets, flew nearly 500 sorties in Operation BINGO. Their targets were electricity transformers feeding the Brenner Pass railway line. The Kittyhawks and the Thunderbolts between them claimed eighteen direct hits on the main buildings and twenty-three on the transformer installations.[29]

To keep the Brenner Pass open for supplies, the Germans concentrated anti-aircraft guns along its length. At the start of November 1943 there were 366 flak guns located at its key staging centres of Innsbruck, Bolzano, Trento and Verona. It was said to result in a flak barrage similar to that encountered at Messina. It contributed to the total of 713 Allied aircraft lost to flak in 1944.[30]

From the last week of November through to Christmas and the year's end, the weather closed in even more. Where missions could be mounted, low cloud, rain, mist, fog and snow in varying degrees meant that many sorties were unproductive. In the final two weeks of December, many DAF squadrons were effectively grounded on six of the days. When the weather prevented operations in Italy, often very poor visibility from multiple layers of cloud up to 20,000 feet, better conditions sometimes prevailed over the Adriatic and in Yugoslavia. This allowed DAF squadrons to assist the Balkan Air Force to hit infrastructure, road and rail traffic in support of the partisans.[31]

On one occasion when conditions were favourable for an operation over Yugoslavia, Captain Mike McCarthy led three sections of his 64th Fighter Squadron of the 57th Fighter Group in a raid on Split Harbour. Although McCarthy was wary of being intercepted by Bf109s and Fw190s from the Luftwaffe base at Mostar, they crossed the Adriatic without challenge.

On their approach to Split, as they had found before, the flak was very heavy. McCarthy saw a freighter moored to the dock and lined it up. He pushed the nose of his Thunderbolt down in a steep dive and aimed at the ship's funnel. Ignoring the flak bracketing his aircraft, McCarthy gave the vessel a burst of fire before releasing his bombs at the desired height and speed.

The bombs hit and exploded right next to the funnel. McCarthy's wingman also hit home, and the other sections followed up with more. Further explosions on the freighter signalled that it was carrying ammunition, and it quickly sank.[32]

During December 1944, despite the worsening weather, each squadron of the 57th Fighter Group managed to average about ninety missions for the month, and more than 600 sorties. On 13 December Captain Mike McCarthy led 64th Fighter Squadron in a dive-bombing attack on an enemy barracks. It was the squadron's 1,000th mission.[33] The same day, that other constant and unconquerable enemy of the Allies struck once again.

On 13 December came the first really serious fall of snow, the thermometer fell as low as fifteen degrees Fahrenheit, and even the fast mountain streams from the heights froze over. The cold, dry weather was less miserable for the men than the mud and the rain, but the mountain blizzards became a serious danger and the tracks, now sheets of glassy ice, were as difficult for vehicles as when they had been a foot deep in mud. Once again as transport became immobilized, supplies of any kind could only be moved by mules. The jeeps drove up as far as they could, then transferred their loads to mules. The final stretch was on men's backs to the forward positions. More and more the Allied troops in Italy were starved of ammunition, in favour of the Allied armies in north-west Europe advancing on Germany. In contrast the Germans were increasing their artillery firepower, exploiting their shorter supply routes and the narrower front lines.[34]

After losing squadrons to Operation ANVIL, when DAF received the news that they were also losing their AOC, AVM Dickson in another transfer out of Italy, it must have confirmed to them that their efforts were now viewed as subordinate to the air war in north-west Europe. To assist with the air campaign in the skies over Germany, AVM Dickson was recalled to London, to be succeeded by AVM Foster. Although from afar the land and air campaigns in Italy seemed disappointing, AVM Dickson's appointment showed that he had further enhanced both his own, and DAF's reputation.[35]

In Europe all eyes were on the Allied armies breaking out of Normandy and battling through northern France. At the same time, yet relatively unacknowledged, the ultimate titanic struggle of the Italian campaign was rapidly approaching. It would pit, so to speak, an unstoppable attacker against an unbreakable defence. The Germans would wait now in the water-logged Po valley and in those Tuscan mountains. While Allied armies in north-west Europe continued their gains towards the German heartland, the Russians also pushed the Germans back relentlessly. In comparison, it seemed to some that the Italian campaign was stuck in a stalemate. There was a fear that spring could bring a resumption of a battle of attrition.

Notes

 1. NA, Kew, AIR 27/987, ORB, 145 Squadron RAF.
 2. Thomas, op. cit., pp. 73–4.
 3. Neillands, op. cit., pp. 344–63; Evans, op. cit., pp. 158–61.
 4. Ford, op. cit., pp. 229–30; Evans, op. cit., pp. 158–61.
 5. Owen, op. cit., pp. 259–61.
 6. Bowyer, op. cit., pp. 190–1; Thomas, op. cit., pp. 73–4.
 7. Veteran's account, F/Lt Rod McKenzie; Duke, *Test Pilot*, pp. 94–6.
 8. Thomas, op. cit., p. 75.
 9. Dundas, op. cit., pp. 146–50.
10. Thomas, op. cit., p. 75.
11. Owen, op. cit., pp. 262–3.
12. Neillands, op. cit., pp. 364–8.
13. Owen, op. cit., p. 264.
14. Ibid., pp. 318–19.
15. Ibid., p. 266.
16. Thomas, op. cit., p. 76.
17. Owen, op. cit., pp. 269–70.

18. Ibid., pp. 270–3.
19. NA, Kew, AIR 27/987, ORB 145 Squadron RAF.
20. Thomas, op. cit., p. 76.
21. NA, Kew, AIR 27/987, op. cit.
22. Ibid.
23. Owen, op. cit., pp. 270–3.
24. Brookes, op. cit., p. 116; NA, Kew, AIR 27/987, op. cit.
25. Dundas, op. cit., pp. 151–2.
26. Ibid.
27. Owen, op. cit., pp. 270–3.
28. Ibid., p. 274.
29. Ibid., pp. 277–8.
30. Brookes, op. cit., p. 132
31. Owen, op. cit., p. 279.
32. McCarthy, op. cit., pp. 59–60.
33. Molesworth, op. cit., p. 105.
34. Ray, op. cit., pp. 176–9.
35. Owen, op. cit., p. 280.

Chapter 15

Could an air blitz open up Eighth Army's path to the River Po?

From the start of January 1945, until the next major offensive to be launched sometime in the spring, around 75 per cent of Allied air operations were to be of an interdiction nature. In late January the weather imposed a near total standstill. Heavy snow fell, curtailing operations of every kind, and each airfield had to wait for the blizzards to end before using manpower to clear the runways.

One day in early March when the weather was favourable, DAF activity illustrated a typical twenty-four hour period of DAF interdiction operations. In the evening twilight six Bostons and eight Baltimores, of 232 and 253 Wings respectively, lifted into the air to bomb a factory and stores depot. On their return journey they undertook road and rail reconnaissance before touching down before dawn next day at their home airfield. Other Bostons and Baltimores hit road, rail and barge routes, including Monselice and Rovigo in the Po valley that night. Also, not untypically, one of the Bostons did not return.

On that same evening a combined bomber/fighter-bomber raid was mounted to exploit reconnaissance intelligence on a concentration of rail traffic. Formations of Marauder bombers from No. 3 Wing SAAF, Thunderbolts from the 79th Fighter Group, Spitbombers from 244 Wing, Mustangs and Kittyhawks from 239 Wing descended on to an estimated 800 wagons on a line near Conegliano. A locomotive and 129 of the rolling stock were claimed destroyed or damaged. Bridges at Ponte Longo, Gorizia, Montereale and Cittadella were knocked out or damaged. In the same twenty-four hour period DAF Spitfires flew as escorts for Marauder and Mitchell bombers. In operations over the Balkans, Thunderbolts and Mustangs used rocket fire to destroy or damage fifteen locomotives, 106 wagons and fifty vehicles. For DAF airmen, both aircrew and ground staff, it was just another day.[1]

While there seemed to be no end to air interdiction operations, for Allied armies in the mountains of the Gothic Line, and in the south-eastern Po valley, the winter stalemate also remained a battle of attrition going nowhere. New thinking was required, not only to take the initiative and break through, but to prevent the Germans from moving some of their divisions back to confront the Allied armies fighting in north-west Europe. The Po valley is wedged between Lombardy and Venetia in the north, and the Tuscan Apennines in the south in the region of Emilia-Romagna.

At its core the Roman road, the Via Emilia, runs as a spine for 150 miles north-west from Rimini on the Adriatic to cross the Po at Piacenza. In summer the Emilia-Romagna can suffer a scorching heat, while in winter the Apennines' winds bring a bitter cold. Emilia-Romagna was the wedge which separated the German and Allied armies and, as winter began to wane, the region threatened to become a killing ground to rival Cassino and Anzio, to which it was already being compared.[2]

*   *   *

In the face of the awesome strength of the German defences, General McCreery of Eighth Army, together with General Clark who was now commander of 15th Army Group, put a very high priority on deception ploys and associated operations. From both intelligence sources and air reconnaissance, the enemy's positions appeared to be impregnable, unless assaulted by an overwhelming numerical advantage. Facing the Allies' seventeen divisions, nine in Fifth Army and eight in Eighth Army, was the Germans' Army Group C, which across its Tenth and Fourteenth Armies, and the Army of Liguria, could call upon twenty-seven divisions. All experience suggests that an attacking army could not succeed against an enemy defender favoured by the terrain, and against such an adverse ratio of force strength. And McCreery thought similarly:

> It really was a ridiculous situation. Not only were we battle weary, depleted, depressed, out-numbered and generally mucked about, but we who could least afford to find manpower, were being asked to send whole formations to France and Greece, and at a time I may add, when we were being ordered simultaneously to nail down sufficient divisions of the enemy, to make a worthwhile contribution to the whole war effort. . . .
>
> But during all this agonizing period we had some things going for us. We had aerial supremacy. The support we had there was derived from the Desert Air Force, which I believe to be the most skilled tactical air power in the world. It was the key to our survival and to our attack.[3]

McCreery's views really referred to the whole of Allied air power and its superiority in Italy. But for him and Eighth Army it was the ever present and responsive DAF, which had been with them through the desert wastes of North Africa, the invasion of Sicily, and the long hard slog through the Italian mainland, since the war began.

It is estimated that the approximate DAF strength and dispositions at the start of the spring offensive, Operation BUCKLAND/WOWSER, in April 1945 included the following formations[4]:

Wings	Squadrons	Aircraft Type/Details
232	55, 223 RAF	Baltimores, medium bombers
239	112, 250, 260 RAF 3 and 450 RAAF	Kittyhawks, Mustangs and Thunderbolts, fighters and fighter-bombers
244	92, 145, 601, 73, 417 RAF 1 SAAF	Spitfire fighters
285 Reconnaissance	2 PRU, 208 TR RAF 40 TR, 60 PR SAAF 1437 Flight SR	Fighter-bomber, and reconnaissance
324	72, 93, 111, 152, 243 RAF	Spitfire fighters
3 (SAAF)	12, 21, 24 SAAF	Bostons and Baltimores, medium bombers
7 (SAAF)	2, 4, 5 SAAF 600 RAF	Spitfire fighter-bombers Beaufighters and Mosquito, night-fighters
57th Fighter Group, USAAF 12th Air Force	64th, 65th, 66th, 319th	Warhawks, Mustangs and Thunderbolts, fighters and fighter-bombers
79th Fighter Group, USAAF 12th Air Force	85th, 86th, 87th, 316th	Warhawks, Mustangs and Thunderbolts, fighters and fighter-bombers

Lieutenant General Sir Richard McCreery had taken over command of Eighth Army in October 1943. He was a long-time supporter of DAF from his time in North Africa, when he served on the staff of Auchinleck and Alexander. On 19 December he had met with the new AOC-in-C of DAF, AVM Foster, to raise some concerns regarding air-army support operations. McCreery was unhappy about the way in which DAF was allocating its priorities for operations in close support of Eighth Army. By the close of their discussions there was a meeting of minds, and an understanding and agreement between the two new commanders on the Eighth Army–DAF partnership. It was cemented further on Christmas Day when McCreery dined with Foster in the DAF Mess.

It was well recognized that DAF was pre-eminent in innovative techniques and tactics to provide close army-air support on the battlefield. The new rapport between McCreery and Foster would soon put DAF to its ultimate test. It would be asked, with the rest of Tactical and Strategic Air Forces, to rise to its greatest challenge.[5] In short, Allied air power must make up for a numerical deficiency in ground forces compared with the enemy, and provide the cutting edge to win the coming battle.

* * *

A common view at the time held that, to break through German defences still in front of Fifth Army in the Tuscan Apennines, and facing Eighth Army in the Po valley, was nigh on impossible. It would require more divisions, horrendous losses of men, and reserves of troops to exploit any breakthrough, which the two Allied armies did not have. Furthermore, to make it worse, as the snows melted in the mountains, and rivers rose, the Germans were flooding large tracts of the Po Valley's low-lying land to limit the Allies' options for attack.[6]

The Allies faced a complex dilemma. They must wait for the drier weather of spring, although this was fraught with other risks. The better conditions and firmer terrain would not only enable both Allied armies to exploit their advantages in supplies, equipment and vehicles but better visibility for aerial bombing and army-air close support would allow full use of the Allies' trump card – air superiority. But the timing of the offensive was all important. Waiting for an improvement in the weather was just one factor. The attack must be commenced before the Germans were able to strengthen their entrenched defences further and, through doing so, a possibility that they might decide to transfer some divisions to north-west Europe. There was even a fear in McCreery's mind that the German Armies could retreat north across the Po up into the Alps, before he launched the attack. Above all Fifth and Eighth Armies must be well prepared and ready with their force concentrations and deployments.

On 24 March General Clark issued orders for the plan of attack to commence in early April. Phase 1 required Eighth Army to cross the Senio, Santerno and Reno rivers in the east, then break through the Argenta Gap to its north. In Phase 2 a few days later, Fifth Army would surge down from their central mountain positions into the Po Valley and strike for Bologna. The goal was to surround, then destroy or capture, all German forces south of the River Po. The language of Clark's orders conveyed the offensive's objective, as a final conquest of the Italian campaign. However, one single phrase in Clark's order, 'If fully successful,' betrayed an underlying doubt.[7]

General Alexander's Special Order of the Day in early April was also full of his typical confidence, even claiming that the battle for the River Po, 'will end the war in Europe'. At the same time, the ever optimistic and confident Alexander could not conceal some apprehension creeping in to his words: 'It will not be a walk-over; a mortally wounded beast can still be very dangerous.'[8]

The battle for the Po would begin on 9 April. The plan called for Eighth Army's four divisions of V Corps, to drive across the Senio and Santerno rivers, and make the all-important first, and major, incision into the German defences. General von Vietinghoff's Tenth Army, despite losing two divisions to the western and eastern fronts, confronted Eighth Army with four divisions of I Parachute Corps, and three divisions of LXXVI Panzer Corps.[9] First the

Indian and New Zealand divisions would cross the Senio and then advance another eight miles to establish bridgeheads across the Santerno. Next 56th and 78th Divisions would exploit the crossings, and drive another ten miles north to break through the Argenta Gap.

The high level of preparation and training for the offensive was such that, the officers and men who were charged with leading the attack, were confident of success. Morale appeared to be higher than at almost any time in Italy, and the desertion problem of 1944 had virtually disappeared. Later after the war some men would disclose that, inside they held misgivings and feared a disastrous defeat. Numerous canals and rivers, each protected by high earthworks and dykes, hid well dug-in German defences, which must first be overcome, merely to reach the south bank of the Po. The attack could founder at any one. Even if the Po could be reached and crossed, it was feared that, like so many previous river crossings, the Germans would escape again to fight once more on its north side, and subsequently melt away in retreat up into the Alps.

So as to give their armies south of the Po even more protection, the Germans had flooded vast areas of the Po valley. The result was that a corridor of high ground about four miles long and up to three miles wide, was bordered on its west side by the flooded land south of the River Reno, and on its east by Lake Comácchio, which adjoined the Adriatic Sea. This narrow corridor carried the only route north, Highway 16, from Ravenna across the rivers Lamone, Senio, Santerno and Reno, through the small town of Argenta, and onwards to Ferrara and the Po. It was to become famous around the world as the culminating clash of the Italian campaign, the battle of the Argenta Gap.[10]

There were many in the infantry who had some scepticism about the outcome. The pattern of the many previous river crossings, when the Germans withdrew to a new defensive line, could be repeated once again. And it was not just one more river crossing. It was a battle which required at least half a dozen canal and river crossings before even reaching the mighty Po itself.[11]

This concern also occupied McCreery. By making use of two small aircraft, a Beech C-45 Expeditor provided by the USAAF, and a two-seat Taylorcraft Auster as used by the Royal Artillery for air observation, McCreery undertook many personal reconnaissance flights. On one of these flights McCreery, was able to see where commandos using the Buffalo amphibious vehicles could make a preliminary and diversionary attack across Lake Comácchio, to land north of the Reno river. It would turn the German left flank, and open up the way to the Argenta Gap. These reconnaissance flights over the battle area by McCreery, could be made with little risk of interception by the Luftwaffe, simply because of the air superiority and domination of the skies won and sustained by DAF.[12]

At the beginning of April DAF issued orders for its own role in the impending attack. Group Captain Dundas, with his Wing Commander of 244 Wing,

New Zealander Ron Barry DFC, were summoned with their counterparts of other wings, to a meeting at DAF HQ. Dundas had been promoted in November 1944 to succeed his predecessor, Brian Kingcombe, who had been posted back to UK. At the age of only twenty-four Dundas was in command of 244 Wing's five squadrons, about 100 aircraft and pilots, the ground crews of repairs and maintenance, in all about 2,000 men. Despite being ever more stressed and fatigued, Dundas threw himself into the job. Determined to enhance the wing's performance in supporting the army, he and Barry introduced a second bomb-rack for the Spitfire, allowing it to carry two 500lb bombs.

At the DAF HQ meeting Dundas heard of the overall plan for Fifth and Eighth Armies, Operation GRAPESHOT, in which it was intended to hit the Germans with the largest yet opening air blitz. It was planned to be greater than that suffered by British and French troops prior to Dunkirk. This unprecedented air-to-ground onslaught would help Eighth Army cross the river Senio which, although more of a stream, was protected by high flood-banks against spring floods. Close air support would then maintain continual attacks on enemy positions in the Army's path. Interdiction operations were also planned to destroy all road and rail bridges across the Po, the aim of which was two-fold. First, their destruction would cut or seriously curtail the enemy's supplies to the battlefield. The second goal was to prevent any retreat by German forces across the Po. Of course the air blitz and the sustaining of close air support, depended upon the weather providing good flying conditions.[13]

*   *   *

In addition to the possibility of bad weather, another new threat was worrying the Allied High Command and DAF planning staff. In January in France the Luftwaffe had used jet propelled aircraft, the Me262, in an attack on the Allies' forward airfields. Over Forli on 2 April in the Eighth Army area, the vapour trail of an Arado 234 Blitz jet bomber was seen. There had been no early warning, and flying at around 35,000 feet at an estimated 430 mph, it carried out an extensive reconnaissance. Anti-aircraft batteries did not possess the latest radar and other equipment to track the Ar234, and Allied air forces had no aircraft with comparable performance. On 5 April another Ar234 made a reconnaissance flight over the Ravenna area. Although once again there was no early warning, anti-aircraft guns were able to engage the intruder.[14]

On Sunday 8 April the weather was poor with high winds, grounding many aircraft on their airfields on the Adriatic Coast. General Clark telephoned McCreery to tell him that the next day would be fine with good flying conditions for the start of the offensive. Later that afternoon, McCreery was sitting reading his Bible, when he was visited by an old friend and officer in a cavalry regiment, Wilfred Lyde. They had a relaxing chat about things other than the coming battle, and Lyde thought it helped McCreery cope with the great pressure and personal strain he was under.[15]

The morning of 9 April was a sunny spring day with a cloudless sky. Allied air forces, as they had done before the battle for Cassino, continued with their regular operations.[16] Routine aerial strikes and reconnaissance, artillery shelling and fire onto German positions was maintained just as normal. For the Germans it must have seemed just like any other in the near six-month stand-off. After a few weeks without rain, and with the ground now firm, they should have been alert for an Allied attack.

Activity was far from normal that morning in Eighth Army. During the night and the morning of 8/9 April, all front-line troops were pulled back a few hundred yards from the Senio. It seemed that the Germans saw little of this. DAF air superiority imposed in effect a No Fly Zone on the Luftwaffe and the ANR, who would have had little or no intelligence from air reconnaissance. The morning passed as so many had before. Even supposing the Germans had begun to suspect a major offensive, in the time available there was little they could have done.[17]

At 1.50pm, out of the blue, an unsuspected air blitz began to rain down upon the German positions. The Allied Strategic Air Force, and the Tactical Air Force, including DAF, commenced an unprecedented onslaught. For more than an hour and a half, 825 heavy bombers dropped 175,000 fragmentation bombs, 1,692 tons of explosives, on enemy gun positions, and on defences which blocked Eighth Army's planned attack points.[18] German gun positions on the east of Imola were enflamed by some 24,000 20lb incendiary bombs deposited by 624 medium bombers.[19]

Simultaneously around 1,000 fighter-bombers, of which some 740 were from DAF, carried out pinpoint, low-level strikes on machine-gun and mortar positions, ammunition dumps, artillery batteries, command posts, HQ positions, and anything trying to move.[20] An artillery bombardment followed for forty-two minutes, which was a normal pre-cursor before a ground attack, which the Germans would now have been expecting.

However, before they could emerge from their dug-outs, they were immediately hit for a further ten minutes by another wave of fighter-bombers, flying so low they barely appeared to clear the floodbanks and dykes. Without a pause, four more identical waves of artillery bombardment, followed by fighter-bomber strikes in similar duration, went in. From beginning to end the battering would last around five and a half hours. It was what we now popularly term 'shock and awe'.[21]

During the afternoon all the fighter-bomber wings dived on enemy positions from Imola to the Reno, rocketing, strafing, and dropping fuel tanks filled with incendiary jelly to fill trenches and dug-outs with a liquid fire. On the V Corps front successive waves of Spitbombers of 244 Wing in more than 120 sorties broke across the Senio during ten-minute lulls in the artillery barrage. Four times the Spitbombers hit German positions on the north bank. Although Eighth Army troops had been pulled back a considerable distance, on some occasions fighter-bombers were directed by Rover mobile units onto locations where the targets were only 500 yards in front the Army's front lines.[22]

After the fifth round of artillery shelling, when the Germans heard the fighter-bombers roar in once more, those enemy troops still unscathed must have continued to huddle heads down in their trenches and underground shelters. Many would have thought the alternating waves of shells and bombs would never end, and the paralyzing nightmare would pound on into the night.

This time, however, the wave of fighter-bombers was a dummy run, screaming low over the Senio without dropping a single bomb. After hour upon hour of incessant shelling and air strikes, it was enough to keep the Germans underground, each man no doubt grateful that he was not receiving a direct hit. While the planes flew in mock attack overhead, right on cue 2nd New Zealand and 10th Indian Divisions drove forward with portable pontoon equipment, unseen and unheard, to make vital crossings of the Senio.[23] It was a culminating master stroke of deception, laid on by the DAF–Eighth Army partnership, which had been so well renewed, and reinvigorated by General McCreery and AVM Foster.

At 7.20pm, as dusk began to darken the sky, the main ground attack commenced. Dykes were blown apart and temporary bridges of portable pontoons and even huge bundles of branches were hurried into place to allow the first tanks to cross the Senio. Some flame-throwers were used from the Allied side to destroy close-in German positions, prior to the infantry moving off. Despite the preceding massive bombardment, the Germans threw themselves into a fierce fight back. And while Eighth Army was across the Senio, next to come was the Santerno river, and this time without any element of surprise. The goal of the Po was still a long way away.

Flying Officer Salt was flying that late afternoon and evening with an army observer above the battlefield:

> Flame throwers of the 8th Indian and 2nd New Zealand Divisions, leaning against the Senio stop-banks, poured a grim barrage of flame at the hapless enemy in dug-outs. All along the line little flashes of flame flickered through the evening haze. The mighty roar of the barrage ceased abruptly at regular intervals for just four minutes, when fighters swept in to strafe the German positions and dive-bombers hurled bombs at their vital points.[24]

Yet with the air blitz the Allies had declared their hand. Alexander's planners had clearly realized the dilemma posed by the Santerno river. Before a critical mass of force and forward momentum would be generated the

German defences on Santerno could bring the offensive to a shuddering halt on only the second day. The attack must get across the Santerno, then accelerate to quickly reach the Argenta Gap before the Germans could bring forward and concentrate more of their forces there.

Once again the support of air power was seen as the only possible way ground troops might do it. During 10 April some 1,200 aircraft, of which DAF fighter-bomber squadrons were a core, continuously bombed and strafed a ten-square-mile area beyond the Santerno to clear a path for Eighth Army's planned crossing. The destruction from the aerial bombardments forced German troops into their dugouts, while Allied infantry advanced to cross the river. This brought an extra unforeseen benefit. The German telephone lines to their front line command posts had been destroyed by the strategic bombing, preventing effective direction of their artillery and tactical movement.[25]

From Forli, from dusk to dawn, eighty-three Bostons and seven Mosquitos took off or landed every two minutes. From Cesenatico, another sixty Baltimores rose into the air, not to attack bridges and pontoons, but gun positions running from Castel Bolognese to Bagnara, from Imola to Massa Lombardo, bombing closer to our troops than DAF had ever attempted at night.[26]

* * *

From 9 to 25 April Group Captain Dundas' 244 Wing flew more sorties than any other DAF wing, although the others were racking up similar volumes. From first light until late in the day aircraft were taking off in fighter-bomber operations. Usually they were in four- or eight-aircraft formations, sometimes in squadron strength; on one occasion on 18 April Dundas led a three-squadron 'Timothy' raid. Besides the pressure being endured by pilots, all air force support services faced immense demands around the clock. Aircraft ground crews, the armament sections in the squadrons, and the wing maintenance unit reached a level of excellence beyond any reasonable expectation.[27] Some extracts from the operations of Nos 92 and 145 Squadrons give an insight into the intensity of sorties flown, and both the damage inflicted and losses incurred, by the whole of DAF on a daily basis.

The squadron leader of 92 Squadron RAF, South African Major John Gasson DSO DFC, and like Dundas another Spitfire ace, had only celebrated his twenty-first birthday in February 1945. Previously he had been promoted to command 92 Squadron by Dundas, who thought Gasson the bravest man he knew, and an outstanding fighter pilot and leader.

Operations Record Book No. 92 Squadron RAF – April 1945 (summarized selected extracts):

11 April: At 1140 in response to a Rover Paddy request, Group Captain Dundas led a four-aircraft bombing attack against an enemy strongpoint.

Two bombs overshot by 10 yards, one undershot by 20 yards, and for the fourth No Result was observed. Pilot Officer P. Smith was hit by anti-aircraft fire in the bomb-dive, and his Spitfire exploded as it hit the ground. Smith was reported missing, believed killed.

At 1640 Major Gasson took off in hazy weather up to 5,000 feet, leading six Spitfires in a TIMOTHY Operation. Five houses were bombed with four direct hits, and other houses in the area bombed and strafed.

April 15: At 1400 four Spitfires led by South African Captain R. Jacobs attacked Tiger tanks, scoring two direct hits followed by a huge explosion, with two near misses. A subsequent strafing attack blew up another Tiger tank, and left others smoking.

At 1440 Major Gasson took another four aircraft into an attack on the Tiger tanks. After one very near miss, and two near misses, one tank was seen to fall down the side of an embankment, and lying at an angle of 40 degrees with its gun muzzle in the mud. It was later confirmed as destroyed.

April 16: At 1210 Major Gasson took off in a six Spitfire formation in response to a request from Rover David. In the Medicina area where the enemy was in full retreat, the attack scored 5 direct hits on a house, and destroyed 2 4-tonner vehicles, 1 3-tonner vehicle, 4 ammunition carriers, 1 light tank, a horse drawn wagon with 10 soldiers, two cars, and 3 motor cycles with side-cars.[28]

In place of Squadron Leader Neville Duke in 145 Squadron RAF, Squadron Leader G.W.F. 'Dan' Daniel took command. Daniel was a veteran from the desert, the third-ranked Spitfire ace in the Mediterranean theatre, and led 145 Squadron into April's ferocious battles in support of Eighth Army.

Operations Record Book No. 145 Squadron RAF – April 1945 (summarized selected extracts):

2 April: In response to a Rover Paddy request Group Captain Dundas led the 244 Wing squadrons in a bombing attack against a crossroads target, which was surrounded by German slit trenches. Because Eighth Army troops were very close, the utmost care was taken to drop all bombs in the target area. Following the attack more than 100 enemy troops surrendered immediately. Later that day Flight Sergeant A. Garth led a four aircraft formation, and sank a 140-foot barge near Piave.

6 April: At 0735 Flying Officer R.D. Franks took off in a group of six Spitfires in an armed reconnaissance operation. On their return Franks' aircraft was seen to be streaming glycol, presumably from anti-aircraft fire. Franks reported that he was about to bale out, but did not do so before his Spitfire burst into flames, and he was lost into the sea.

9 April: Led by Squadron Leader Daniel, the squadron flew 20 sorties in a TIMOTHY operation attack against enemy positions 100 yards in front of our troops along the Senio River. All bombs were dropped in the target area among slit trenches and dugouts, which were then strafed with cannon and machine-gun fire.

12 April: In 28 sorties the squadron destroyed two tanks and a number of buildings. The Wing's success was overshadowed by the loss of Wing Commander R. Barry DFC, who, while leading 417 Squadron on a close support target, blew up in his bomb dive through an unknown cause.

13 April: Flight Lieutenant G.T.Y. Melville led six aircraft in a bombing and strafing attack against a tank and some buildings. W/O J.R. Moffat, a New Zealander, after being hit by flak, then hit some high tension wires. His aircraft then hit the road, spun, cart-wheeled, and caught fire. It is feared he was killed.

17 April: At 1710 in the evening Flight Lieutenant A.R.M. Hammet led three Spitfires in response to a request from Rover Paddy. A tank was seen to go into a building. At 1740 it was bombed, with two direct hits causing a large red flash, which destroyed the house. The tank was probably destroyed.[29]

On 17 April the infantry battle for that narrow sliver of land near the town of Argenta, the Argenta Gap, was stalling and in danger of bogging down. The Germans must surely have been able to predict what would come next. Around noon the following day Eighth Army troops were pulled back a little way, to allow DAF Kittyhawk and Mustang fighter-bombers to pound German positions in a TIMOTHY operation. Argenta was then soon taken and so it continued.

Operations Record Book No. 145 Squadron RAF – April 1945 (summarized selected extracts):

19 April: In 28 sorties most targets were mortar positions bombed and strafed. Flight Lieutenant D.J.S. Wood destroyed a house, bringing praise from Rover David.

20 April: During 28 sorties flown in close support, 3 houses and one Nebelwerfer position were destroyed, and one tank, two vehicles and 5 barges damaged.

26 April: In 20 sorties between the Po and Adige Rivers, one vehicle and one motor cycle destroyed, a flame throwing tank and many other vehicles damaged.

28 April: With 601 Squadron, attacked a German convoy of some 200 vehicles north of Vicenza, destroying more than 50 and many more damaged.

During April 145 Squadron flew 730 operational sorties, in nearly 1,000 hours, dropping 440 500lb bombs, with each pilot averaging about 1.5 sorties every day. Among the squadron's claims of targets destroyed or damaged were: 139 vehicles, eighty-five barges and other vessels, one locomotive, five guns, five tanks and many buildings. Unable to be estimated were the thousands of enemy troops killed or wounded in the air-to ground attacks, or subsequently taken prisoner by Allied troops. Fourteen Spitfire Mk VIII aircraft were lost. From a squadron strength of around sixteen pilots over the month, two were believed killed, one missing, and one wounded.[30]

While DAF fighter-bombers pounded German forces during the day, the hours of darkness were not forgotten. The night-fighters of 600 Squadron, now operating Mosquitos, were out every night. In the first week of April area patrols were operated in the Udine-Corizia-Trieste region, in support of bombing raids by the Bostons of 232 Wing. Otherwise nightly operations were mainly defensive patrols against Luftwaffe intruders.

Operations Record Book No. 600 Squadron RAF – April 1945 (summarized selected extracts):

> April 2: At 2150 in the Lake Comácchio area Flight Lieutenant Jack Ingate was vectored onto a bogey. This proved to be a friend, another Mosquito of 256 Squadron.
>
> April 13: At last light Squadron Leader Hammond and Flying Officer Moore intercepted two Fw190s. The leading Fw190 was shot down and destroyed. After a chase the second was damaged in the starboard wing before getting away.[31]

Besides the victory by Hammond and Moore, the only other detection of enemy intruders during April were a Ju87 chased on 11 April, and some Fw190s pursued on 19 April, without engagement. Yet the high number of uneventful patrols by the night-fighters of 600 Squadron without contact with enemy aircraft, showed how DAF had come to even own the night sky.

On 26 April when 57th Fighter Group flew thirty-three missions, Captain Richard L. Johnson and Lieutenant Roland E. Lee of the 66th Fighter Squadron were aloft on the day's twentieth mission in their P-47 Thunderbolts. In response to a call from Rover Joe, they were strafing enemy vehicles when they were attacked by a lone Bf109. The Bf109 made two passes at Lieutenant Lee, who each time succeeded in evasive actions.

On a third attack by the 109 Captain Johnson was able to cut in. The enemy aircraft tried to climb and weave away. Johnson held on, keeping the 109 in his sights, only to find his guns failed to fire. After this Lee managed to close to about 500 feet of the 109, firing a burst into its fuselage. As the 109 began to go into a death spin, its pilot baled out. It was the final kill of the war for the 57th Fighter Group.

Lieutenant Lee's victory took the 57th Fighter Group's total for the war to 184 enemy aircraft destroyed, with twenty probables and seventy-nine damaged. On 29 April they suffered their final combat casualty. Lieutenant Aikens V. Smith of 65th Fighter Squadron died after baling out.[32]

The above stories and selected extracts from DAF squadrons' operational records are just a very small sample of the massive number of air-to-ground sorties, probably around 35,000 to 40,000 in April, and of the maelstrom of destruction unleashed by DAF day after day. But, like Eighth Army on the ground, there was a price to be paid.

Over the month of April 244 Wing lost nine pilots killed, and three missing out of about eighty pilots at the beginning of April. Three more were wounded or injured, bringing the casualty rate for the month to 22.5 per cent. Many more survived being shot down and baling out, and forced landings. One of the nine pilots killed from 92 Squadron on 12 April was Wing Commander Barry, deputy to Group Captain Dundas. Barry was the last Spitfire ace to die in Italy and the Mediterranean theatre. Dundas spoke of that time as being punch-drunk, consumed with a ferocious mind-set to finally have done with this enemy, and described April 1945 as 'that blood-stained month'.[33]

* * *

The total number of Allied aircraft, bombers, fighters and fighter-bombers, in operation over the battle areas, including escorting fighters and reconnaissance aircraft, was close to 5,000.[34] The Germans later claimed that the heavy bombing by the Strategic Air Force did not demoralize their troops. To assess which type of aerial attack caused most destruction and casualties would be impossible. There is some evidence, however, that the fighter-bomber attacks in close air-to-ground attack, so well performed by DAF Squadrons, inflicted the greatest disruption and psychological impact on German troops.

The commander of the German 98th Division, General Reinhardt, a veteran of the Eastern Front, said the constant air-to-ground war from the fighter-bombers was the worst bombardment he had ever experienced. Planes peeled off in turn from their 'sky cab-ranks' to strike anything they could see, a vehicle, a tank, even to strafe a single German soldier.[35]

For three weeks from 9 April DAF fighter-bombers pounded German forces mercilessly. It was maintained from dawn to dusk every day with little pause. Later in the month retreating German columns were brutally slaughtered.

* * *

In one key area the Allies were particularly fortunate. Their other normally implacable enemy, the rain and cloud so frequent in Italy's winter and early spring, deserted the battlefield. There was no significant bad visibility to protect the enemy's ground forces.

What was it like on the ground? What was the reality of the losses being incurred by the German armies from this daily battering from the sky? One airman, Australian Flight Sergeant Stan Watt, of No. 450 Squadron RAAF in 239 Wing, found out for himself. Watt had completed his tour of operations in March 1945 when he was given two options. One was to return to Egypt as a flying instructor. Watt opted for the alternative, which was to join a Mobile Operations Room Unit (MORU), specifically as the CO of MORU Rover Paddy. After only one week's training, Watt took up his role in command of some eighteen Eighth Army men, close behind the front lines. He was stunned by the large numbers of dead to be seen, mostly as a result of anti-personnel cluster bombs. Piles of dead bodies were grouped along the road, awaiting mechanized burial in mass graves.

The ground was desolate mud, with the odd ruined building, and scarecrow trees devoid of leaves. All the birds had long gone. Watt found the continual noise deafening, bombs exploding, shelling, rocket fire, and the constant scream of Allied fighter-bombers. In freezing rain, lying in the open in a bed-roll, always wet, there was little sleep. It seemed every night the Germans would open up with rockets, brought up to the front in trucks, before pulling them back before daybreak.

One April afternoon following the commencement of the Allied offensive Watt directed four Spitfires to attack some German panzers. After destroying two of them, the Spitfire pilots radioed back to Rover Paddy. Watt heard that they had spotted some very large concentrations of enemy forces, which were defended by heavy flak:

> They reported at least a thousand German trucks, self-propelled guns and tanks milling around on the south side of the Po with no bridge left standing for them to make a crossing. I called up every available aircraft in the Cab-rank. Within fifteen minutes the dive-bombers had begun their deadly work. It was a massacre. For the rest of the day successive squadrons each spent ten minutes raking the vehicles with machine-gun fire and dropping their bombs. When their bomb racks and magazines were empty, they returned to base, re-armed and flew back to the fray. The attack was finally called off when night fell and the planes were unable to see their targets.

Next morning Watt was able to drive through drizzling rain over part of the battlefield from which surviving German troops had retreated. What he saw was total devastation:

> Bodies were hanging out of vehicles, or splayed like rag dolls across the ground. Wisps of smoke still drifted lazily from burnt out trucks. Flies were already buzzing, disturbing what would otherwise have been an

unearthly silence. One soldier appeared to have taken a fighter's cannon shot in his stomach, causing it to burst like a watermelon.

Watt later estimated the dead to number between 800 and 1,000.[35]

* * *

The air blitz by DAF fighter-bombers on 17 and 18 April, added to the artillery and outflanking gains by other forces to the east and west, finally allowed Eighth Army to break the enemy's defences at Argenta.[36] In a final incisive breakthrough of the war in Italy it was perhaps symbolic. As Montgomery had stressed they must, in August 1942 before the second battle for El Alamein, Eighth Army and DAF had fought to the end as one. It was also fitting that it was the DAF fighter-bomber, first pioneered in early 1942 in the desert, which struck a telling blow to bring about a tipping point at the Argenta Gap, and gave the German forces not a moment's rest until the end.

Fifth Army had launched its offensive from the centre of the Tuscan Apennines on 14 April, and by 22 April had taken Bologna and reached the River Po at San Benedetto. Next day, 23 April and perhaps appropriately it was St George's Day, Eighth Army occupied Ferrara on both sides of the Po. The motorized and armoured units of Fifth and Eighth Armies, swept on into northern Italy, taking Modena on the 23rd, Mantua on the 24th, Piacenza and Genoa on the 27th, Padua on the 29th, Turin on the 30th, and on 2 May, Milan, Venice and Trieste, where Yugoslav partisans had arrived a day earlier.[37]

All the bridges across the Po had been destroyed by Allied air forces. Air interdiction had first cut off the German armies' supplies, then left them with no way out. They were trapped. On 2 May staff of General von Vietinghoff, at the Caserta HQ of the Supreme Allied Commander Mediterranean, signed the surrender of all German Armies in Italy, to Field Marshal Alexander. On 4 May all German armies in Germany, Holland, and Denmark surrendered to Field Marshal Montgomery.[38] The speed of disintegration of enemy forces, and the rapid exploitation by the Allies' Fifth and Eighth Armies in the last days of April, was made possible by air superiority. Allied air power, with DAF the battlefield enforcer, dominated the airspace.

Notes
1. Owen, op. cit., pp. 282–5.
2. Morton, *A Traveller in Italy*, pp. 108–9 and 208–9; Evans, op. cit., p. 198
3. Harpur, *The Impossible Victory*, pp. 124–5.
4. Saunders, *The Fight is Won – Royal Air Force 1939–45, Vol. III*, p. 401; Dundas, op. cit., p. 140.
5. Mead, *The Last Great Cavalry Man*, pp. 165–6.
6. Harpur, op. cit., pp. 124–5.
7. Ibid., pp. 154–5.
8. Ibid., pp. 156.

 9. Linklater, *The Campaign in Italy*, p. 419.
10. Squire and Hill, *The Surreys in Italy 1943–45*, pp. 62–6.
11. Harpur, op. cit., pp. 157–9.
12. Mead, op. cit., pp. 173–7.
13. Dundas, op. cit., pp. 154–9.
14. *History of HQ 12 AA Bde*, op. cit., pp. 12 and 16.
15. Mead, op. cit., p. 178.
16. Owen, op. cit., p. 300.
17. Harpur, op. cit., pp. 157–9.
18. Owen, op. cit., p. 300.
19. Saunders, op. cit., p. 230.
20. Brookes, op. cit., pp. 148–9.
21. Harpur, op. cit., p. 158.
22. Owen, op. cit., p. 301.
23. Harpur, op. cit., p. 158.
24. Saunders, op. cit., p. 230.
25. Brookes, op. cit., p. 149.
26. Owen, op. cit., p. 301.
27. Dundas, op. cit., p. 159–62.
28. NA, Kew, Air/27/747, No. 92 Squadron RAF.
29. NA, Kew, Air/27/987, No. 145 Squadron RAF.
30. Ibid.
31. NA, Kew, Air/27/2062, No. 600 Squadron RAF.
32. Molesworth, op. cit., pp. 114–16.
33. Dundas, op. cit., pp. 159–62.
34. Brookes, op. cit., pp. 148–50.
35. Harpur, op. cit., p. 159.
36. Ayris, op. cit., pp. 141–6.
37. Saunders, op. cit., p. 231; Doherty, op. cit., p. 221.
38. Saunders, op. cit., p. 231.

Epilogue

On the morning of 3 May 1945, the day after the German surrender in Italy, the respective commanders of Eighth Army and DAF, General Sir Richard McCreery and Air Vice Marshal William Foster, exchanged personal communications. Those messages illustrated what was perhaps the greatest of all the many DAF achievements.

It was McCreery who first sent a personal signal to Foster, which included the following:

> In this the hour of our complete victory, I feel my first duty is to convey to you and all the officers and men under your command, my heartfelt gratitude for the magnificent support that the Desert Air Force has rendered to the Eighth Army throughout our long association. This last great battle has been won as a result of complete confidence and co-operation between the Eighth Army and the Desert Air Force.
>
> The Desert Air Force has achieved a degree of efficiency in close support of the ground forces that has never been equalled in any other partnership.[1]

And McCreery ended his message with:

> I am confident that ... the results that have been achieved on the battle-fields of Africa and Italy will long be quoted as a perfect example of inter service co-operation.[2]

In a handwritten letter Foster replied:

> Thank you very much for your generous signal, and doubly so for your private note to me. It is a great thing for me to know that the work of my men has fulfilled its purpose, and earned such praise.[3]

Foster finished his response with:

> With you, I too hope that the combined Eighth Army – Desert Air Force results in this campaign, will provide an abiding foundation for Army – Air understanding, wherever it is needed in the future. I'd like finally to say that I think the Eighth Army is extremely fortunate in its commander.[4]

In the final battle in Italy for the River Po, the lead-in air blitz and sustained air-to-ground bombardment were pivotal to assist the Allied armies' victory on the ground. The final battle which broke the German armies in Italy demonstrated that the vision espoused by Auchinleck and Tedder, had been followed to the end. When Montgomery had taken command of Eighth Army in August 1942 he had confirmed his trust in this strategy, and said that Eighth Army and the DAF 'must fight hand in hand. It is one battle, not two'.[5]

The personal remarks of McCreery and Foster to each other on 3 May showed that in their hearts they believed that the unity of Eighth Army and DAF had been the key to victory. DAF had fought with Eighth Army as an integral part of one entity, yet at the same time maintained its independence as an air force to do all the other things an air force must do, as Tedder had insisted.

Air Chief Marshal Slessor of the RAF summed up the Italian campaign, when he said that 'if there had been no air force on either side, the German Army could have made the invasion of Italy impossible'.[6]

From the embryonic beginnings in 1940 in RAF Eastern Command in North Africa, the air force groups, wings and associated squadrons that became designated as the Desert Air Force fought an air war against the Italian and German air forces for five years. Over those years they won and sustained air superiority until the final victory. In that time they pioneered numerous innovations and 'firsts', which were copied in most other theatres of the Second World War, such as:

- Winning the air war first, to achieve air superiority.
- The first trial and development in combat of the fighter-bomber.
- The capability of squadrons to maintain combat operations on the day on which they re-located forward or back to new airfields close behind the army's front lines.
- Air interdiction of the enemy's communications and supplies to the battlefield.
- Establishing what is now called a 'No Fly Zone' before a major offensive, as at El Alamein.
- Interception and destruction of enemy ground attacks, as at Ksar Rhilane.
- Close air/army support through forward air controllers, first trialled at El Hamma.
- An air blitz coordinated with, and prior to, an army offensive.
- The 'Rover David Cab-rank' of fighter-bombers over the battlefield, called up by the army through mobile operations rooms.
- Development of dedicated fighter-bomber squadrons in an air-to-ground war.
- The first multi-national air force.

The list of pioneering 'firsts' by DAF seems remarkable. Not only was DAF the leading air force in introducing and implementing these techniques, tactics and strategies, it deployed them often simultaneously, and flexibly, in support of ground forces in long, gruelling campaigns. The formative years of DAF in the desert instilled adaptability to harsh conditions, where the variety of challenges and the hardship of operating demanded fortitude of spirit. These attributes became engrained in the ethos of DAF.[7]

One of its most important achievements flowed indirectly from its success and is often overlooked. The dominance of DAF first in North Africa, then in conjunction with other Allied air forces in Italy, allowed Allied armies to re-deploy over long distances in rear areas, without Axis air forces spotting, attacking or disrupting their movements. This enabled Allied armies to con-centrate for an offensive with impunity from enemy interference, and very often bestowed the benefit of surprise for the attack.

The development of the fighter-bomber role in the air-to-ground war by DAF became perhaps not only the most physically visible impact but also the most psychologically damaging on the Axis forces. The ever increasing destruction which was wrought on German forces in Italy reached a crescendo in April 1945. General von Vietinghoff, C-in-C of the German Army Group C in northern Italy, thought the fighter-bombers to be the most destructive weapon used against them in the final battle:

> They hindered practically all essential movement at the local points. Even tanks could not move during the day because of the employment of fighter-bombers. The effectiveness of fighter-bombers lay in that their presence alone over the battlefield paralysed every movement.[8]

And General von Senger of XIV Corps stated:

> We could still move when required at night, but we could not move at all in the daytime due to air attacks. It was the bombing of the river Po crossings that finished us.[9]

The role of the fighter-bomber, and related tactics learned from DAF, were also used to great effect by other Allied tactical air forces in the Normandy invasion, and the subsequent advance into Germany. Although the tech-nology has advanced beyond any comparison, the principle and power of the fighter-bomber can be seen in modern multi-role combat aircraft. Perhaps its most recent manifestation was in the operations of NATO aircraft, which laid the foundation for the overthrow of the Gaddafi regime in Libya. It is ironic that it was there in the Libyan desert that the fighter-bomber was first pioneered by DAF.

The achievements of DAF over five years is also demonstrated by the subsequent career success of each of its commanders. In January 1943 AVM Tedder became deputy to Eisenhower at the latter's request, and AOC-in-C

Mediterranean Air Forces. Then, in December 1943, when Eisenhower became Supreme Allied Commander for the Operation OVERLORD invasion of Normandy, Tedder went with him as his Deputy. Subsequent DAF commanders, Coningham, Broadhurst, and Dickson, followed in successive transfers to very senior air force appointments for the north-west Europe offensive. This recognition and promotion of DAF commanders was no mere coincidence.

In a related perspective, the achievements of DAF leaders and their strategies owed everything to what was accomplished by all of its officers and men in whatever role or period of time they served. From 1940 to 1945 it was they who suffered, died, were wounded, maimed or taken prisoner, but who made the enterprise a success. As AVM Foster said in his letter to McCreery, 'it is the quality of the youngsters who actually do the job, and the enthusiasm of the maintenance crews who keep their aircraft going for them, that gets the results'.[10]

The first-hand accounts and stories from DAF airmen in this book are but a very small sample of some of those youngsters who, in all roles and services of DAF, did their job and got those results. And some are still with us in their later years to tell of their time in the legendary Desert Air Force.

Notes

1. Private collection, McCreery, communications between Gen McCreery and AVM Foster; Owen, op. cit., pp. 308–9.
2. Ibid.
3. Ibid.
4. Ibid.
5. Chalfont, *Montgomery of Alamein*, p. 193.
6. Owen, op. cit., p. 255.
7. Owen, op. cit., pp. 307–8.
8. Ibid., op. cit., pp. 303–4.
9. Ibid., op. cit., p. 305.
10. Private collection, McCreery, op. cit.

Some Statistics

War statistics can be mind-numbing and, at the same time, so horrific. Some, however, can help to illuminate the scale and effort that was expended, and the following few statistics I think do that.

On 1 April 1945 the Allies could call upon some 12,500 aircraft in the Mediterranean theatre. Of these around 4,400 were fighter-bombers, or others deployed in the air-to-ground war. Assuming a 75 per cent service ability rate or higher, this amounted to at least 3,300 flying operational sorties in close support of the Allied armies. This dwarfed an estimated 130 serviceable aircraft of the Axis air forces.[1]

In the month of April the Allies flew close to 66,000 operational sorties, a daily average of 2,200. In dropping 48,000 tons of bombs on enemy forces, 402 aircraft were lost.[2] As Axis forces retreated towards the River Po, in the four days of 21–24 April nearly 6,000 Axis vehicles were destroyed, and the majority of those by Allied air power.[3]

During 1944 the Allied air forces lost 713 aircraft to Axis anti-aircraft fire.[4]

Earlier, over the first six months of 1943, the Allies gained air superiority in North Africa, and began to dominate the Mediterranean airspace. In preparation for the invasion of Sicily in July, month by month air raids increased dramatically on the Axis' main rail centres, principal ports and communication hubs in Sicily and southern Italy. The weight of bombs dropped per month, increased from approximately ten tons in January 1943, to some 2,600 tons in July. This bombing campaign brought about a reduction in the number of the enemy's rail trucks from some 120,000 per month, down to around 60,000 per month.[5]

Without in any way inferring any sense of some kind of league table, the overall statistics of the following two DAF squadrons are worthy of note.

No. 3 Squadron RAAF (P-40 Tomahawks and Kittyhawks, P-51 Mustangs)

Group Captain Dundas thought that No. 239 Wing RAF was the best fighter wing in the DAF. So it is not surprising that one of 239 Wing's squadrons, No. 3 Squadron RAAF, was the highest-scoring British Commonwealth squadron in the Mediterranean Theatre, with 246.5 enemy aircraft destroyed, comprising 217.5 shot down and twenty-nine destroyed on the ground. In its fighter-bomber operations 3 Squadron destroyed 709 tanks or motor vehicles, twenty-eight water vessels, and twelve locomotives.

It was in Italy that 3 Squadron painted the Australian Southern Cross on the rudder of each of its aircraft, a practice which it continues to this day.[6]

No. 600 (City of London) Squadron RAF (Beaufighters and Mosquito night-fighters)

Bearing in mind that the operations of No. 600 Squadron RAF were predominantly in the night-fighter role, their overall tally is remarkable:[7]

	Destroyed	Probable	Damaged
Enemy aircraft	165	13	34
Motor Transport	16	–	15
Locomotives and Wagons	3 locos	–	10 various
	21 various		
Shipping	1 boat	–	1 boat
			6 barges

Spitfire Aces

Perhaps the last word should go on a few statistics relating to the Spitfire fighter pilots. The incomparable Spitfires, and the skill of their pilots, were dominant in the defensive fighter role for winning the air war and maintaining an ascendancy over Axis fighters. This was a major factor in allowing so many fighter squadrons, including Spitfires as Spitbombers, to operate in the fighter-bomber role.

The top ten scoring Spitfire aces of the campaigns in North Africa and Italy, with five victories or more were:

Pilot	Service	Theatre Claims	Total Claims
Duke, N.F.	RAF	20	27
Mackie, E.D.	RNZAF	16	20
Daniel, S.W.F.	RAF	16	16
Hugo, P.H.	RAF	10	17
Taylor, J.S.	RAF	13	13
Maguire, W.I.H.	Rhodesia	12	13
Hill, G.U.	RCAF	10	10
Hussey, R.J.H.	RAF	9	9
Turkington, R.W.	RAF	9	9
Ingram, M.R.B.	RNZAF	7	8

The above table excludes shared victory claims, probable victories and claims for damaged enemy aircraft.[8]

Notes

1. Brookes, op. cit., p. 153.
2. Brookes, op. cit., pp. 150–2.
3. Ibid
4. Brookes, op. cit., p. 154.
5. Tedder, *Air Power in War*, pp. 108/9.
6. Australian War Memorial (www.awm.gov.au).
7. NA Kew. AIR 27/987/April 1945, ORB No. 600 Squadron RAF.
8. Thomas, op. cit., p. 86.

Glossary

AA	Anti-aircraft
ACM	Air Chief Marshal
AI	Air interception radar
AM	Air Marshal
AOC	Air Officer Commanding
AOC-in-C	Air Officer Commanding-in-Chief
AVM	Air Vice Marshal
Cab-rank	Small formations of patrolling fighters and fighter-bombers on immediate call by radio for close army and tactical support
C-in-C	Commander-in-Chief
CO	Commanding Officer
DAF	Desert Air Force (previously WDAF – Western Desert Air Force)
FG	Fighter Group (USAAF)
FS	Fighter Squadron (USAAF)
GOC	General Officer Commanding
IFF	Identification Friend or Foe; airborne radio identification device
JG	*Jagdgeschwader* (Fighter Wing)
LG	Landing Ground
Luftflotte	Air Fleet
MAAF	Mediterranean Allied Air Forces
MASAF	Mediterranean Allied Strategic Air Force
MATAF	Mediterranean Allied Tactical Air Force
MORU	Mobile Operations Room Unit
MT	Motor Transport
NASAF	North-West African Strategic Air Force
NATAF	North African Tactical Air Force
NWAAF	North West African Air Forces
NWATAF	North West Allied Tactical Air Force
OP	Observation Post
ORB	Operations Record Book
OTU	Operational Training Unit
PR	Photographic Reconnaissance

PRU	Photographic Reconnaissance Unit
PSP	Pierced Steel Plate
RA	Royal Artillery
RAAF	Royal Australian Air Force
RAF	Royal Air Force
RCAF	Royal Canadian Air Force
RNZAF	Royal New Zealand Air Force
SAAF	South African Air Force
SASO	Senior Air Staff Officer
TAC	Tactical Air Command (USAAF)
TAF	Tactical Air Force
TBF	Tactical Bomber Force
Tac-R	Tactical Reconnaissance
USAAF	United States Army Air Forces
WDAF	Western Desert Air Force
WDF	Western Desert Force

Bibliography and Sources

1. Official Records and Publications

Daniell, David Scott, *The History of the East Surrey Regiment, Volume IV*, Ernest Benn Ltd, London, 1957.

Doherty, Richard, private copy from HQ 12 Anti-Aircraft Brigade, *History of HQ 12 AA Bde*, 1945, np.

Herington, John, *Air Power over Europe 1944–1945*, Australian War Memorial, Halstead Press, Sydney, 1963.

Herington, John, *Air War Against Germany and Italy 1939–1943*, Australian War Memorial, Halstead Press, Sydney, 1954.

Linklater, Eric, *The Campaign in Italy*, His Majesty's Stationery Office, London, 1951.

No. 3 Squadron RAAF, www.3squadron.org.au

RAAF, *RAAF Saga – The RAAF at War*, Australian War Memorial, Canberra, ACT, Australia, 1944

Roy Smith (AASC No. 5), *Air Support in the Desert*, Ref Major General John Malcolm McNeill, 1983–6, King's College, London.

Ray, Cyril, *Algiers to Austria, a History of 78 Division in the Second World War*, Eyre and Spottiswoode, London, 1951.

Saunders, Hilary St George, *The Fight is Won, Royal Air Force 1939–45*, HMO, London, 1954

Smith, Lieutenant Colonel H.B.L., and associates, *The Cassino Battles*, the Queen's Royal Surreys' Association Museum, Clandon Park, West Clandon, Guildford GU4 7RQ.

Squire, Lieutenant Colonel G.L.A., and Hill, Major Peter, *Algiers to Tunis, The 1st and 1/6th Battalions The East Surrey Regiment in North Africa 1942–43*, The Queen's Royal Surreys' Association Museum, November 1993, Clandon Park, West Clandon, Guildford GU4 7RQ.

——, *The Surreys in Italy 1943–45*, The Queen's Royal Surrey Regiment Museum, March 1992, Clandon Park, West Clandon, Guildford GU4 7RQ.

National Archives, Kew, London

AIR 27/399/17, Operations Records Book (ORB) September 1942 (Summary), No. 38 Squadron RAF.

AIR 27/399/19, ORB September 1942, No. 38 Squadron RAF.

AIR 27/399/20, ORB October 1942 (Summary), No. 38 Squadron RAF.

AIR 27/399/21, ORB October 1942, No. 38 Squadron RAF.

AIR 27/746, ORB January 1944 (Summary), No. 92 Squadron RAF.

AIR 27/747, ORB January 1944, No. 92 Squadron RAF.

AIR 27/821/38, ORB August 1942, No. 104 Squadron RAF.

AIR 27/821/40, ORB September 1942, No. 104 Squadron RAF.

AIR 27/821/41, ORB October 1942, No. 104 Squadron RAF.

AIR 27/821/44, ORB November 1942, No. 104 Squadron RAF.

AIR 27/987/16, ORB August 1944, No. 145 Squadron RAF.

AIR 27/987/17, ORB August 1944, No. 145 Squadron RAF.

AIR 27/987/18, ORB September 1944 (Summary), No. 145 Squadron RAF.

AIR 27/987/19, ORB September 1944, No. 145 Squadron RAF.

AIR 27/987/32, ORB April 1945 (Summary), No. 145 Squadron RAF.

AIR 27/987/33, ORB April 1945, No. 145 Squadron RAF.

AIR 27/987, ORB May 1944, No. 600 Squadron RAF.

AIR 27/987, ORB April 1945, No. 600 Squadron RAF.

WO 204/7739 'Explosion at Bari: Redeployment of shipping at ports in the rest of Italy (period December 1943 to February 1944).

National Archives of Australia

www.naa.gov.au – barcode no. 5243743, F/O LB McDermott, No. 413011.

2. Other Sources

Alexander, Field Marshal, Earl Alexander of Tunis, *The Alexander Memoirs*, Cassell & Co. Ltd, 1961.

Annussek, Greg, *Hitler's Raid to Save Mussolini*, Da Capo Press, 2006.

Arthur, Max, *There Shall be Wings*, Hodder and Stoughton, London, 1993.

Atkinson, Rick, *An Army at Dawn: The War in North Africa, 1942–43*, Henry Holt & Co., 2002

——, *The Day of Battle: The War in Sicily and Italy 1943–44*, Henry Holt & Co., 2007.

Avery, Max, with Shores, Christopher, *Spitfire Leader*, Grub Street, London, 1996.

Ayris, Cyril, *Kittyhawk Pilots*, Stanley M. Watt, Western Australia, 2002.

Barnett, Correlli, *The Desert Generals*, William Kimber & Co. Ltd, London, 1960.

Baumbach, Werner, *Broken Swastika*, Robert Hale Ltd, London, 1960.

——, *The Life and Death of the Luftwaffe*, The Noontide Press, 1991.

Belogi, Marco, and Leoni, Elena, *Pantelleria*, After the Battle No. 127, 15 February 2005, Battle of Britain International Ltd.

Bierman, John, and Smith, Colin, *Alamein*, Penguin Books, London, 2003.

Bowlby, Alex, *Countdown to Cassino-Battle of Mignano Gap,1943*, Leo Cooper, London, 1995.

Bowyer, Chas, and Shores, Chris, *Desert Air Force at War*, Ian Allan Ltd, 1981.

Bowyer, Chas, *Men of the Desert Air Force*, William Kimber & Co. Ltd, London, 1984.

Brookes, Andrew, *Air War over Italy*, Ian Allen Publishing Ltd, 2000.

Carver, Field Marshal Lord, *The War in Italy 1943–1945*, IWM, Pan Books, 2002.

Chalfont, Alun, *Montgomery of Alamein*, Weidenfeld & Nicholson, London, 1977.

Chant, Chris, *Aircraft of World War II*, Amber Books Ltd, London, 1999.

Clark, General Mark, *Calculated Risk*, Harrap & Co. Ltd, London, 1951.

Clark, Lloyd, *Anzio*, Headline Publishing Group, London, 2006.

Crosby, Francis, *A Handbook of Fighter Aircraft*, Imperial War Museum, Hermes House.

Cunningham, Admiral Viscount Cunningham of Hyndhope, *A Sailor's Odyssey*, Hutchison & Co. (Publishers) Ltd, 1951.

d' Este, Carlo, *Bitter Victory, The Battle for Sicily 1943*, Aurum Press Ltd, 2008.

——, *Eisenhower, A Soldier's Life*, Henry Holt, New York, 2002.

Docherty, Tom, *Swift to Navigate: 72 Fighter Squadron in Action, 1942–1947*, Pen & Sword Books, Barnsley, 2009.

Doherty, Richard, *British Armoured Divisions & their Commanders*, Pen & Sword Books, Barnsley, 2013.

——, *Eighth Army in Italy 1943–45: The Long Hard Slog*, Pen & Sword Books, Barnsley, 2007.

Duke, Neville, *Test Pilot*, Grub Street, London 1992.

Dundas, Hugh, *Flying Start*, Stanley Paul & Co. Ltd, London, 1988.

Eisenhower, Dwight D., *Crusade in Europe*, Heinemann, London, 1948.

Ellis, John, *Cassino, the Hollow Victory*, Aurum Press, London, 2003.

Fenby, Jonathan, *Alliance*, Simon & Schuster UK Ltd, London.

Follain, John, *Mussolini's Island*, Hodder and Stoughton, London, 2006.

Ford, Ken, *Battleaxe Division*, Sutton, Stroud, 1999.

Hamilton, Nigel, *Monty – The Battles of Field Marshal Bernard Montgomery*, Hodder & Stoughton, London, 1994.

Harpur, Brian, *The Impossible Victory*, William Kimber & Co. Ltd, London, 1980.

Holland, James, *Together We Stand – North Africa 1942–43: Turning the Tide in the West*, Harper Collins 2003.

Infield, Glen B, *Skorzeny: Hitler's Commando*, St Martin's Press, New York 1981.

Infield, Glenn, *Disaster at Bari*, MacMillan Publishing Co, June 1971.

Kesselring, Albert, *The Memoirs of Field Marshal Kesselring*, Lionel Leventhal Greenhill Books Ltd, London, 1996.

Leckie, Robert (Editor), *The World War II Reader*, iBooks, inc World War II MHQ, Simon & Schuster, New York, 2001.

Lewis, Norman, *Naples '44*, William Collins & Sons Ltd, London, 1978.

Liddell Hart, Basil H., *The Rommel Papers*, Collins, London, 1953.

Lucas, Laddie, *Wings of War*, Hutchinson, London, 1983.

Macintyre, Ben, *Operation Mincemeat*, Bloomsbury Publishing Plc, London, 2010.

Majdalany, Fred, *Monte Cassino, Portrait of a Battle*, Longmans, Green and Co. Ltd, 1957.

Masters, David, *So Few*, Eyre & Spottiswoode, London, 1945.

McCarthy, Brig Gen Michael, *Air-to-Ground Battle for Italy*, Air University Press, Alabama, 2004

Mead, Richard, *The Last Great Cavalryman*, Pen & Sword Books, Barnsley, 2012.

Montagu, Ewen, *The Man Who Never Was*, The Camelot Press Ltd, 1953.

Montgomery, Field Marshal the Viscount Montgomery of Alamein, *El Alamein to the Sangro*, Collins, London, 1958.

——, *The Memoirs*, Collins, London, 1958.

Moorehead, Alan, *African Trilogy*, Hamish Hamilton, London, 1944.

——, *Eclipse*, The Text Publishing Co, 1997.

——, *Montgomery*, Hamish Hamilton, London, 1946.

Neillands, Robin, *Eighth Army From the Western Desert to the Alps, 1939–1945*, John Murray (Publishers), Hodder Headline, London, 2004.

Nesbit, Roy C., *The Armed Rovers – Beauforts and Beaufighters over the Mediterranean*, Pen & Sword Books, Barnsley, 2012.

Odd Bods UK Ass, *ODD Bods at War 1939–45*, Veritage Press Pty Ltd, Gosford, NSW 2250, Australia.

Odgers, George James, *Pictorial History of the RAAF*, Paul Hamlyn Pty Ltd, 1977.

Orgill, D., *The Gothic Line, The Autumn Campaign Italy 1944*, William Heinneman Ltd, London, 1967.

Owen, Roderic, *The Desert Air Force*, Hutchinson & Co Ltd, London, 1948.

——, *Tedder*, Collins, London, 1952.

Parker, Matthew, *Monte Cassino*, Headline Book Publishing, London, 2003.

Peniakoff, Lt Col Vladimir, *Private Army*, Jonathan Cape, London, 1950.

Perrett, Geoffrey, *Winged Victory – The Army Air Forces in World War II*, Random House, New York, 1993.

Pöppel, Martin, *Heaven & Hell, War Diary of a German Paratrooper*, Spellmount Ltd, Staplehurst, 1988.

Richey, Paul, *Fighter Pilot*, Orion Books Ltd, London, 2001.

Roberts, Andrew, *Masters and Commanders*, Penguin Books Ltd, London, 2009.

Rommel, Field Marshal Erwin, *Rommel and his Art of War*, edited by Dr John Pimlott, Greenhill Books, London, 2003.

Shores, Christopher (with Hans Ring & William N. Hess), *Fighters Over Tunisia*, Neville Spearman Ltd, London, 1975.

Shores, Christopher, *Mediterranean Air War, Vol. 1*, Ian Allan Ltd, Shepperton, Surrey, 1972.

Tedder, Marshal of the RAF Sir Arthur, GCB, *With Prejudice*, Cassell & Co., London, 1966.
——, *Air Power in War*, Hodder & Stoughton, London, 1947.
Terraine, John, *The Right of the Line*, Pen & Sword Books Ltd, Barnsley, 2010.
Thomas, Andrew, *Spitfire Aces of North Africa and Italy*, Osprey Publishing Ltd, Oxford, UK 2011.
Vader, John, *Spitfire*, Macdonald & Co (Publishers) Ltd, London, 1970.
Wellum, Geoffrey, *First Light*, Penguin Books, London, 2009.

3. Private Collections
Broadhurst, private collection – Communication from ACM Sir Harry Broadhurst to General Sir Charles Richardson.
McCreery, private collection – Communications between General Sir Richard McCreery and Air Vice Marshal William Foster.
Doherty, Richard, *Eyes in the Sky – The Gunner Air Observation Posts: The Beginnings*, August 2012, np.
Woodhouse, Lieutenant Colonel J.W., '*Memoirs*', unpublished (Ref Michael Woodhouse).

4. Veterans' Accounts
Bevis, Flight Lieutenant Lewis S.: Pilot, RAF Transport, Hurricane fighters.
Ingate, Flight Lieutenant Jack: Pilot, No. 600 (City of London) Squadron RAF, Beaufighters and Mosquito night-fighters.
Jensen, Flight Lieutenant Frank: Pilot, Nos 230 and 284 Squadrons RAF – Sunderlands and Wellingtons in Air/Sea Rescue.
McKenzie, Flight Lieutenant John: Navigator, No. 459 Squadron RAAF – Wellington bombers.
McKenzie, Flight Lieutenant Rod: Pilot, No. 3 Squadron RAAF – Kittyhawk fighters, and Nos 145 and 601 Squadrons RAF, Spitfire fighters.
McRae, Squadron Leader Bill, DFC AFC, Malta George Cross (Fiftieth Anniversary): Pilot, Nos 148 and 104 Squadrons RAF – Wellington bombers
Ormsby, Gunner (OFC) John J.: 25 Battery, 9th (Londonderry) HAA Regiment RA (SR), interview with Richard Doherty, October 1993.
Paterson, Flight Lieutenant Ron: Pilot, No. 152 Squadron RAF – Spitfire fighters.
Richardson, Sergeant Alec: Pilot, No. 3 Squadron RAAF – Kittyhawk fighters.
Russell, Flying Officer Tom: Pilot, No. 3 Squadron RAAF – Kittyhawk fighters.
Stocks, Squadron Leader William S. 'Bill' Stocks, DFC: Pilot, Flight Lieutenant No. 221 Squadron RAF, Wellington bombers, and Squadron Leader No. 28 Squadron, Liberator bombers.
Watt, Flight Sergeant Stan: Pilot, No. 450 Squadron RAAF – Kittyhawk fighters.
Wiggins, Wing Commander Lloyd, DSO DFC: Pilot, No. 38 Squadron RAF - Wellington torpedo-bombers, and Squadron Leader No. 455 Squadron RAF (1944/45 Langham, UK) – Beaufighters (rocket-equipped) in anti-shipping.

5. Travel Sources
Over recent years the author made a number of visits to Egypt, Tunisia, Sicily and Italy. In addition recourse was made to a wide range of historical, geographical and travel sources on those countries, which included the following:

Eyewitness Travel Guide, *Egypt*, Everyman Guides, London, 2000.
Eyewitness Travel Guide, E. & A. Lisewscy, *Tunisia*, Dorling Kindersley Ltd, 2005.
Diana Darke, *Travellers' Tunisia*, Thomas Cook Publishing, 2005.
Tomkinson, Michael, *Tunisia*, Michael Tomkinson Printing, 2006.

Benjamin, Sandra, *Sicily, Three Thousand Years of Human History*, Steerforth Press, 2006.
Eyewitness Travel Guide, *Sicily*, Dorling Kindersley Ltd, 2007.
Insight Guide, *Sicily*, Discovery Publications, 2007.
Eyewitness Travel Guide, *Italy*, Dorling Kindersley Ltd, 2007.
Insight Guide, *'Italy'*, Discovery Publications, 2007.
Morton, HV, *A Traveller in Italy*,
Morton, HV, *A Traveller in Southern Italy*,
Publicazioni Cassinesi, *The Abbey of Montecassino*, Montecassino, 2005.

Index

Part 1: Military, Naval and Air Forces
(including Formations and Aircraft)

Part 2: General

Part 3: Airmen by Nationality